A Fish Supper and a Chippy Smile

Also by Cathryn Kemp:

Painkiller Addict: From Wreckage to Redemption

'We Ain't Got No Drink, Pa': A Little Girl's Struggle to Survive in 1920s South-East London

A Fish Supper and a Chippy Smile

Love, Hardship and Laughter in a South-East London Fish-and-Chip Shop

HILDA KEMP AND CATHRYN KEMP

This edition first published in Great Britain in 2015 by
Orion
an imprint of the Orion Publishing Group Ltd
Carmelite House, 50 Victoria Embankment,
London EC4Y 0DZ
An Hachette UK Company

1 3 5 7 9 10 8 6 4 2

A CIP catalogue record for this book
is available from the British Library.

ISBN 978 1 4091 5842 4

Typeset at The Spartan Press Ltd,
Lymington, Hants

Printed and bound by CPI Group (UK) Ltd, Croydon, CR0 4YY

The Orion Publishing Group's policy is to use papers that
are natural, renewable and recyclable and made from wood
grown in sustainable forests. The logging and manufacturing
processes are expected to conform to the environmental
regulations of the country of origin.

www.orionbooks.co.uk

Hilda Kemp
29th July 1921 – 18th February 2003

Acknowledgements

I am indebted to my father, Albert Kemp, for his encouragement, anecdotes, and for driving me to and from Bermondsey to relive his past and research our family's background.

My gratitude also goes to Val Johnson, Hilda's sister from Ted's second marriage, as a source of family stories and legend, and for her unswerving support.

Ron Johnson, Hilda's youngest brother, added his memories and stories, many of which were painful, but told with his persistent good humour. Dad, Val and Ron, you are all so like Hilda! Thank you all so much for your many kindnesses.

Lee Ricketts lent me a precious photograph of Hilda with her mother Emily in Spa Road, and Val shared her photographs as well.

I want to thank the Imperial War Museum and the London Docklands Museum for invaluable background information.

I wish to thank my agent Jane Graham Maw at Graham Maw Christie Literary Agency and Publishing Director Anna Valentine at Orion.

I reserve the final thank you for Hilda herself. She was a great lady, and it has been a strange pleasure inhabiting her world and her heart for this, the first book of her memoirs. I love you, Nan.

Cathryn Kemp is an award-winning writer and former journalist on national newspapers who wrote her own memoir in 2012. *Painkiller Addict: From Wreckage to Redemption*, published by Piatkus, reveals how she fell ill with a life-threatening illness and became hooked on her painkilling medication. The book is a gripping true story that offers a deeply personal window into one of the biggest medical scandals of this century – drug addiction aided by hospitals and doctors. It is a horror story as well as a love story, a survival story and a battle for dignity and freedom.

Unlike the vast majority of addicts, Cathryn chose not to remain anonymous and has talked publicly about her addiction. Now living and working in Sussex, she is currently setting up the first UK charity to raise awareness of addiction to medicines, called the Painkiller Addiction Information Network (PAIN). Find out more at www.painkiller-addict.com

In 2015, Cathryn wrote *'We Ain't Got No Drink, Pa'*, the true story of her grandmother's childhood in the slums of 1920s Bermondsey.

Introduction

Letter to Albert, Brenda and Christine, February 2003

I know I haven't got long. The doctors keep telling me I have the constitution of an ox, but I see the pity in their eyes and I know my time is coming. I meant to write to you so many times but somehow I never got round to it. My Bert always used to say I could talk for England, but when it came to writing letters I was always lost for words. But I want to find the words now because they are all I have left to give to you all. And I'm not going senile, I know that Brenda and Christine are dead; Brenda left me as a little girl, when she was barely able to tie her own shoelaces, and Christine, you left me when I was an old woman.

No mother should ever live to see the death of a child, let alone two of her children, but I did, and the horror of it stays with me even now while I'm laid up 'ere like a proper lady in my hospital bed, waited on hand and foot. And no, I never lost my East End accent, though God knows I tried to bring you up to be better than me, to talk 'posh' as I used to say to my friends in the fish and chip shop. They'd chuckle at me, thinking I had 'ideas above my station', as I was nothing more than a chippy girl, but I always knew life could be better, and I wanted that so desperately for you all.

Neither of you has ever left my heart; I have talked to you every day since you left me, and this is my last conversation – for a while at least, until we are reunited.

I gave birth to three babies, and only one is left to follow me. Only Albert, or Little Albie as I called him, survives me. Who could have foreseen that? The world can be a cruel and harsh place but I have lived such joy, had such laughs and loved so fiercely that I can't say I didn't live life to the full – even if my heart was broken many times over. As you know, I haven't had an easy life. You three, of all people, know that, but there's so much more I would have told you if I'd had the time or the courage. When I think of you, I think of your childhoods, filled with innocence and protected from the harshest realities of life. We didn't have much, but what we had we shared, and what we didn't have – well, we didn't miss much. These were the things I wanted to give you; I wanted you to know love and security because I never had them. I knew what it was to grow up in desperate poverty, to have to scratch around for a penny to buy bread, to feel the seeping cold of a foggy dockland night with only a thin blanket and a too-small coat to cover me, to share the filthy mattress on the iron bed with my brothers and sisters, fighting for space while huddling up to keep warm, to watch my mother give us the only food she had and not know if any of us would eat again the next day. I know what it is to feel hunger – not the impatient growl of a tummy that has missed a meal: proper hunger, the type that aches in your soul as much as your belly; the type that tries not to remember when we last ate, or predict when we'd eat again. That feeling never leaves a person. It's why I always kept a few chocolate bars in stashes hidden around at home. You three always laughed at me for that. I don't blame you, I understand how it must have looked silly, even a bit crazy to you, but I could never lose that feeling that we might never eat again and that was how I coped with it. You see, I couldn't find it in me to trust again. Once gone, trust is gone for ever, however much we pretend otherwise. I never wanted you three to feel that insecurity, but I know I wasn't always able to keep you from it. There were times when you were growing up that I had to hide the fact I hadn't eaten so there was enough food for you to eat that day, despite working for Wally in the chippy, dishing out food and friendly banter with my customers. I know that you found me out, Little Albie, when you caught me mopping up the gravy from your plate with your half-eaten slice of bread after you'd finished your meal. I saw you watch me, and you knew that was all I'd eaten that day. I would have done anything to spare you that sight. But I am proud that I didn't repeat the mistakes my parents made in other ways. I brought you up to know love, so much love. I hope you feel the love in your heart as you read this, as what I have to say won't be easy to read. But I want you to know who I am, and who I was brought up to be, because this is all I have left of the past, and the memories haunt me in vivid Technicolor, as if they happened yesterday.

I want you to know me because I gave you life. My history is, in some strange way, your history too. I just hope that my beloved husband Bert and I stopped history repeating itself; but only you can be the judge of that.

This is hard to write, but my family life, my childhood, was one of chaos and fear. Every day was a battleground, a fight to survive and a fight to be safe. My pa was a hard drinker and a hard hitter as well. Many, many times I felt the force of his fists after a night on the grog. I did what I could to protect my younger brothers and sisters, and my ma, who was always ill and often pregnant with another child, but in doing that I took on a force stronger than myself. 'That Man' – that's how I have always referred to my pa – That Man had the devil in him. He would earn a few pennies being a bare-knuckle fighter in the Old Kent Road, down Hackney Marshes or by the docks. He honed those fists into fighting machines and it was me and my ma who bore the brunt of them at home. He would always celebrate a win or commiserate a loss by drowning his sorrows. And he had a lot of sorrows to escape if his love for the beer was anything to go by. If *only he'd drowned himself proper – Lord knows I would never wish harm on anyone, yet I'd wish it on him a thousand times over and feel no guilt. He was a drunk, a womaniser and a brute. At closing time one of us would be sent to the pub by Ma to get him. He'd make a show of it, carousing, swearing to his drinking friends that he wouldn't be under the thumb but he'd come home all the same, stinking of booze, reeking with dark anger and the proof, if he'd not known it till then, that he was a failed man: a casual dock worker by day, a hardened street fighter by night and a lousy drunk to boot. My nose still bears the proof of his rages; broken so many times that I lost count.*

It was my darling Bert who saved me; it was he who decided he was going to get me out of there. And it was my Bert who gave me my babies, you three, and it doesn't feel so long ago since I held you all in my arms and fed you, hearing you breathe and suckle in the long night hours . . . I'm wandering in my mind. Where was I? Yes . . . I remember.

Time. It doesn't feel like so long ago that there was too much of it. Time spent kicking our dirty, broken shoes against the tenement step in Bermondsey where I was born, kicking bottles down the cobbled streets, dodging the milk cart or the rag and bone man. There were days when time stretched before us and we forgot our troubles and the fact we were hungry, cold and dirty; days when we ran wild down at the docklands, jumping onto barges and stealing coal, racing through the dank back streets of South-East London like water rats, feeling like we were as free as the gulls that called every morning when the fishing boats chugged up the slimy, brown waters of the Thames. You wouldn't believe it but we loved London. 'Once a Londoner, always a Londoner', Ma would say and she was right. We left London in the end, as you know, but I always missed it. Dark, filthy, crime-ridden Bermondsey, where you knew your neighbours, you kept your eyes down and your ears shut as defence against the gangs at war in our streets. You never went to the police and you all kept each other's secrets. Those times are gone and maybe it's best that way. Secrets have a way of coming back to find us, just when we think we're safe from them.

I'm sorry if this letter feels like that but I need to tell my story, and the story of all our lives during the misery and hardship of those days. I wanted all three of you to be different, to live better lives away from the smog and the trouble, live in peaceful places where no hard men from the local gang would come knocking, where children could run free then be tucked up safe and sound in a loving, warm home. Perhaps these were pipe dreams after the start I had in life, but I always knew I wanted to make a 'normal' family with a kind father for you, warm clothes and the feeling of being loved. Is there a better feeling in the world? I hope you had that feeling, especially you, Brenda, as you lived such a short life. Even now, I miss the smell of your hair as I dried you down after your bath, and I can still feel you snuggle into my arms for a bedtime story. It breaks my heart all over again every time I think of you, and I remember so much. They tell me that it's part of being an old woman, that time has no meaning except to bring back the ghosts of the past. Memories seem more real than the reality of each day.

I've got no complaints in 'ere. The nurses are good to me, the doctors make jokes and scribble notes on their clipboards, which I suppose is meant to do me some good. I know my time is up, though. They bring more of the drips, which hang by my bedside like clear, bloated bladders – oh, my Bert would've loved that. He'd have laughed so much, seeing me in 'ere, his 'Duchess' lording it over the surgeons, getting my meals three times a day and painkillers at bedtime. He'd have said I was living like a proper duchess at last.

My Bert.

How can two words convey so many emotions? He was my

5

true love, my first and only sweetheart, and I loved him dearly for nearly 60 years until he passed away. It was three years ago, but every day I still speak to God and ask, 'Why take him? Why take my Bert? You've had my Brenda – ain't that enough for you?' Then, of course, He took Christine from me as well. I talk to Bert most days, sometimes my memory of him is so powerful I could almost believe he's just walked out of the room and will come back in with a mug of cocoa and two Garibaldi biscuits on a tray, like he used to every evening. We'd listen to the wireless together before turning in for bed, and we were happy. I wanted you to know that happiness which nourishes a person right to the pit of their souls. It was the kind of love that swept me away and at the same time kept me rooted in living a good life, and making a home for you, my three babies.

Little Albie, there's only you left and so I dedicate this to you. I know you carry your sisters in your heart, and that's where they should be.

I must stop now. My head feels light, as if I'm not really 'ere any more. I know it won't be long, and so all I can say is that I love you as fiercely as I did the day you were all born, squalling and wailing as you were placed in my arms.

My legacy to you isn't riches, it's a wealth held in your heart for ever.

Your loving mum,
Hilda

CHAPTER I

Frying Tonight

1951

'Oi, 'ilda, the sign outside says you're frying tonight, but I ain't seeing nothing done in ere!' The voice, which accompanied a loud cackle, cut through my daydream, startling me into remembering where I was: standing with my back to the door of Wally's Fish and Chip Shop, where I worked.

The shop had just opened for business, at 5 p.m., and already there was a queue of hungry customers on the cobbled street in Bermondsey, south-east London.

'Sorry, Mavis, I was miles away. Don't know what's got into me today,' I replied, before quickly tying my apron round my waist, which was already thickening from the new life growing inside me. 'Bit distracted, must be this hot weather.'

With that I smiled to myself. I knew full well it wasn't the weather or the strain of working long hours serving customers and frying fish. I knew it was my third, longed-for pregnancy that was making me dreamy: the child that would complete my family, alongside my eldest boy Albert, five, or Little Albie as I liked to call him; my darling girl, Brenda, who was nine months old; and now this little one, still just a twinkle in the night sky but making its presence felt already. At least I wasn't nauseous like I was with Brenda. Then, the smell of the oily cod and the chips being coated in greasy brown vinegar would turn my stomach. I lost count of the times I would have to mumble an excuse to Wally, the owner of the shop and my boss, and stumble to the outside lavvy in

7

the tiny, dirt-streaked yard to throw up what remained of my breakfast before I could carry on serving my regulars with a smile and a laugh.

Yes, this time was definitely better but, even so, I had a job to do and I would never forgive myself if I wasn't pleasant and charming to the women from the nearby estate, who relied on the shop each Friday evening for a quick, hot supper after a long week working their fingers to the bone with chores and child-rearing.

There was little enough round our way in respect of luxuries. Most of us scraped by each week, sometimes having to use 'Uncle's' (our name for the pawn shops that dotted our busy streets) to get by. Life was an endless round of washing, cooking, cleaning and shooing away children as we scrubbed floors and doorsteps. Our husbands went to work wherever they could, returning home at night, expecting to put their feet up and be served their dinner. There was little respite – except for the weekly Friday-night treat of a natter in the chip-shop queue, and the promise of a steaming hot dinner of crunchy battered fish and golden chips. That was our idea of luxury!

'So, what will it be today, Mavis?' I beamed at my favourite customer. 'Your usual?'

'You know me too well, 'ilda – always the same for us. My Alfie don't like change, you know that. 'e'll have skate an' chips, the kids'll have rock an' chips, an' I'm watching my figure so that'll do us.'

'Comin' up!' I said, grabbing the metal spoon and burying it deep into the pile of freshly cooked potatoes, scooping out a great pile of glistening yellow chips and pouring them onto the stack of newspaper pages. With one deft action, I grabbed the metal prong from the warming shelf above the fryers and hooked out a resplendently oily skate which I placed on top. I dropped the tongs back onto the metal shelf with a clatter, and with a quick series of folds wrapped the meal into submission. Yesterday's rag became today's dinner plate!

I did the same again with the next order, knowing that tonight the kids would eat, her husband would eat, but Mavis would have to make do with whatever was left from their only hot meal of the day.

I glanced around quickly to see that Wally wasn't watching me. Wally, a short, thin man with dark hair combed over the bald spot on his head and kind eyes, was chatting to his shorter, plumper wife, Betty. Seeing he was distracted, I quickly heaped an extra scoop of chips onto Mavis's second bundle, wrapping the whole lot in yet another page from that day's *South London Press*, giving her a sly wink as I did so.

Mavis looked back at me and nodded her thanks. That was all that needed to be done – there was no point saying anything. Mavis was worn down by life. She had wispy hair and a thin, haggard-looking frame. Her movements were tense, prickly. We'd become friends over the years I'd worked at the chip shop, as she was a regular customer when her husband Alfie was in work. When he wasn't, which was more frequent recently, she'd pop by anyway for a chat before opening time. She had twin boys. She called them her babies but they had just reached school age. Her husband drank heavily, which was the reason he was in and out of work. Money was so short that she'd only been able to afford one pair of shoes for the twins, so they went to school on alternate days. Lord knows how she got away with it.

I knew how hunger felt. I had gone without my dinner many times so that Albie and Brenda would have enough to eat, and my husband Bert would have something in his belly before starting his early morning shift as a delivery driver for Coca Cola. I sighed as I recalled the pangs of hunger at bedtime, suppressing them with hot tea; the lies I told my Bert, and the kids, that I was watching my weight, when of course I was not eating so that there would be enough food on the table to feed my family. These were hard times, and there were hard choices to be made, and they always fell to the women of the house to make them. It didn't seem fair, but then life wasn't, was it? Just for a second I was reminded of another time, much longer ago, when regular meals were like Father Christmas – possible but not probable. Those were the days I felt the soreness of real, aching hunger.

I was born in July, 1921. I grew up in the slums of Bermondsey, living in two rooms with Ma, Pa and four siblings. Pa – Ted Johnson – was a casual docker who never knew from one day to the next if he would work. On top of that he was a drunk; a man who spent the little money he earned in the dingy, dirty, drinking holes near the docks. He would drink our food money away, then return home, roaring drunk and filled with bile, and then subject Ma – Emily – and me to violence and beatings. He ate the little food we had, and drank the little money we had, then he went out and boasted about what a great man he was. Well, I hated my pa, and that's not something I'd say about anybody else but him. He had been a prize fighter in the army, and used the power in his large, veiny fists to fight bare-knuckle down by the docks or in The Ring, a notorious hang-out for fighters, criminals and illegal bookies in Blackfriars. There, he'd fight for money, then spend his winnings buying rounds for his so-called 'friends'. No, I freely admit it, I *hated* Pa. He knew how to land a punch on an opponent to cause maximum damage, and by God he gave me some beatings. I was just a child, and many was the time I turned up for school with black eyes, or a limp where he'd inflicted hurt on me. Yet, even though everyone in the neighbourhood knew what was going on, no one ever stepped in to stop him. And no one would now. In our part of the borough, it was not the done thing to intervene between a man and his family, however much he hurt and frightened them. There was, and still is, a conspiracy of silence. People didn't want to 'interfere', it just wasn't the done thing. My children have known only gentleness from their father – they've been lucky they don't have to suffer violence like that.

It's because of Pa that I knew the sharp pangs of hunger. I knew what it was to feel the cold, and not know when the next meal would be. So when I saw Mavis sacrifice her food so her children could eat, I couldn't help myself. It was wrong of me to give extra chips. I knew that Wally's business wasn't a charity, and that he had to make a living like the rest of us, but my nature was always too soft-hearted. I couldn't bear seeing Mavis and her kids suffer, and a handful of chips would hardly break the bank so I risked it for her and for others when I could. It was all I could really do, to help. My Bert tells me I'm a soft touch several times a day. He always says I'll let anybody tell me a sob story, but it's who I've always been. I brought up my siblings as my mother's right hand: I washed their faces, tucked them up in bed, read them bedtime stories and soothed away their night terrors.

But all that happened in another time and place.

I shook my head to try and release the thoughts from my mind, hoping they'd fly out and settle somewhere else instead. I always did that to try and clear my head, but it rarely worked. I so desperately wished I could forget the things about my past I wanted to forget.

I leaned over the counter and slipped the two warm parcels, one distinctly fatter than the other, into my friend's string bag. 'How are things, Mavis?' I asked tentatively, quietly, hoping she'd hear the gentleness in my voice and guess at the compassion I felt for her, for all us mothers dealing with hard choices and difficult lives.

Mavis's face was lined with worry. Her wispy brown hair was tied back in the turban all us housewives wore, and she was dressed in a faded, flowery pinafore and a pink cardigan, despite the heat of the day. She had always been thin but today, as the sunlight filtered in through the large front window of the shop, she looked gaunt. Her cheekbones stuck out, and I wondered how long it had been since her last proper meal. 'Oh, well, you know, things are the same. Alfie's waitin' to start 'is new job, just a week or so to go now...'

Mavis's voice trailed off, and for a brief moment I could see how much it had cost her to tell me even this brief snippet of their lives. For a moment neither of us spoke. There was no need to. I knew that a week waiting for a job was an indescribably long time when you had mouths to feed. She and Alfie had three children under the age of five, yet Mavis looked years older due to the strain of surviving, and the worry of living hand-to-mouth. I noticed her worn shoes and her darned stockings, her unwillingness to give up in the face of destitution. And it *was* destitution: if there was no money in the house then people didn't eat, I knew that well enough.

'What's his new job?' I asked, hoping it was true and Alfie really did have some means lined up to earn a decent living. His last job driving for a tallow works hadn't worked out, again. Alfie was known for being a drinker. He had a reputation for not turning up to work some mornings, and it cost him and his family dear. As a result, he was turned away from jobs so frequently I was surprised that he'd been offered a new position.

'Oh, it's a good one, this time,' Mavis replied, her eyes looking brighter with the hopefulness of the poor. ''e's got a gig drivin' the meat van which goes round all the butchers in the East End, collecting the fat and offal. We shan't 'ave a worry in our 'eads once 'e's workin' there.' Mavis smiled, avoiding my eyes, and I wanted to believe her so much it hurt.

'Of course things will get better, dear. They 'ave to, don't they?' I murmured, my hand veering to Mavis's woollen sleeve with the slightest of touches. It was all I could do to give her comfort, to let her know she wasn't the only one who experienced the helplessness of seeing a man drink away the family money. Even so, a feeling of powerlessness swept over me. I couldn't help her – all I could do was give what little I could by understanding a hint of her plight, a plight that was so ordinary around here it hardly counted.

'You ladies goin' to natter all day? I'm runnin' late enough as it is, an' my old man will skin me alive if I don't get back in time with 'is dinner!' The moment disappeared as if it had never been, cut away by the cross words of my next customer, Violet.

'Alright, Vi, I'm comin'. No need to get shirty,' I said crossly, knowing the small moment of intimacy with my friend was lost. 'Mavis, that'll be four shillings, please.' I wished then I didn't have to charge her. I felt awkward as I watched her open her purse and carefully count out the money. As she put the coins into my hand I arranged my face into a falsely jaunty smile. Mavis looked away. I knew that sometimes being jolly was too much to bear. Feeling helpless, I turned to the till, pressing on the buttons that released the drawer for the money with a sharp jolt. The coins clattered into the metal trays and I shut it with force. The damn thing always stuck. I looked up to say, 'Goodbye, dear, and give those babies of yours a kiss from me,' but Mavis was already out of the door, hurrying home with her precious cargo, back to hungry mouths, and the leftovers – if she was lucky.

Sighing, I turned to Violet, who was listing her order. She was a boisterous woman who lived a few doors down from me. She was plump and loud, and had a skinny, hen-pecked husband and five snotty-nosed children who ran wild on the estate. 'Sorry, dear, you're going to have start over. Don't know what's wrong with me today – my head's all over the shop.' With that I smiled to myself again, and I was back to thinking about my baby, the one who would restore the good times, who would bring sunshine into our lives, I was absolutely sure of that.

Later that evening, after the last customer had finally left, just after 10 p.m., and I'd washed the floor down with soap suds, I started thinking about Mavis and all the women I knew who kept their households together. As I brushed the bits of batter leftovers from the warming trays, popping a few crunchy pieces into my mouth as I worked, I mused on how lucky I was with my Bert. He was a good, decent, upstanding man whom I'd met when I was a young woman of 20, and him a fresh-faced soldier of 21.

I'd been evacuated to Braunston, near Coventry, during the war. Bert Kemp, or Albert as he was really known, had been sent to Weedon Barracks for two weeks' leave, and it was there that I met him at a dance. By the time he'd been posted back to North Africa with the Royal Electrical and Mechanical Engineers, or REME for short, in support of the Eighth Army, we were in love, and he had promised to marry me on his return – *if* he returned – from the fighting.

Four long years I waited for him, and when he finally returned, he was true to his promise.

We were married in August 1945 in Victoria Park, east London, and we settled into married life, living with his parents, Dolly and Albert Snr – who we called Pop – in

Bow. The start of our life together wasn't easy. Of course, we barely knew each other. My good, decent, upright Bert was also a stubborn, cautious, rather rigid man who wanted to eat the same dinner of meat and two veg every night, and who made love to me in the same stolid, earnest way every night. It was definitely not a torrid, passionate relationship, and many women might have been miserable without romance to create drama in their lives. I never lost that feeling of being safe with him, though, and that's what saw me through the difficulties of our first year adjusting to each other. I dare say he'd been as shocked as I was to find himself with a spouse he barely knew except for a few stolen nights of love in the dim, distant past. I expect I was a disappointment to him in some ways, though he never said so, as he was always a gent towards me. I loved him for being so different from my pa: he went to work every day, he was always on time, always keen to help and he worked hard to keep a roof over our heads. Every night he polished his only pair of shoes, making them shine for the next day's work. He had pride in himself, I'll say that for my Bert. I knew how lucky I was to have a man who rarely drank, and who preferred to stay at home each evening with me and our two children rather than go to the pub like most men round our way.

I threw the remaining chips, which had gone soggy now, into a bundle and offered it to Wally, my boss, who had been counting up the day's takings. I stood next to him, by the white-tiled wall of the back of the shop, and drew pleasure from the gleam of the cleaned metal surfaces and sparkling, pale blue Formica worktop.

Wally looked tired, but was evidently pleased. He turned round to me. ' 'ere's yer money, 'ilda. Well done, girl, we did well tonight.' He beamed. He was such a kind, gentle man; I was lucky to work for him.

I held my hand out for my money; I didn't need to count it. Wally was as honest as the day was long. He'd never think to cheat me out of a penny. I knew all my wages were there in full in the brown envelope I put into my bag.

'You get off, girl. I'll see yer tomorrow.'

I smiled at my boss, gratefully. He never kept me long after closing as he knew I wanted to get back to see Bert and have our late dinner together. I reached for my coat and hat. Despite the heat, it would've been unthinkable to walk the streets of Bermondsey without proper attire. It just wasn't the done thing! As I said a bright 'Cheerio!' to Wally, I turned the sign on the door round to 'Closed'.

Stepping out onto the street, I exhaled, suddenly feeling tired. It had been a long day. I'd started work at 4 p.m., after giving the littl'uns their tea and making sure Bert was home before leaving them with a quick kiss and a promise to bring back the leftover chips. It was a thirty-minute walk from the Redriff Estate in Rotherhithe to the fish and chip shop, which was situated just off the Old Kent Road. On nights like this, with the warm air and shining moon far above me, it wasn't an unpleasant walk, but even so I felt I was dragging my feet behind me with exhaustion. *It must be the baby*, I thought to myself. Every day I seemed to feel more and more tired and I was only a few months gone. But I loved walking through the familiar streets of my childhood at night. It was mostly quiet, the bustle of the daytime roads becoming quieter, as if deserted, with only the sounds of pianos being played in the pubs that lined the alleys of south-east London, and the hum of voices inside them filtering out onto the cobbled streets. I could almost see myself and my brothers and sisters in my mind's eye, kicking against the pavements with our hobnailed boots, avoiding a beating from Pa by skimming stones down at the Thames waterside, or hailing ships as they moored against the great walls of the dockyards, churning the brown waters in their wake. I breathed in that familiar scent of my beloved Bermondsey: the soot and coal from the factories, the bitter stink of the tanneries and the sweet vanilla smell of the biscuit and custard factories.

I turned into Rotherhithe New Road and continued home towards Rotherhithe, where we lived in a tenement building on the Redriff Estate, near Greenland Wharf, where the timber yards were situated. There was still plenty of bomb damage along the route, even though the war had ended six years earlier. The docks had been obliterated during the Blitz, the whole area decimated by wave after wave of German bombers, each raid releasing the stench of scorched spices and the medicinal smell of herbs as bombs rained down on the cold-store warehouses lining the waterfront. I'd narrowly escaped with my life more times than I could recall, dodging the explosions as I raced into London Bridge underground station for shelter, or into our Anderson shelter in the backyard of our house in Spa Road. They had been frightening days, but the war spirit had driven us onwards: everyone looking after each other, or so it seemed. Those days were gone now, of course, leaving the familiar grudges and complaints of neighbours as they resettled into 'normal' life after our victory. The docks were silent, the huge gates locked and the ships that still docked there – many fewer than in my youth – lay silent and dark against the moonlit sky.

As I walked along, I scrabbled inside my bag for my door keys. In the old days, we never left our doors locked: no one had anything to steal, and everyone knew everyone else, so there was no use for keys or locks. It was unheard of! Times had changed. *And not always for the best*, I thought to myself, as I rounded the corner into Redriff Road and headed towards our block of tenement flats, which loomed over the bombed-out carcasses of buildings. I knew my Little Albie played on those sites, despite my many warnings, but boys would be boys. I whistled my frustration as I puffed my way up the stone steps.

I turned the key in the front door and walked in, depositing my coat and hat on the hat stand. 'I'm home, luv,' I called out. 'I've got a few chips to share. They'll be cold by now but never mind, they'll still taste alright.'

'That you, 'ilda?' came Bert's familiar voice. He would be sitting in the parlour, in his chair by the unlit hearth, probably with his newspaper spread in front of him and his slippers on.

'Who else would it be?' I chuckled, putting down my bag on the wooden kitchen table, then bending down to take two plates from the cupboard.

Even though Bert'd been home since 4 p.m., it was up to me to fix our dinner and wash up afterwards, before washing his shirt, the children's clothes and my blouse ready for tomorrow. At times like those I thought of my ma, Emily, who spent her life washing and cleaning, then waiting up for her scoundrel husband to return from the pub. Again, I sighed, but this time in gratitude for the kind man in the other room. Despite his faults he was my Bert and I loved him dearly.

I squeezed past a wooden chair to get to my cooker. The kitchen was small but I felt very proud to have a proper stand-up cooker, rather than the old coal-fired range I used to cook on for Ma and my siblings. Our furniture was spartan, and consisted mostly of second-hand utility goods, bought with coupons once we'd successfully applied for a furniture permit. Bert and I had scraped together the money to buy ourselves a cooker, a kitchen table and chairs, plus a couple of beds, small wardrobe, cot and an armchair for Bert where he'd sit in the evenings. They were all second-hand, but after the filthy stained mattresses and cold iron beds I'd slept on as a child, this almost-new furniture made me feel like a queen living in the height of luxury. Well, Bert did call me his Duchess. He had since we were courting. He always said I should've been born to better things and I always disagreed with him, saying what could be better than a good man and a cosy little home of our own?

I leaned against the cooker for a moment, feeling the first flutterings of this latest, our third baby, moving inside me. It was time to tell Bert he was going to be a father again. 'I'll tell 'im tonight,' I vowed to myself.

I cooked his supper, dishing up the last of the beef stew from last night's meal and plonking the majority of the chips onto his plate. On mine, I ladled a small spoonful of stew and a few chips. I could wipe the gravy with a piece of bread and that would do me. It was more important to keep Bert's energy up as he worked 12-hour days on the delivery lorries, starting at 4 a.m. each morning.

Placing the plates on the table I called out, 'Your dinner's ready, Bert.' I could hear the shuffle of his slippers as he moved into the kitchen. He grabbed my waist from behind and planted a kiss on my cheek. 'Get off you, soppy 'a'porth!'

I blushed. He was always demonstrative with me when we were in private – it was one of his many endearing qualities. 'Now, get yer dinner down you 'cos I've something to tell you,' I said, arching my eyebrows.

Bert looked back at me. His lovely, freckled face looked quizzical but he evidently decided against asking any questions; that, or he was probably starving hungry. He drew out a chair, first making sure to pull one out for me.

I could never quite get used to Bert's gentlemanly ways. His red hair – it earned him his nickname 'Ginger' amongst his pals from Bow – was greased back in the style of the day with Brylcreem. He wasn't a tall man, but he was stocky and well-built, with twinkly eyes and such a handsome face. It took my breath away every time I looked at him. What did I do to deserve such a good-looking fella? How come he'd wanted to marry me, a girl from the slums?

By now, Bert was polishing off his dinner, scooping up the remains of his meat and gravy with a slice of buttered bread. The kettle whistled on the stove, and I got up to make us both a nice cuppa. I saw Bert glance at my figure as I moved. *I bet he's guessed*, I thought, but I wanted to string out the moment, savouring the last delicious moments of anticipation before telling him. *'e'll be pleased, won't 'e?* I thought to myself. I knew that money was a struggle and this baby was one extra mouth to feed, but surely the thought of a new little bundle to show for our love couldn't be a bad thing?

For a moment I froze: it hadn't occurred to me that our new child could be anything other than a delight, but times *were* hard, and Bert's money only went so far, despite the scrimping and saving I did on a daily basis, and the hours I put in at the fish and chip shop.

Bert must have seen the worried look on my face because he put down his slice of bread, looked me squarely in the eyes and said, 'Come on now, 'ilda, what is it?'

'Oh, Bert,' I replied, nervously. 'It's a baby ... I mean to say, we're 'avin' another baby!' I looked up at him, peeping up from under my eyelashes, bracing myself in case it wasn't the welcome news I'd thought it was.

I had longed for a third child to complete our family, despite being the grand old age of thirty, and I'd assumed Bert did too, but now I wasn't so sure.

Bert said nothing.

I gulped and looked down, picking at a knot of wood on the table with my finger.

I felt Bert before I heard his words. He grabbed me into a big bear hug and began whispering softly in my ear: 'Duchess, I couldn't be 'appier.'

And with that I turned into his embrace, knowing that I had the best man any woman ever had, and no queen, or duchess, could ever be happier than I was at that moment.

CHAPTER 2

Birdsong

7 August 1945

I stretched my arms and yawned. Sunlight streamed in through the single window of the terraced house. I lay for a moment, lazy and warm, hearing the sounds of the house awakening around me: the coal fire being scraped clean, the sound of water being pumped in the dirt-streaked yard. I was lying in a small, iron-framed double bed covered with a greying but clean sheet. There was a single wooden chair in the corner, which was draped with my stockings, brassiere and blue cotton dress, and a pair of army trousers and jacket. A single grey woollen sock lay in one corner of the room, the other being out of sight. There was little ornamentation apart from the clothes. The window had a ragged net curtain to spare our blushes from the other families using the single lavvy in the yard or collecting water. The wallpaper of the room was stained with brown blooms of damp and peeled down the walls in mournful strips. Despite the bleakness of my surroundings, I had never felt happier in my life.

I'd been living at Dolly and Pop's house in Bow, east London, since escaping from a vicious beating by my sadistic father. I had fled from our home in Braunston, to where we'd been evacuated, leaving behind my ailing Ma and siblings. Ma had begged me to leave, saying that Pa would not stop tormenting me until he killed me. It had broken my heart to leave my family but I knew she'd been right and so, clutching my suitcase and gas mask, I left without looking back, to return to my birth place: the dirty, bombed-out, collapsing city of London.

From the minute I stepped off the train at Euston Station I felt my spirits soar. I was home, back where I belonged, with only an aching heart and tear-stained face to remind me of my beloved Ma.

I would never see her alive again.

If I'd known that as I stepped off the train into the seething mass of people, I might have turned tail and fled back to the security and comfort of her arms, to breathe in the smell of talc and carbolic soap that clung to her brown hair. I was a grown woman of 24, my life ahead of me, but I still felt safe in her arms, with her gentle words and loving kisses peppering my forehead. She was a saint, a martyr to her marriage – and I was determined never to become like her, however much I adored her. She spent her life in domestic slavery to a man who drank away the money, leaving her and her children to starve. I had seen her beaten to a bloody pulp by the man who had promised to love and honour her, and he'd been as brutal to me. Many beatings, harsh words and scant love. I had vowed as a child never to marry a man like Pa; I would stay a spinster for ever rather than fall for a man with dubious charms and hard fists.

As I travelled through the rubble of our once-great city, I marvelled at the hardy spirit of Londoners who picked their way through the devastation to go to work. It didn't look like a city that would win the war, in fact London looked as if it would never recover its former glory – a shambling wreck of a city beset by shortages and rationing, a grey pallor of smoke hanging over the jagged roofline that had been fashioned by German bombers.

Like a refugee Jew fleeing Nazi persecution, I had arrived on Dolly and Pop's doorstep with one small suitcase and the clothes I was standing up in. Bert's mother and father had taken me in without a murmur, showing me such kindness I loved them instantly with the kind of passion only a battered young woman can harbour.

Bert's parents had sheltered me until their son came home from the war, almost two years after I'd arrived, and we could get married. Even though Dolly and Pop lived in the same grinding poverty of our class and time, I saw only their many kindnesses and love. I didn't notice the oily walls, the grease-streaked windows, the grey light and huddle of the terraced house they lived in. Especially not now my Bert was back. I'd have moved into the trenches to be closer to him, and thought nothing of the mud, rats and squalor.

There came a grunt, then a strangled snore, and movement beside me. *Gawd, I keep forgettin' I'm a married woman!* I laughed to myself, as I remembered it was my Bert lying beside me, and not one or all of my four siblings. I'd grown up sharing a bed, firstly with Ma, Pa and my brother, Les, and sister, Joanie. Then, when the family grew, I shared a filthy, lice-infested mattress with my younger brother Ron, and baby of the family, Patsy, as well. I was used to sharing a bed, but for the life of me, I wasn't used to sharing it with my husband!

Bert and I had got married three days earlier. He'd finally come home to me – albeit for a 28-day leave – to make me his wife. Our time was limited, though. He hadn't officially been demobbed yet and had to return to his barracks with the REME. I stole a glance over at him. A tuft of his red hair showed above the blanket, and he snored again. I resisted the urge to giggle and pulled the covers up to my neck. I was stark naked underneath them, and I suddenly felt shy. For the first two nights after our wedding at St Mark's Church in Victoria Park, my handsome husband had been too drunk to do his manly duty, if you know what I mean. I hadn't minded – I needed a few days to get used to the idea that I was someone's wife now, and not plain old Hilda Johnson any more. I knew what went on between men and women beneath the sheets. I'd grown up sleeping in the same bed as Ma and Pa, who had one child after another. I knew what men's urges were, and how their wives had to submit to it, or get a beating, which was why I was so surprised at how gentle and shy Bert had been with me. It was so different from Pa's noisy rutting, and Ma's silent submission. With me, Bert wanted to make sure I was happy, that I was enjoying our bed-sharing, and he'd said lovely things to me as he'd undressed me, calling me his 'beautiful 'ilda'. Well, I hadn't expected that! I'd been bracing myself for an onslaught, and it had caught me off-guard when Bert showed yet again that he cared how I felt. He'd kissed me, nibbled my ears and somehow, despite the fact neither of us had had carnal relations before, we'd managed it. Then managed it again, then again until we decided we both liked it, very much indeed! Blow me down with a feather, I hadn't expected that!

I stifled another giggle at the memory. It was only a few hours ago, but I'd become a woman in the truest sense last night. I felt my cheeks flush red at the thought of our love-making. Bert moved again, then his arm appeared from under the sheet. 'Come 'ere, Duchess,' he said, his voice gruff with sleep. I snuggled into his arms, and all at once felt secure. All the embarrassment disappeared in a moment as I lay my head on my husband's shoulder and placed an arm over his body, feeling the tickle of his chest hair against my skin.

'You both decent in there?' came Dolly's voice up from the hallway. 'Yer breakfast is ready. 'urry up or it'll get cold!' she bellowed.

I was grateful she hadn't tried to knock and come into our room, even though it was her house we were 'honeymooning' in.

Bert turned round to kiss me then, with a quick movement, pulled his arm from under me and jumped out of bed. He had no qualms about revealing his naked body. He pulled on his army trousers and a clean shirt, whistling to himself as he moved. 'Come on, girl, up yer get. You don't want to miss Mum's sausages,' he said.

Typical of a man to think about his stomach, I thought. 'You go down, Bert, I'll follow in a minute,' I replied, not wanting to step out from the cover of the sheets. Even though Bert loved me – I could be absolutely sure of that – I was still nervous about being so thoroughly naked in front of him.

'Alright, Duchess, just don't be long.' And with that he dropped a lovely swift kiss on my forehead and left the room, taking the steep wooden stairs down two at a time.

I wasn't long behind him. In the kitchen, Dolly was bustling over the range, the sizzle of fat sausages filling the air, making the small window that looked onto the grimy yard steam up. I blushed as I entered the room, feeling I must look different now I was a properly married woman, no longer a girl, but if anyone noticed they didn't show it. Dolly threw me an apron and told me to dish out Bert and Pop's meal while she poured steaming hot tea into four cracked cups. Bert's younger sister, Dorothy, lived at home, but had already left for work at an office nearby while Bert's younger brother, Frank, was still waiting to be demobbed somewhere at sea in the Navy. That left Dolly, Pop, Bert and me to eat our late breakfast together.

Bert gave me a wink as I dropped two sausages onto his plate. Time was running out for us, as Bert had to be back in barracks in a few days' time, and there were a few things we needed to do together before he left. We had to register for our own house with the council, we also needed to apply for our Household Buying Permit as furniture was strictly rationed.

I also wanted to go by my father's flat to check on my siblings. He had moved back to London after Ma's death the year before. Her tragic life was cut short by beatings from her husband and the grind of hard work and poverty. She was at peace now, but I wanted to check on her 'baby', Patsy, a young girl of nine. But I daren't go there without Bert to protect me from my pa, and so I'd asked him if we could go that day.

Bert had raised an eyebrow. He knew that temperamental old bastard's rages, and how I'd spent my childhood cowering in fear of my life as he used his fighting skills to batter his wife and eldest daughter. I knew Bert would think 'Why go back? Why give him the satisfaction?' But I had to make sure that Patsy, my youngest sibling who lived with him and his new fancy woman, Phoebe, was okay. Ron, who was now a strapping lad of 16, was living with our ma's sister in Forest Hill after a short-lived lodging with Pa in Walworth. I'd seen Ron at my wedding, of course, only a few days before, and his cheeky smile and ready laugh had been a tonic for my worries about having abandoned them all to Pa. I hadn't had much of a chance to say hello or find out his news, except to discover that he'd been kicked out by Pa for daring to tell him straight how badly he treated Phoebe. Pa had roared at my brother to pack his bags. That, at least, was a relief. That Man couldn't hurt him while he was under another person's roof. *If Ron's living in Forest Hill with our aunt then he'll be okay,* I'd thought to myself. *'e's escaped at last.* At least Pa had never laid a hand on Patsy. Even so, I had missed her and Ron terribly and worried about them constantly. My wedding had been the first time I'd seen them since Ma's funeral, and I hadn't yet been to see where Pa and Patsy were living. As far as I knew, Les was still overseas awaiting demob, but I knew even when he did return he'd never come to seek out his father, not after the time Pa burnt him with his cigarette end. Joanie had married her Sid and was living up in Braunston, as far as I knew.

I'd begged Bert to go, and, reluctantly, he'd agreed. I was ecstatic at the thought of seeing my sister, but I was also wary, as only a victim of Pa's beatings could be. How would I feel seeing him again? My stomach churned at the thought. I remembered so clearly the sound of his hobnail boots announcing his arrival each evening when I was a young girl. Hearing him stumble and weave in them as we waited inside our tenement rooms for the explosion of his temper. I didn't even have to close my eyes to conjure up the memories of the quick, sharp thud of his fists as they hit my face. I felt faint thinking about it, but I had to have courage and face him again. I'd been brave so many times in my short life, this was only one more time. Luckily for me, I had Bert to cling to. Surely Pa wouldn't start a fight with me if Bert was around?

I barely took three bites of my sausage, I felt so nervous. Dolly patted my hand, obviously thinking that it was the newness of married life that had robbed me of my appetite. I smiled at her, hoping to reassure her, and gulped my tea instead. It was sweet and hot and instantly I felt a little better, almost ready to face That Man.

When we'd finished, the men sat and read the paper at the kitchen table as Dolly and I cleared up. It was Tuesday, the day after Dolly's wash day, and the zigzag of washing lines in the yard sagged low to the flagstones with heavy sheets, clothes and underwear. I wrapped my hair up into a turban and went out to take the washing down.

As I removed the pegs, I heard the sound of birdsong coming from nearby. I looked up into the small patch of blue sky above me. I couldn't see a bird, but it sounded like a blackbird, like the ones I'd heard some mornings in the countryside around Braunston. I stood, transfixed. It was a sound of such sweetness, such lyrical beauty that it took my breath away. The fear of seeing That Man dissipated; there was just a tiny bird singing for the pure, primal joy of it. Feeling like my soul had been cleansed, along with the clouds of sheets and shirts, I redoubled my efforts, pulling them from the line, feeling like my marriage, my life, had somehow been blessed that day.

Later, I stood in front of Dolly's only mirror in the hallway, which had been cluttered up for so long with the sand bucket and water pump in case of incendiary bombs. Tugging my beret, I pulled it sideways, but somehow I looked too jaunty. *It's bound to annoy Pa like that*, I thought. I pulled it flat across my head but resembled a female version of a casual docker like Pa used to be, so I discarded that look as well. Just when I thought, *Blow this, I'll go without a hat!* I pulled it to the back of my head. The dark blue beret framed my dark brown hair. My brown eyes looked back at me from a face that wasn't exactly pretty (my broken nose from Pa's fists put paid to that), but looked nice, pleasant and cheery. I smiled back at myself. Then remembered what we were about to do. My face fell.

We were catching a bus into town, then catching another bus out to Walworth in south-east London, where my pa now lived. I had started to write a letter to him so many times, telling him we were coming, but just couldn't put pen to paper. I didn't want That Man to think he deserved any warning, any polite letters. He wasn't human in my eyes. I'd seen him burn my brother Les with his cigarette ends, I'd seen him smash my heavily pregnant ma in the face before turning his fists, and his belt, on me. I'd seen him check his reflection in the mirror, jiggle the coins in his pocket and throw Ma a wink before going out to meet a floozy and buy a round for his friends. No, Pa wasn't worth a piece of paper or the price of a stamp. So Bert and I were going, without warning.

Of course, part of me hoped he'd be out and we'd have to come home instead.

Bert appeared behind me. He'd brushed his hair back, and wore his now-familiar army cap at an angle. His uniform was spotlessly clean, his army boots shiny. I looked at us in the mirror. We made a nice couple and again, it struck me how lucky I was.

He took my hand and, without a word, we stepped outside. It was a warm day, the sky streaked with white clouds, and there was a gentle breeze. We walked in silence, enjoying the feel of being together, until we reached the bus stop. Bert took out some change and smiled at me, squeezing my hand tight. I tried to look cheerful, but inside me there was a riot of emotion. There was the terror of seeing Pa, the excitement at seeing Patsy, and there was also sadness. The sadness was because I could never fix our family, however hard I tried or however much I prayed to God to make Pa stop his drinking and his violence. My prayers had never worked. He had made our lives a torment, and I could only be thankful that I was now away from him, living my own life at long last. And I was proud to be going back to my family as a married woman, a woman with a future. My goodness, how grown up I felt!

It was nearly 11 a.m. by the time we stepped off the bus

and looked around the main high street in Walworth. Even though I'd grown up in nearby Bermondsey, I had never travelled much beyond the borough boundaries, and I'd never set foot this side of south-east London. Much of the area had been bombed out. Several shops still had their windows missing, but with signs up announcing they were still open for business.

I squeezed Bert's hand even tighter as we walked down Chapel Road to Manor Place, where Pa's tenement was situated. It wasn't cold, but I felt a slight shiver down my spine as we approached his street. Part of me wanted to baulk like a skittish horse.

Before I knew it, Bert and I were standing outside 410 Chapel Road. It was a five-storey tenement and towered over us. Several children were kicking their heels in the street, while two women gossiped as they scrubbed the steps of the neighbouring property.

Suddenly a window was flung open on the fifth floor, revealing the sounds of a loud argument. A woman was screaming, 'You bastard, you've been 'avin' it off with 'er, I know you 'ave! Don't you dare deny it!' and then a rough man's voice bellowed his reply, 'You shut yer mouf, you fat cow. You don't know nothing about it, an' so what if I've noticed a pretty gal. You're mad, you are, you don't know what yer sayin'. I should 'ave you carted off to a loony bin.' The woman's voice rose up a decibel, if that was possible: 'You're a heartless bastard. I don't know why I ever left my 'usband for yer. Maybe you're right, I need my 'ead examinin'!' This was followed by, 'Shut yer fuckin' mouth!' as the man's swift response boomed into the street.

By now the children had stopped kicking their heels and were staring up at the open window with undisguised glee, while and the women had stopped their talk and were nudging each other.

I blushed, embarrassed. The sound of Pa's voice was unmistakeable. There was another scream, then the sound of the woman sobbing loudly.

Bert looked at me and said, 'We'd better get up there, 'ilda, before they kill each other.'

I blinked, then nodded my reply. I don't know why, but inside I'd had a fantasy that maybe, by now, Pa, at the ripe old age of 44, might have settled down, calmed himself a little. That he might even be happy living with his new woman. With a sigh, I acknowledged that men like Pa didn't change. They never learned and they carried on inflicting the same terrible damage to those around them, with no regard for anyone's feelings apart from their own.

We walked up the five flights of wooden steps. As we reached the top of the building the staircase grew darker and darker; by the time we reached the top it was almost pitch black. I felt like we'd reached the dark heart of the building. It was like stepping into an animal's lair. I was wary, on edge. I glanced at Bert but he looked calm and focused. Perhaps the horrors of war had given him a steely core.

My husband rapped sharply on the door. I shrank back behind him, wishing we hadn't come. The shouting stopped. Bert rapped again. There was the sound of a chair scraping along the floor then footsteps.

I could make out a length of string coiled through a hole where the key fob should have been. Reaching around Bert, I pulled on the string and the door moved inwards and there was Pa.

His face was in semi-darkness. I could make out the bulk of his short, well-built frame. He slicked back his dark hair and his voice came out as a rough growl. 'Who is it? What d'you want?' I could feel myself tremble, but when I spoke my voice sounded clearer and louder than I expected. 'It's me, Pa. It's 'ilda. I've come to see you an' Patsy with my Bert.'

Bert said nothing. He drew himself up and stared back at my pa.

For a moment Pa looked like he would like to shut the door on us, but in that moment's hesitation, the woman's voice came from the back of the flat, 'Who is it, Ted? I ain't got any money if it's the butcher – 'e'll 'ave to wait till Friday for 'is bill to be paid.'

'It ain't the butcher, it's 'ilda,' said Pa.

'Aren't you goin' to invite us in?' I asked, sensing that we weren't exactly welcome guests.

'Come in, then,' said Pa, grudgingly. 'I didn't recognise you, 'ilda. Must be yer new married life that's good fer you.' He sounded cross that I looked so well.

I bit back my response that it was only because I didn't live with him any more. That definitely wouldn't have helped the situation.

Warily, Bert and I stepped over the threshold. The flat was small, with two doors that presumably led into the bedrooms and a living area that contained a tiny kitchen with a gas cooker, a range fire and a sideboard. There was a simple wooden table in the centre of the room with three chairs. Bert and I took one each, while my pa took the other, leaving the woman who was presumably his new wife, Phoebe, standing by the window. The walls were a dull brown, presumably from the municipal paint that Pa stole from whomever he was working for. He was a painter and decorator now, and the tiny scullery to the left of me was crammed with pots of brown paint and a few tattered paintbrushes. There was an old settee and little decoration except for a strangely extravagant velvet tablecloth that draped down the sides of the table in a kind of fabric swoon.

There was a squeal and suddenly Patsy was in my arms. ''ilda! You came back to us!' she said, making my heart sink into my boots.

'Just for a visit, Patsy, luvvie. Oh, it's good to see you, 'ow are you? Are you eatin' proper? 'ow's school goin'?' I kissed her and hugged her. She clung to me just a little too tightly. *It must be hard for her*, I thought, *living without her mother, with Pa and his new woman friend*. I disengaged Patsy and held her at arm's length to get a good look at her. Her clothes were clean if tatty, her face was rosy and she looked well, if a little skinny. 'You're growin' up so fast! And into such a beauty!' I exclaimed.

Patsy had inherited our pa's dark hair and big eyes. She giggled and cuddled back into my arms.

'Won't you make yerselves at 'ome?' came the woman's voice. She was a large lady with fair hair, wearing the uniform all housewives wore: a flowery pinafore. She looked ruffled. Her hair had stray wisps and her left cheek had a bright red slap mark across it.

'Looks like we got 'ere in the nick of time,' whispered Bert to me.

'I'm Phoebe, pleased to meet you. I was so sorry to 'ear about yer mother, Emily.' She said. Her face was kind-looking, though her eyes were red with the telltale sign of tears. But she looked like she really meant what she said.

I was momentarily taken aback but instantly warmed to her. She had a caring look about her; in fact, she reminded me of Ma. She had that same gentle quality that shone from her, despite the privations and troubles she lived with. Why she'd ended up with a man like my pa was anybody's guess.

Pa had drawn up his chair and was sitting, leaning on

the back of it, staring at me like I was an alien from another planet.

'Nice place you got 'ere,' I said, faintly. While it was a small flat it looked clean: the floors had been swept and aside from the depressing brown walls, the place looked well cared for. That was something, at least.

Patsy sat next to me, her small hand curled in mine.

'So, 'ow's Ron, then? Where's 'e livin' now?' I said to make conversation, knowing full well he'd got fed up of Pa's rages and moved out.

'Livin' with yer aunt,' snorted my pa. Even if I hadn't already known that, I would have known that he meant my ma's sister rather than his family. Pa had little contact with his parents or siblings. He'd left home, joined the army and, as far as I knew, had never gone back to see his father or his stepmother, despite the fact they'd only lived streets away from us in Bermondsey. We'd grown up hearing how his stepmother had abused him by pouring boiling water over him as a punishment, and how he had been forced to beg on the streets of Blackfriars by his father from the age of six. He hadn't had an easy life, which made his behaviour understandable, if not excusable.

'Oh,' I said, nodding my head. I didn't want to ask any more questions as it was obviously a sore subject for Pa, but then what wasn't?

Phoebe bustled around her kitchen, bringing a teapot to the table and laying out a few biscuits on a cracked plate. Times were still tough, I could see. No doubt Pa's money from his new work was being slung down his throat in the pubs most evenings.

We sat at the table, Bert coughing awkwardly, as Phoebe poured the tea. I smiled my thanks, all the while hoping my beating heart would quieten down. I didn't want my old man to know how frightened of him I still was. I'd seen him at my wedding only days earlier but it felt like a different time. I'd been so pleased to see Ron, Joanie and Patsy that I'd been able to ignore the sight of That Man in his best suit standing in the church like he belonged there. And now we were seated round his table, just like old times: his woman with a slap round the face to show for her efforts, the neighbours witnessing his temper and young Patsy and me cowering from him.

I sighed. Pa looked over at me. I could see he wanted to say something, his face a picture of sour temper.

'Lookin' down on us, 'ilda, are you?' he sneered.

'ere it comes, I thought. 'No, Pa, why d'you think that?' I replied, averting my eyes, trying to head him off.

But he wasn't to be mollified – his temper was still up from his argument with Phoebe, I could see the signs. He twitched as he spoke. Rubbed his hands across the black stubble on his chin. *I'm goin' to get it*. I knew him too well.

'You come in 'ere, without a bye-yer-leave, and you look down on yer own father.' He was off, his voice rising as he spoke until it became a snarl. 'You always did think you were too good for the likes of us, yer family. Stuck-up cow, why don't yer go back to yer new life an' leave us alone. We don't want you 'ere, stickin' yer nose in, lookin' at us like we're no good.' He was shouting now.

I caught sight of the net curtain as it moved gently in the breeze from the open window, reminding me that I was to be the next player in the theatre of my pa's life, his neighbours as our audience.

'I won't 'ave you speak to 'ilda like that. She's my wife an' she worries about what 'appens to all of you.' Bert stood up as he spoke. His voice was still as calm as the rest of him, but there was a hint of menace. He had no qualms about standing up to my old man. His figure was as straight as a soldier's should be, his head raised high, and he stared at my pa without a blink, forcing Pa to look away.

But Pa then rose slowly from his chair. It was the confrontation he'd been itching for. 'An' who the 'ell are you to tell me what to do in me own 'ome?' Pa moved towards Bert, standing directly in front of him. Nose to nose they stared. I could hear Patsy start to cry and Phoebe shush her but I couldn't take my eyes off them. Pa's face grew redder and redder. He looked like he would explode. 'Now why don't you take that silly cow and get the fuck out of my fuckin' 'ouse. I ain't goin' to take cheek from you or anyone. Go on, get the fuck out of 'ere, an' don't you come back in a hurry. If I catch either of you 'ere again, I'll skin you both alive, I will!' Pa jabbed Bert's uniform with one of his stubby, grime-etched fingers.

'Let's go, Bert. We ain't welcome 'ere.' I took my husband's arm and threw a look to Phoebe that I hope showed her how sorry I was to rile my pa again. I knew it would most probably be her that would take the brunt of Pa's mood once we had gone.

Bert stepped back, and I prised him out of that flat. I couldn't even say goodbye to Patsy. We stumbled back down the dark stairs, and didn't look back till we reached the bus stop. I was almost retching with the old terror and I was heartbroken to leave Patsy in there with That Man. I wanted to bring her home with me and look after her myself, but I knew Pa would never allow it.

'There must be something we can do...' My eyes searched Bert's face. He looked back at me. He looked weary, as if That Man had stolen the day's joy from him. 'There must be something,' I repeated, as if saying it again would make any difference.

CHAPTER 3

Promises

May 1946

The pain hit me with the force of a surging wave. I heard a long, deep moan and realised it was coming from my mouth. Clutching hold of the iron bed-frame, I bent over as the pain rose again, swelling and heaving until it reached a crest and, mercifully, collapsed, leaving me panting with fright. *Looks like the baby's comin!* I barely had time to acknowledge the truth of it before another of the surges began. There was little more than a few minutes between my contractions.

With a whimper, I grabbed the bed-end with both hands, feeling like the tidal loop of the Thames had nothing on the pull of this baby being born. I cried out for help but my voice was feeble. Dolly was downstairs somewhere, probably in the kitchen. Would she hear me if the wireless was on? Bert was at work as an 'iron fighter', his nickname for his job as a scaffolder. He'd been demobbed months ago, and was doing whatever work he could to put food on the table. I prayed to God that someone was in the house.

I'd been changing mine and Bert's bed when the first pains had hit me. I'd thought nothing of it even though they felt stronger than the pretend contractions I'd been having recently – I wasn't due for another couple of weeks. But, very quickly, the pains had become urgent and I felt the first prickles of fear as I realised it wasn't going to be a long labour – the pains were too intense for that, I was sure of it.

'Dolly! I'm 'avin' the baby!' I shouted as loud as I could. Then the next spasm reared up and I was lost inside the agony, feeling like I was in the grip of a surging pain that had overwhelmed my body and was pushing me into dangerous and terrifying territory.

At that moment Dolly rushed in as fast as her small, heavy body could carry her. I saw her mouth form a perfect shape of an 'o', and she immediately barked orders down the stairs to Dorothy, who had popped back home for her lunch. 'Go and ring for an ambulance, dear. 'ilda's 'avin' the baby! Go as fast as you can!' I don't think I'd ever heard Dolly raise her voice before. With that, she smoothed down her apron and looked me up and down, assessing the situation. 'Now, dearie, you're alright, I'm 'ere an' I've 'ad three babies an' no 'arm ever came of me. Don't look so scared, it's all perfectly natural,' she said, smiling.

Well, I could've laughed only my body twisted into the next contraction, and the world seemed to go dark for the next minute. I could hear myself shouting now. I felt disconnected from the sound, as if my voice was unattached from my body, taken over by this sensation. I was inside the wave now, concentrating on riding it to its conclusion, all the while feeling like my hold on it was slipping. 'Oh, Gawd, I ain't never felt anything like this before, Dolly!' I cried, feeling just like a small girl again.

I felt Dolly take my arm and guide me towards the stairs. Slowly, we inched down them, me bent double like an old woman, till we reached the kitchen. Weak sunlight filtered through the tatty net curtain at the scullery window. Dolly steered me into a kitchen chair. I gripped the table for support.

'Sit yerself down 'ere, 'ilda, and wait for the ambulance. It won't be long. Before you know it, you'll 'ave yer own little baby an' be enjoyin' a nice cup of tea.'

Dolly meant well, but the pain was beating down into my

spine and a cuppa was the last thing I needed right now. With a groan I shifted my pain-racked body, trying to find a comfortable position, but it was impossible.

'Now, you wait 'ere, an' I'll go an' pop me 'ead out an' see when this ambulance is comin'. We don't want it to miss the 'ouse. Will you be alright, duckie?' Dolly asked, cocking her head to one side.

I nodded my reply, not trusting myself to speak. I was panting now as the pains came, bowing my body into each rolling contraction. This baby was well and truly on the way, and there was nothing I could do about it, except pray.

At that moment, I thought of my ma and how I wished she was alive to be here with me. Suddenly the torture of the pains felt like nothing compared to the great, aching loss I felt for my mother every single day. She had been dead for less than two years and there wasn't a day that went by that I didn't miss her. She had been everything to me, and now she was missing the birth of her first grandchild. I felt a sob escape from my heaving body.

My face was wet by the time Dolly bustled back in with a pile of fresh linens. Observant as only a mother could be, she at once saw the tear tracks on my face. 'There's no need to cry, my dear, it'll all be over in a jiffy.'

I nodded in reply. The loss of my beloved mother would never be healed, I knew that in my heart. Ma had been my best friend and my comfort. Her wisdom, patience and fortitude had got me through the terrors of my childhood. She had sheltered me from Pa's beatings as much as she could. I had loved her with every cell in my body, every heart beat, and I wanted her with me so much, I thought I'd burst with sadness. I heard a wail and knew it was coming from me again but this time I didn't care who heard it. I wanted my mother, and she could never come back to me.

Dolly patted my hand, seemingly at a loss to help. Dear Dolly. She was the kindest, most warm-hearted mother-in-law in the world, and yet nobody could replace my mother at a time like this.

The moment didn't last long. The next pains ripped through me and I clung to the wooden table, scarred from years' of use, for dear life. Dimly, I heard the sound of footsteps outside, then a man's calm, clear voice said, 'Now, where's the mother-to-be?'

I opened my mouth to reply, but instead came a long 'Oooooooh!' sound as the next contraction hit me.

'Good, that's it, keep breathing and we'll have your baby out in no time,' said the voice in an efficient manner. I didn't look up. I was too intent on panting through the pain. A strong arm held me tightly and guided me towards the front door. Everything went dark again as the pains went through me.

I'd had some explaining to do to Bert when I realised I was pregnant, I remembered, with a grim smile to myself. This baby had come along almost nine months to the day after our honeymoon nights, and must've been conceived that first consummation. I giggled to myself, then puffed with all my might as another contraction swept over me.

Ten minutes later, I was being wheeled quickly through the doorway of a large, looming building. 'St Andrew's Hospital, luvvie. You'll be alright.' With a whistle the man walked off and in a flurry of voices I found myself travelling down a long narrow corridor, past a ward filled with women, into a small room with a single window. It was then the urge to push hit me. But I couldn't just yet...

'Come on then, Hilda, it's time to get onto the bed. Give me your hand, will you, Mrs Kemp?' Another faceless voice. This one had a stern, authoritative manner. The nurse who had spoken, and Dolly, heaved me onto the bed, settling me back against the pillow. I squeezed Dolly's hand tightly.

'This baby's coming fast! Won't be long now, Mrs Kemp.' Both Dolly and I looked up at that, and I almost burst out laughing. I was still unused to being called by my married name.

'Exactly which Mrs Kemp are you referrin' to?' said Dolly, laughing. 'I'd say my child-bearin' years are well an' truly over!' she cackled.

'Mine might well be if this is what birth is bloody like!' I shouted, and we all looked at each other and broke into laughter.

'That's it, keep your spirits up, Mrs Kemp. You're almost there. We'll have this baby out by the time your husband gets back from work!' The nurse smiled. Although she was brisk and efficient, she seemed nice enough.

'Thank Gawd for that!' I said, more brightly now.

The next contraction seemed to last for ever. Time seemed to loop in on itself. I don't know how long I was lying there. The next thing I heard was the stern voice saying, 'Push, Mrs Kemp! Come on, I can see the baby's head, won't be long now.'

The room seemed to back away from the bed. The epicentre of my world was this pain, these animal-like surges.

'Come on, dear, almost there. Now, keep panting like I showed you.' And with that the nurse started the mechanical breathing, looking into my eyes to encourage me. I copied her with punchy intakes of breath. 'The baby's crowning. Just keep still, keep steady. Keep breathing. Good girl.' The nurse peered over my bent legs. 'Now, when I tell you, I want you to push as hard as you can – can you do that for me, Mrs Kemp?' I nodded. Anything to get this baby out! 'Now, hold steady. That's it, now ... PUSH!' With that I pushed into the contraction as if my life depended on it. 'Nearly there! The head's out – one or two more pushes and your baby will be in your arms!' The nurse looked up at me, her eyes bright.

'I can't, I'm too tired, I can't do it!' I moaned, my forehead slick with sweat. I'd been in labour for five long hours by this point. Not quite the quick birth I'd imagined!

'Now then, 'ilda, don't you go givin' up on us. Yer baby's nearly 'ere, an' that's my grandchild, so no messin' about. Do what the nurse tells you,' bantered Dolly, holding my hand tightly.

'Ooooooooh!' I shrieked, as another contraction hit me.

'PUSH! Come on, Mrs Kemp, the baby's nearly out, one more big push . . .' And with that, there was the sensation of a great release, and a baby's first cry filled the room.

My heart swelled with relief. My baby was healthy and strong if the cry was anything to go by. I said a breathless prayer of thanks and raised my head up, craning my neck for a first look at my child.

'It's a boy! Well done, Mrs Kemp, he's a beauty!' crowed the nurse. I never thought to ask her name. It was a shame as, later, I'd liked to have thanked her properly. I collapsed back on the bed, onto the pillows. My body felt spent, like a cake that comes out of the oven too fast and collapses.

'Oh, isn't 'e a big boy!' cried Dolly.

'Ten pounds exactly,' said the nurse, wrapping the bundle up and placing it in my arms.

I looked down at my baby boy. His face was screwed up, red as a beetroot and he was bawling with all his might. Tufts of bright ginger hair stuck out from his head, and he rooted towards my breast like a little creature seeking nourishment. I stared at my little boy in sheer, unadulterated wonderment. How could we have made something so perfect? I'd carried him for nine long months, talking to him, dreaming about him, waiting to meet him at last, and here he was. A perfect son. *I will have a lifetime to get to know him*, I thought, with something close to bliss. My eyes filled with tears, and my heart with love. Is this how Ma had felt when I was placed into her arms for the first time? Is this why she made all the sacrifices she did for us? In that instant, I knew why she'd refused food so we could eat, spurned new clothes so we could be warm, worked all the hours God sent and never complained. Because this love, this astonishing, pure love, was all-encompassing, so wide, so deep, that I knew in a moment I would do anything to protect him. 'Love' was too small a word for how I felt as I gazed down at him, watching him suckle against me.

' 'e knows what 'e's doin'!' Dolly said with a laugh, and we all chuckled.

'My goodness, what a racket! 'e's got 'ealthy lungs!' I said, in wonder. I could hardly believe I was holding my very own little boy in my arms. I turned to Dolly and smiled. 'You'd better let my Bert know – 'e won't want to miss a second with 'im.'

'Don't worry, I gave Dorothy strict instructions to make up a sandwich for Albert and send him over here the minute he gets in from work.' Dolly smiled back, and we both gazed at the squally little boy who was now sucking greedily.

By the time my Bert crashed through the doors of the ward I'd been transferred to, I was dozing, my boy beside me in a cot placed next to my bed. Dolly had left a couple of hours ago, back to cook dinner for her husband's return from work. I'd needed her support during my labour but I'd been glad for a few hours alone with my son, our son.

Bert woke me with a kiss on the top of my head. I opened my eyes and smiled lazily. ' 'e's in 'is cot. Your son is waitin' for you to give 'im a cuddle.' I yawned, stretching my arms and wincing as the movement caused yet more dull aching in my poor, bruised private parts.

I shifted up to look at Bert. He was standing looking into the cot, his face a picture of shock and wonder. 'You can pick 'im up, Bert. Go on – 'e can't wait to meet 'is pa.' I smiled in encouragement.

'I don't want to 'urt 'im,' said Bert gruffly.

'You won't, luv. 'e's a bouncin', bonny boy, just like 'is father was when 'e was born.'

With that, Bert bent over and reappeared with our baby in his arms. He came over to the bed and perched on the edge of it. 'Well, I never,' he said, with an amazed expression. I could've cried seeing the look of pride that lit up his face. 'I'm a father,' he said, simply. His voice was quiet, his eyes shiny with tears, and he swallowed down his emotion with a great gulp.

'What shall we call 'im?' I asked, touching the soft skin on his little head and feeling his strong pulse beat through his fontanelle. For some strange reason, we hadn't yet discussed names. I think both of us were too afraid that something would go wrong, and spoil the new life we were building together. I laughed as the baby curled his fingers round my thumb and clung on with a surprisingly fierce grip.

'Albert. I want 'im to have the family name,' Bert replied. 'What d'you think, Duchess?' It was common in the East End to name the first-born son after his father, and his father before him, and so on.

I looked down at our boy, who had started to root for his milk again, and nodded. 'Little Albie. That's what we'll call 'im, so we don't get confused between you, Pop and the baby!'

'Little Albie. Well, it suits 'im down to the ground.' Bert laughed, and he reached over to me and gave me a kiss.

'An' 'e's a proper cockney, like his dad. 'e was born within earshot of Bow Bells.'

'Not really.' Bert chuckled. 'There ain't any bells to ring no more – they melted them down durin' the war!'

At that moment a different nurse, a younger woman with fair hair but with a similar starched uniform, walked up to the bed. 'Now, enough of that laughing in here, if you please,' she said. 'And how is Mother?'

It took me a second or two to realise she was talking about me! It had been nine months almost to the day that I became a 'Mrs', and now I was a 'mother'. I gasped, as if somehow catching my breath would slow things down. So much had changed in such a short time.

'Time for me to go.' Bert winked. He gingerly placed Little Albie in my arms, gave me a cheeky kiss in full view of the nurse, and left.

I watched him go. In the space of five, short years I'd gone from a slum girl, living on the banks of the docklands, my skin a map of bruises, to being a married woman, with a husband who loved me and a little baby of my own. All those years I'd prayed that one day I'd be able to leave the Bermondsey squalor and make a life for myself, and I never once thought my prayers would be answered. I saw my life now as nothing short of a miracle, and no bossy nurse was going to spoil my mood.

'Time to check you and the baby over. Then he'll go into the nursery ward with all the other babies. You can't have special treatment in here,' she said, with a voice as starchy as her uniform.

'Yes, nurse,' I said, meekly. But I was smiling inside at how lucky I knew myself to be as I submitted to her examination.

47

*

It was two days later that Pa came to visit. I suppose I should have realised he'd come but, even so, it was a shock to see him in the ward, surrounded by brisk efficiency and the smell of disinfectant. I hadn't seen him since that visit to his flat. If I'm honest, I'd have been happy never setting eyes on him again, but he'd come, and I had to deal with it.

He stood at the end of my bed and I took a moment to appraise him. His hair gleamed black with the boot polish he used to cover the grey, but his face bore the telltale signs of a life badly lived: his nose looked thick from too many fights and was peppered with broken red lines from the beer he drank nightly. His stocky, once-muscular frame had run to fat and he looked bloated.

His manner was formal, uncomfortable. I had no wish to relieve him of his discomfort, and so I waited until he spoke. ' 'ilda, I've come to see you an' me grandson.' His voice was low and rough, and he slicked his hand through his hair. I'd seen that gesture a thousand times. It signified that he was ill at ease.

'So I see,' was all I said, my mouth a thin, tight smile that was not reflected in my eyes. Around us the normal bustle of the ward was in progress: nurses hurried here and there, bringing metal bed pans or injections to their patients. A couple of women moaned softly. There was a noisy family at one end visiting a woman who'd given birth to twins that morning. I looked up at my pa. I refused to look away, and his eyes darted sideways first, giving me a sense of victory, however small. 'This is Little Albie,' I said, not wanting to give him any ownership as 'his' grandson. *And 'e's not your anything*, I swore to myself. *'e's mine and Bert's an' 'e won't ever be yours as long as there's breath in my body.*

' 'e's a beauty – a big boy. Goin' to be a fighter one day,

48

like 'is grandpa,' said my pa, and instantly my hackles rose. *Over my dead body*, I thought, still smiling that awful tight smile at him.

Pa shuffled his feet. Inside a hospital he looked diminished, nervous. This was not his territory, surrounded by women and their business of bringing life into the world. All Pa ever did was tear the life out of his wife and children, rip the happiness and security of our worlds away from us so we always learned that things inside a family can be more brutal and dangerous than anything lurking outside it.

' 'ow's Patsy?' I asked. 'Is Patsy doin' alright at school?' Pa flicked his eyes my way again, and muttered something about bringing Patsy up here one day soon. 'I'd like to see 'er,' I added, feeling that sadness again from having left her, Joanie and Ron with Pa when Ma was dying.

'Well, I'd better be off. Just wanted to see the little man for meself. Give yer 'usband my best,' Pa said, as he put his flat cap back on his head. As he turned to leave, I saw him eye up one of the young nurses. He touched his cap by way of a goodbye then sauntered out of the ward, seeming more like his old, arrogant self again.

It was only when he'd vanished that I felt my body relax. I had forgotten that I had lived my life in a permanent state of anxiety and tension as a child, worrying about what mood he'd be in and how drunk he'd be each evening when we heard the sound of his boots on the staircase. I realised I'd been clutching Little Albie to me so hard he'd woken up and started to moan a little. 'Shush there, my darlin'. All better now. The nasty man 'as gone away an' I promise I'll never, ever let 'im be alone with you as long as we both live. You've nothing to fear from 'im, by Gawd – I promise you that.' As I rocked Little Albie back to sleep, I also promised him that I'd be the best mother I could be. I'd follow my ma's example, loving him and protecting him from anything or anyone who threatened our lives. He would never go hungry, and he would never feel the sickening fear that I lived with every day of my childhood, as long as there was blood in my veins and breath in my body. Those were my vows to him, and I would keep them whatever might happen in our future together. I told him I'd chosen the best pa in the world for him, that he had a proper father, one who would love him as long as he lived.

If I did nothing else, I'd always be grateful I'd managed that.

With that, and a snuffle, my baby boy fell back to sleep, and I wiped away the single tear that moved with slow grace down the contours of my cheek.

CHAPTER 4

Moving Out

1947

There was a crash, and a grunt, then the whole pile of boxes slid one by one to the ground with a great thud. 'Watch out, Bert, yer'll kill yerself *and* break all my plates at this rate!' I shouted, cross that the crockery gifted to us on our wedding day by Dolly and Pop could so carelessly handled. 'Be careful – it's not like we're millionaires an' can buy a new set,' I grumbled, my breath forming plumes of steam in the harsh chill.

Bert's ginger hair appeared over the top of one of the boxes, and his face appeared soon after. He gave me a grin and, with a cheeky smile, said, 'Don't get yer knickers in a twist, Duchess, I know what I'm doin'!'

I raised an eyebrow and said no more, choosing to fume off back inside to Dolly's kitchen to wait for the men to move our stuff out. I heard Bert stamp his feet to keep them warm, then the engine of the van roared into life.

Bert and I were leaving his parents' home in Bow and moving to our first flat together. I should've been thrilled at our new-found independence but, instead, I felt a sickening trepidation in my stomach. I was restless and grumpy, and I knew exactly why, though I could do nothing about it. We had talked it through a thousand times.

It made perfect sense for us to go and live in one of the cheap tenement flats next door to my pa and Phoebe.

I had been worrying constantly about Patsy and whether she was coping being brought up by my pa without her

51

siblings around her. Phoebe had given birth to a little girl, Valerie, only a week or so before I'd had my Albie. She was a beautiful little baby girl by all accounts, except she'd been born with disabilities: her arms, fingers and toes had not formed properly in the womb. I'd heard from one of Pa's neighbours that Pa had thrown Phoebe down one of the rickety flights of stairs of their fifth-floor building while she was heavily pregnant, in a terrible repeat of the damage he did to my ma.

Ma had been eight months pregnant when she was shoved down the stairs of our Spa Road home because Pa's dinner wasn't on the table when he got in from a session boozing in the pub. Patsy, my youngest sister, had been born a month early, within hours of Ma's 'accident'. Patsy came out healthy, thank God, but I shuddered to think of That Man's drunken cruelty, and how he was now inflicting it on another woman who'd done nothing wrong, except for the misfortune of loving such a vicious scoundrel. Phoebe had divorced her soldier husband to marry my pa. Much good it had done her. She was now stuck with a cheating bully for a husband, and a baby who would have to live out the consequences of That Man's actions for the rest of her life.

Bert and I had been discussing the idea of adopting Patsy amongst ourselves for a few months, but Phoebe's fall down the stairs had galvanised us into action. We were going to live in a flat next door to That Man to keep an eye on him and to make sure Patsy was being looked after. As I said, it made perfect sense, but the thought of hearing my old man's whistle every evening as he sauntered up the street, coming home from whatever work he'd managed that day, was almost too much to bear. I felt like a small child again, with that same knot of fear in my belly; the fear I'd sworn I'd never have to feel again. But some things were more important, and I couldn't stay away from my family any longer. Both Bert and I hoped that having my husband there would help keep Pa's behaviour in check.

My pa had also got the key to a flat in the same block as ours for Joanie, my eldest sister and her husband, Sid. They would continue their married life down in Walworth. It looked like the family would be together again, and only time would tell if we were all doing the right thing.

'Ready? 'ilda, where are you? We're all set to go! Come on now, don't keep me mate waitin'!' Bert's voice jolted me from my reverie. I looked around, startled for a second. I was sad to say goodbye to Dolly and Pop. They'd been as good as blood family to me and Little Albie, and I was desperately sorry to leave them.

Dolly huffed in, carrying her grandson with her. He was eight months old but already starting to crawl around the house. He was bright as a button and a quick learner. I was as proud as Punch of him.

I hadn't had time to get to know many of the other mothers in Old Ford Street, but several of them stood and waved from their doorsteps as we hurried outside. Bert's pal, Ronald, had lent us his delivery van. We didn't have much in the way of possessions, but we had some sheets, bedding, pots and pans, and all of Little Albie's things, including a teddy bear that he adored. Bert was already inside the vehicle. I hesitated for a moment, then I felt Dolly's hand on my arm, warm against the winter freeze.

'Now, go on then, dearie. You get yerself in that van an' don't think for a minute we won't miss you all. We love you all, but it's time for you to start your own life together.' With that, Dolly smiled. Her wrinkled, round face looked pale, her sandy hair wisps in the breeze. She looked like she'd lived the hard life she had, but all I could see was the kindness that shone from her. I hugged her tightly, not trusting myself to speak. I knew that tears were only a blink away. Her large, solid body enveloped me. Then I said a hasty goodbye. Pop was at work, and so I told Dolly to give him our love. With that, there was nothing left to do but gather my son from Dolly's arms and settle us into the front seat, alongside my Bert and his mate, who was driving us to Chapel Road.

Fighting down the sobs that threatened to engulf me, I waved, trying to make my face look excited and pleased to be moving on. Inside my heart was breaking, but I didn't want Dolly to see my pain. She knew what a wrench it would be leaving the security of her home, but she also knew, in her loving, wise way, that it was time to go.

Only I knew how much the move to Pa's street would cost me in fear and unhappiness.

Ronald pulled up after a bumpy hour-long ride, in our new part of south-east London. The van shuddered to a halt, and the four of us stumbled out as if we'd been travelling for miles. The street was quiet at least, I noted, even though it was early afternoon, though that could've been due to the cold weather. The buildings were the usual tall Victorian tenements. They seemed to lean together over the road, looking down on us and our few boxes. All had their windows clamped shut.

It was the harshest winter in living memory. The wind seemed to howl from Siberia, and along with the rationing, which seemed never-ending, there were shortages of coal and food to contend with. It was the bleakest of times. Many said it was worse than during the war. At least then we all stuck together and we expected the rationing and queues for food as part of the war effort. But the war was over – we'd won, but by goodness it didn't feel like we had. We had a generation of young men slaughtered in the trenches, and no work with which to welcome the survivors home. Coal was more expensive by the day, and we queued for hours to buy even the most basic of foodstuffs. No, it felt like more like we'd lost the war, and this winter and the shortages were our punishment.

I tucked my wool coat round me, shivering with the chill that seeped in everywhere. Despite the intense cold there were several small children with snotty noses and grubby cheeks playing by the kerb. I instantly worried about them wearing such thin layers of clothing in this terrible cold. No vehicles lined the road; it looked like the street had never seen a moving vehicle before. Flecks of snow lightly brushed my face. *Better get inside before the baby freezes*, I thought to myself.

Heads of local housewives poked out of net-curtained windows. I gulped. Then Pa appeared in the doorway of number 41. His hands were in his pockets and he beamed over to us, the picture of fatherly happiness. Bert went over and shook his hand, then Ronald did too. They spoke a few words, their breath forming curls of thick white cloud. Pa seemed impervious to the weather. He stood and rolled a cigarette. He'd barely acknowledged me, and I preferred it that way. No pretence.

'Come on, luv. We'd better get unpacked before Little Albie gets cold,' I said, my voice a nervous squeak.

' 'en-pecked already are yer, Bert?' guffawed my pa.

I smiled my thin smile. 'Bert, you with me?' I said softly.

' 'course I am, 'ilda,' he replied, and placed one of his strong, capable hands on my arm. 'Come on then, Ronald, better get this lot inside or my missus'll 'ave yer guts fer garters!' joked my Bert loudly.

I could've kissed him. It did the trick. All three of the

men started heaving boxes up to the first floor of the flats. I followed in after them.

Our flat was much the same as Phoebe and Pa's: it had a small kitchen and living room where we'd spend the majority of our time as a family. There was a tiny scullery and an inside toilet. There were two bedrooms and a tiny hallway. The walls were painted a grey colour and there were patches of wallpaper here and there from previous tenants. It was cold but clean. I gave it a quick glance – nothing I couldn't clean and polish up in a day.

The previous tenants had left a bed and mattress that didn't look too worse for wear, and we already had a cot for the baby to sleep in. There was an upright cooker and a shelf above the fireplace for storing our bits. That was it. No frills, as they say.

'It'll do,' I said, to no one in particular and, with a flourish, I took out my broom and started to sweep the wooden floor.

Later, after I'd cleaned out the cooker, cooked us a plain dinner of boiled sausages and mash, and put Little Albie to bed, I raised the question of adopting Patsy.

'There's no 'arm in askin' the old bugger, is there?' Bert said, contentedly picking the last of his sausage out from his teeth with a toothpick.

I sighed. 'There's never any 'arm in askin' anything – it's what we'll get as a result that bothers me,' I replied, glumly.

A few months later, as summer finally warmed the tenements and the ragamuffin children playing out on the street, Bert and I were sitting in my pa's and Phoebe's kitchen. Joanie and Sid had popped by before leaving for the market to get provisions for their dinner. Patsy was playing with Little Albie on the floor while the baby Val was asleep in her cot in the smaller of the bedrooms. Pa was leaning back in his chair, eyeing both of us with a calculating look.

'So you want to adopt my Patsy,' he said.

I fought against my rising temper. 'Yes, we want to offer my sister a home so that you an' Phoebe don't 'ave to worry about another mouth to feed,' I said, before realising my mistake.

'You sayin' I can't feed me own family?' Pa instantly leapt to his own defence, moving forwards so his elbows now leaned on the kitchen table.

' 'ilda didn't mean nothing by it. She only meant we'd be 'appy to take Patsy in to make us all the more comfortable.' Bert's voice was steady, but I guessed at how infuriated he must feel trying to make Pa see sense.

'So what's in it fer us, then?' Pa spoke and looked sideways at his wife, who cast her gaze down towards the floor.

'Well, as Bert says, we want to 'elp, an' I miss seein' Patsy every day. It's natural for sisters to be together,' I said.

I didn't want Pa to guess how desperately I wanted to take my little sister, who was a young girl of 11 years old, away from him. From what we could hear from the neighbouring building, Pa's tempers had got worse rather than better. Most days we heard him shouting at his wife. There were screams, the sounds of scuffles and the clang of pots being thrown against the paper-thin walls. It was a wonder the neighbours put up with it but then, once Pa was on the rampage, it was always best to keep out of his way. It broke my heart thinking that Patsy and her half-sister Val were living in the same flat as that monster. How could they not be affected by his rages? I didn't want my sisters growing up in mortal fear and dread, like I had, and so I was determined to get Patsy out of there. There was nothing I could do about Val of course, but I worried about her too. After all, she was my flesh and blood, as well as the rest of my siblings.

I had no problem with Phoebe. She seemed like a lovely woman, and my initial impression of her being like my ma remained. She was all kindness and love, just as my ma had been. It was obvious even from an onlooker like me that she kept her family together, scraping together what was left of Pa's beer money to feed them all and keep them clothed. I saw Ma in her in how she was a magnet for the other abused wives of the neighbourhood, of which there were many. I'd lost count of the times that I popped in with Little Albie to find one of her friends from the tenements sitting at the table with a steaming hot cuppa and red eyes, or a tale to tell of the casual cruelty their menfolk inflicted on them after a night down the pub. Phoebe would listen to her women friends, hold their hand when they got tearful, or add extra sugar, if she had it, to their tea to make them feel better. One woman, Irene, lived two floors above me, and would pop in most days. We never heard a peep from the flat she shared with her husband, George, but we all knew he made short work of abusing her. Often she'd wince when Phoebe offered her a seat, the rumours being that her old man beat her with metal coat hangers. Well, she never said a word about it directly, but I'd seen bruises on her legs and arms that didn't appear there by magic. It was a hard life for the women of south-east London. Every day I thanked my lucky stars that I'd found a good man, in among all the rogues and charlatans that seemed to be the lot of many young women.

It wasn't all plain-sailing though. Bert and I had our rows; after all, we'd barely known each other when we met. The first year of married life was tough. I was determined not to end up like Ma, and it made me defensive about being told when to have dinner ready by. At the same time, Bert was expecting me to be more like his mother in the way she cooked and busied about the house, but I had my own way of doing things; after all, I'd been caring for other people since I was a girl of seven years old. But somehow we worked things through, and Bert had never laid a finger on me, however cross we made each other. In fact, the only time he really shouted at me had been when I was pregnant with Albie – he'd come home from work early and caught me hanging out of the window trying to clean the panes of glass. Well, he'd roared at me to get down and startled me so much I nearly lost my footing anyway! He'd apologised for scaring me, of course, but said I wasn't to clean windows again – that would be his job from now on. How could I object to that! His gruffness made me feel safe; his need to keep me away from dangerous tasks warmed my heart and made me feel protected.

It was a very different story for Irene and Phoebe.

The room had gone quiet, and I looked up to see Pa ease himself back into his chair. His eyes were speculative, cunning. 'So you want Patsy ... alright then, you can 'ave 'er, but I've got a few conditions of me own.' His face was alight now with malice.

'Go on then, Ted, let's 'ear it,' replied Bert, shifting on his seat.

Phoebe stood up to go and put the kettle on, but Pa made a warning gesture and she sank back again in her seat. 'I want 'er back when she's fourteen an' ready to go to work. I've fed 'er an' put clothes on 'er back since she was a baby an' I don't see why you should get 'er money once she's left school.'

I reined back my anger. Fed and clothed her! My ma and then Phoebe had done that from the money left-over from Pa's drinking bouts! Ma had regularly pawned her few possessions, including her wedding ring, to be able to feed us all.

How dare he sit there, so self-righteous, so full of his own good deeds, when I knew the truth of it!

Bert put a steadying hand on my arm. He must've known how close I was to blowing my top. 'All right, Ted, that's fair enough. We'll take Patsy until she's ready to leave school an' go to work, then she'll come 'ome to you, fair an' square.' With that, Bert held out his hand to shake Pa's.

Pa hesitated for a moment, enjoying his bit of power, then shook it. 'Of course, you can't 'ave 'er just yet. Come back in a month's time an' we'll sort out the details,' he added, rolling another cigarette.

I almost choked. 'What d'you mean, we can't 'ave 'er yet? What's your game, Pa?' I spluttered.

'Calm it, 'ilda. Like yer Pa says, we'll come back in a month an' we'll sort it then. We'll be seein' yer. Ted, Phoebe,' said Bert, nodding to both, and steering me out of the kitchen, down the long flights of stairs and into our home.

I almost exploded with rage when we had shut our own front door behind us. 'Just who does that man think 'e is?' I spat, shaking with anger.

But, as ever, my Bert won me over. ' 'ilda, don't you see, 'e does it to upset you. Just don't fall for it. 'e's a difficult man an' we 'ave to play it by 'is rules. Now, why don't you make me a proper cuppa an' I'll light the fire. Then you can tell me all about this royal engagement, an' Princess Elizabeth tyin' the knot. Isn't that what all the 'ousewives round 'ere want to gossip about?' With that Bert chuckled.

I knew he was right about Pa and my reactions to him; I just couldn't see my way to changing the anger that built up in me every time I heard the lies pouring out of That Man's mouth. It was always my weakness. I reacted to Pa with outrage, and that's what gave him power over me.

I also knew that Bert was trying to distract me by

mentioning the engagement of our future queen. Us London-ers loved the royal family and the news had, as Bert said, sent us into a frenzy of speculation about her dress and whether the food and drink at the reception would be rationed the same as for us ordinary folk. 'But 'e'll be chuckling to 'imself about 'ow 'e's the big man in charge of us,' I whined.

'Let 'im,' replied Bert, simply. '' e's nothing to us. And now that cuppa if you will, Duchess – I've got a right thirst on me. So, will Elizabeth's dress be parachute silk like yours was, darlin'?' Bert replied, a grin on his freckled face.

I threw my kitchen rag at him with frustration before bursting into laughter. 'You won't change me thoughts that easily, Albert Kemp!' I replied.

It wasn't a month later, or even two months, that we went back to discuss Patsy: almost five months had passed when That Man finally agreed to have the conversation again. Princess Elizabeth had married her sweetheart Prince Philip, making the country swoon. Bert and I had even nipped along to Buckingham Palace hoping to get a glimpse of the happy couple. We were beaten back by the sheer numbers of people, many of whom had camped overnight on the procession route, and had to listen to the wedding and the celebrations on the wireless instead.

But enough was enough. It was time to face up to Pa.

I was determined that I wouldn't leave that flat without my youngest sister Patsy. We sat again in the kitchen. Phoebe, Val and Patsy were nowhere to be seen. My pa, Bert and I faced each other across the wooden table. I held Little Albie close to me and tried not to look into Pa's eyes.

Bert was the first to speak. 'We've come for Patsy,' he said.

'' ave you now?' replied Pa, his face a picture of menace.

I fidgeted. Why did it always have to be like this?

'You said we could adopt 'er. We've waited six months an'

now it's time to sort this out,' said Bert. I didn't know how he kept so calm. 'Where is she?'

My pa ignored him. 'Well, s'ppose I told yer I've changed me mind? S'ppose I never meant you to take me precious daughter at all. S'ppose your schemin' at my expense 'as come to nothing?' Pa's voice was rough and low. He looked like he was enjoying every minute of this exchange.

The room was quiet enough to hear a pin drop and I was suddenly aware of the sounds from outside: two housewives gossiping, children playing on the road were fighting, a cat miaowed.

'Well, 'ave you changed your mind?' I piped up. Bert had told me to keep quiet and he would handle Pa, but I couldn't help myself.

Pa just looked at me, and slowly lit the ciggie that was hanging out of the corner of his mouth. I watched the small trickle of smoke rise up to the ceiling. It hovered by a big, yellow damp stain.

'You old scoundrel! You never meant for us to take Patsy – you were lyin' through your teeth!' I exclaimed, no longer able to keep my temper in check. I should have known from the start that Pa had no intention to make life better for Patsy. I was shaking, furious. I was heartbroken for her. I knew I was defeated and I could never make amends for leaving her, Joanie and Ron when Ma was dying. Ma had begged me to go but I should've stayed, whatever damage my old man would have done to me. But this was worse than any punch. Pa had lied to us and strung us along, just as he'd done all his life. I'd really thought we'd be able to keep Patsy safe at long last, but it wasn't to be. When would I accept I could never win with Pa?

My father grinned. I was right, he was enjoying his power over my emotions. I stood up so fast my chair tipped over onto the floor and with a 'You bastard!' I swept from the room, the sound of Pa laughing ringing in my ears.

Bert grabbed my arm in the corridor. 'You just 'ad to rile 'im up, didn't you?' His face was cross.

I took one look at him and burst into tears. 'Don't you start on me as well. 'e was never goin' to 'elp Patsy, an' now I'll never be able to 'elp 'er. You don't know nothing about how mean 'e can get, so don't you dare tell me it was my fault!' With that I shook off Bert's arm and ran into the street. My vision was blurred with tears. They were tears I should've shed a long time ago. I always felt like I'd let my family down, running away to save my own skin. I really thought I'd have a chance to make it up to my littlest sister at least by taking her in as my own daughter. I leaned over and felt a huge sob rise up inside me. I walked blindly down Chapel Road and onto the high street, tears running down my face. An elderly woman wearing a brown coat and rollers in her hair touched my arm and asked, ever so kindly, 'Are you alright, dearie?' I mumbled a reply, wiped the tears away and walked on, not wanting to explain this terrible pain I felt.

It was several hours later, when the roads were dark and the crowds had vanished into their homes for dinner, that I walked back into our flat. The fire was lit and, to my surprise, I found Bert in the kitchen with my apron wrapped round his middle. He was holding a plate with a fat paper parcel on it that gave out the distinct aroma of fish and chips. I breathed in and sighed. There was nothing quite like good, old-fashioned chips to heal the soul and provide a simple balm for whatever was wrong in life.

When he heard me come in, Bert turned around, holding the plate aloft in one hand. 'I'm sorry, luv, I don't know what got into me. It's yer pa, 'e makes me mad as hell you know . . .' Bert's voice trailed off as he watched me. 'I got us some supper.'

In a couple of footsteps I was in his embrace, crying into his shoulder as his arms wrapped round me. 'Come on now, 'ilda, maybe it's time we moved on. We can't do nothing 'ere for your Patsy, an' livin' near yer pa 'as made us both miserable. Maybe it's time to go, Duchess – what d'ya say?'

I pulled out of his hug and looked up at him. His blue eyes were so full of kindness and love I choked on a sob, before nodding my reply. It *was* time to go. There was nothing to keep us here. I couldn't fix my pa and make him a better dad. Again, I'd learnt the lesson that I couldn't protect others from him either. And the terrible truth was that our marriage was being affected by living here. We had to go, I could see that now. We'd tried – and failed, and it was time to see the truth of it. 'Will you promise me one thing, though, luv?' I said, peeping up at him.

'Anything, darlin' – anything to see you smile again,' replied Bert, earnestly.

'Promise me you won't wear me flowery apron again. It don't suit you.' I chuckled.

With that Bert grabbed me tighter and, laughing, he bent down to kiss me. 'I promise, Duchess,' was all he said, before his mouth met mine.

CHAPTER 5

As British as Fish and Chips!

1948

'Ow! Get yer 'ands off me, mister!' The sound of a young boy's outraged voice carried across the estate. There was another shout, and a scream, and I bolted to the front door to see what was going on. A harried-looking policeman had hold of one of Tommy Jones's ears, and was dragging him towards the flats in our section of the building. Meanwhile, the boy hollered blue murder.

I leaned over the concrete balcony that ran the length of our floor to get a better view.

'Now, Tommy, if I 'adn't caught you stealin' sweets from old man Harris again, I wouldn't 'ave to drag you 'ome by yer ear,' the local bobby reprimanded the squirming boy loudly. The policeman was a pleasant chap by the name of Gerald, from my home borough of Bermondsey; he looked up and saw me peering from my position on the first floor of the tenements, and raised his eyebrows in a gesture that was all too familiar. 'Got a right one 'ere, Mrs Kemp,' Gerald called up, keeping his tight hold on Tommy as the boy yelled and tried to swipe the officer. 'Might 'ave to take 'im down to the station and teach 'im a lesson 'e won't forget in an 'urry!'

I tutted. Tommy was my neighbour Violet's eldest, a strong-willed boy of ten, who got caught doing something he shouldn't almost daily. Bert, Little Albie and I had only lived on the Redriff Estate in Rotherhithe for a few weeks, but already we knew the comings and goings of most of the people we lived side by side with. After all, there were so many of us living in close proximity that despite the rather grand size of the estate, we all knew each other's business.

It didn't bother me. I'd grown up with seven people to two rooms in squalid tenements near the docksides less than a mile away from where we lived now. Leaving Patsy had been a wrench, but once Bert and I had made the decision, things fell into place. We'd asked at the council offices for housing and, to our delight, we'd been offered this flat. It wasn't big by anyone's standards: the four rooms were poky, but they were ours, and I was away from my pa once again. Of course, I missed Patsy, and I'd hardly seen Ron as he'd been called up for National Service but, as Bert kept telling me, it was time for me to start our married life properly, and what he meant by that was *without looking back*.

My next-door-neighbour Vi had four other children, and another on the way. It seemed she could barely keep track of them all. She never seemed to mind, though. She was a big woman, with thick dark hair, a whiskery chin and a great gulping laugh that shook the rolls of fat that enveloped her. Her family was noisy and always getting into mischief but she was a character, and despite the chaos she brought to my doorstep, we had warmed to each other instantly.

Bert said we could've done worse; on days like this, I wasn't sure. 'I doubt that'd do any good – it'd only upset his father,' I said, shaking my head. Vi's husband John was a slight, wispy man with greying hair and a receding chin. He hovered behind Vi, almost as if he was trying to make himself invisible. He worked at Greenland Dock on the timber wharf, but was out most hours – trying to escape his noisy brood, I shouldn't wonder.

'But it's the third time this week Tommy's been caught trying to steal sweets. 'e 'as to learn it ain't right. I'll 'ave another word with 'is pa tonight an' see if I can't talk some sense into 'im as well.' The policeman disappeared up the stone stairwell below our floor and appeared a few moments later with Tommy still in tow, on the corridor where Violet and I lived in close proximity to each other.

Tommy gave me a great scowl and I laughed in response. 'That won't do you any favours!' I said, laughing. 'Come on now, Tommy, give yer ma and pa a rest from all this nonsense. Why can't you just be a good boy?'

With that Tommy gave me a grimace and stuck out his tongue. I clicked my tongue against my teeth and shook my head. He was a live-wire, that one. I shuddered to think what would become of him in later life.

My own son, Little Albie, was now more than two years old, and he had the sweetest temperament of any little boy I knew. He was shy but a real darling, and I adored him, calling him 'my lovely boy' and singing to him all day as I did my chores. He had been walking for months now. He was a bright boy but reserved in nature, and that suited Bert and me down to the ground. I don't know what I'd have done with a mischievous little devil like Tommy!

I shivered as I stood in my doorway. This winter was tropical compared to the icy blasts we'd endured last year, but standing out on the landing like this was doing no one any good, least of all myself. And with that thought, Little Albie gave a cry from inside the two-bedroom flat we called home. He had woken from his nap, no doubt helped by Tommy's outburst. I nodded to the policeman and hurried back inside, feeling relieved when I could close my own door behind me. It wasn't that I didn't like my neighbours; it was just that sometimes I could've done with a bit of peace.

Little Albie was standing up, gripping the bars of his cot and wailing. 'Shush there, little one, come on now. There's no need to cry,' I crooned. I picked him up and settled him on my left hip. His tears stopped instantly. 'You see, there was no need for any fuss. Now, come on, we need to get your daddy's dinner ready. 'e's been out at work since 4 a.m. this morning an' 'e'll be starvin' when 'e gets in.'

Bert was now working at the Eldorado ice-cream factory in the centre of London. Every morning he got up at 4 a.m. to walk the three miles into the city to start work driving a delivery van; then, every night, once he'd returned the vehicle to the depot, he'd walk the three miles home. We hardly saw him! I had no complaints though, as my old man worked as hard as he could to put food on our table and I loved him for that alone. He always came in with the ravenous hunger of a working man, and I liked having his dinner on the table and piping hot for him on his return so he knew his efforts were appreciated.

But, despite my housewifely concern, there was a part of me that was itching to be out at work again, even though I wanted a larger family. Most of my friends told me I was mad to want to be out working when my Bert could provide for me to stay at home and keep house, but I missed the variety of having a job. I'd loved working at the Peek Frean biscuit factory in Bermondsey as a young woman, then during the war in a munitions factory just outside Coventry. I know I was unusual – most women down our way never questioned their roles as homemakers, but I'd always enjoyed the banter of workplace companionship. I missed the camaraderie and the laughs. I knew being a stay-at-home mother wouldn't be enough for me, but I also knew I would have to choose my words very carefully when I finally plucked up the courage to ask Bert if I could go out and find a job. That's how it was in those days. Being a wife meant asking my husband for permission. And while I knew I was lucky that I had such a decent, solid man, it still stuck in my throat that as a woman I didn't have the freedom to choose for myself.

I sighed, then remembered I was meant to be chopping veg for tonight's hot pot. I always had the cheapest cuts of meat from the local butcher and tonight's supper – a scrag-end of lamb – was no exception. *Some extra money wouldn't go amiss*, I thought to myself, as I clanged the pots onto the cooker and began the next set of chores.

That night, after Bert had eaten and pushed away his plate with a 'Thank you, Duchess, that was delicious,' I introduced the subject of me working. 'Listen, luv, there's something I wanted to ask you ...' I began.

Bert cocked his head to one side, and smiled. 'What is it, Duchess. We can't afford a new coat for Little Albie and that's that. Let's not fight about it now, eh?' He looked tired. There were new lines furrowing his brow. He worked long hours driving boxes of ice-creams around the country then heaving great stacks of them into shops, cafés and restaurants – by the end of the day, I was lucky to get two words out of him. He would eat his dinner, read his paper in the lounge then fall asleep in his chair. Nine times out of ten I'd have to gently wake him so that he could go to bed properly. Yes, he worked like a Trojan for us, and yet there was still never enough money to afford any luxuries. *Providing for us all must be a burden*, I thought. I could see it on his face, though he'd never admit it to me. That thought gave me the courage to continue. A few extra pennies would help ease things a little. It was worth asking. I swallowed and continued: 'Well, you know that during the war I worked in the bombshell factory ... ?'

'Yes, I do know that, 'ilda. Go on,' replied Bert.

'An' you know that before the war I worked packing bis-cuits up at Peek Frean's ...' My voice was a little breathless.

'Yesssssss,' said Bert. 'I think I know where this is goin', but spit it out, girl.' He chuckled though he looked weary.

'Well, I'd like to get meself a little job, just so I can earn us a few extra pennies each week so we could even put some away, maybe have a little holiday somewhere – Southend-on-Sea would be nice. Ma always wanted to go there...' I knew I was rambling but I couldn't stop. 'I've even 'ad a word with Vi next door an' she says she'll take in Little Albie for me for when I'm out at work. She said she doesn't even want payin' – just a few pennies for 'is food an' maybe a bit extra to give 'er 'usband, but she says it's no problem an' she's got so many children that one more an' she won't even notice...' I hadn't even looked at Bert's face to see his reaction. I hadn't realised how much getting a job had meant to me until I'd started to speak.

With a huge great sigh I sat down – I'd been pacing the kitchen as I ranted at Bert, and with a tight smile ended with, 'Please, Bert, will you think about it?'

His laugh was the last thing I thought I'd hear. 'Look, as long as it makes you 'appy, Duchess, then I'm all for it. If it don't work out, you can always stop.' And with that he got up, deposited his plate on the ceramic sink and walked into the lounge.

Blimey, that was easier than I thought it'd be! I thought to myself, blinking as I imagined the new possibilities a nice little job would bring us. A holiday. Maybe even a radiogram! We'd both wanted one since we'd got married as we shared a love of big-band music, but what with Little Albie needing clothes and having to buy second-hand utility furniture for the flat, we hadn't scraped together enough money yet. Oh, and I could buy a new wool coat for Little Albie from the Provy lady! Thank goodness for the Provident Financial! We had no other way of affording to buy clothes for Little Albie and ourselves apart from the doorstep lender: every week I'd give the Provy lady a few pennies to pay off whatever we'd purchased, and every week she'd mark it in her little book and we'd pass the time of day.

At that moment, to my surprise, Vi's head poked around the kitchen door. 'Not disturbin' you, am I? I 'ear you saw Tommy with the policeman today. What's 'e been up to, then? I don't know what I'm goin' to do about 'im, I really don't. An' 'e of course won't tell me nothing about what 'e's been up to . . .' And with that Vi laughed, not looking the slightest bit perturbed about her wayward son.

'I was miles away, Vi,' I replied, smiling. 'I didn't 'ear the door go. Bert let you in, did 'e? I've got nothing much to report. Tommy was caught stealing sweets again, or that's what the bobby said to me.' I got up and started busying myself with cleaning the plates and pots. 'Fancy a cuppa? Sit down as I've got something to tell you an' all. I may be takin' you up on that offer of lookin' after Little Albie!' With that I gave a delighted laugh, and put the kettle onto the heat. Things were working out after all.

Everything did start falling into place. It wasn't even a week later that Enid, who lived three doors down from me, popped by one afternoon to borrow a cup of sugar. She was a haggard-looking woman with dark brown, straight hair tied back in a severe knot off her face. Her eyes were a piercing blue, but she always looked neat and well dressed. She lived with her husband Reginald, but we had little to do with them normally as they kept themselves to themselves. I didn't even know what Reginald did for a living. The couple had no children and I often wondered if that was why she didn't join in with the neighbourhood gossiping and casual friendships of the estate. I never asked her. I didn't want to pry, but my instincts told me she'd wanted children of her own, and either couldn't have them, or her husband hadn't wanted them. That's how it was for some women, and we all had to bear our burdens as best we could. I welcomed her into my kitchen, pleased that she'd wanted to pop by. I felt sorry for her, if truth be known, and wanted her to know she had a friend in me if she ever needed one. It was during our conversation over a cup of tea that she mentioned there was a fish and chip shop not too far away that needed an extra pair of hands. She told me Vi went there when her old man had a good week at work, even though there were chippies closer to our estate. It was a good one, insisted Enid, and a good place to work by all accounts.

Well, I'd never considered working in a chippy before, but the more I thought about it the better it seemed. I wanted to work with people, that I was sure of, and the hours would suit my home life well. Apparently, you didn't start at a chippy till the late afternoon, so at least Little Albie would only have to be with Vi for a couple of hours at the most until Bert got home from work. The more I thought about working in a fish and chip shop, the more I liked the idea. The meal had always reminded me of the good times of my childhood, dodging the bombs that rained down on London, tucking into hot battered fish and fluffy, golden chips before the sirens went off again. I giggled to myself thinking how Bert would manage by himself with our son! *There's no 'arm in popping by one afternoon to 'ave a look at the place*, I thought. *Just to see 'ow friendly the boss is*.

The next day I pulled on my wool coat and my beret, making sure to check myself in the mirror before I left the flat. I hadn't said a word about the fish and chip shop to Bert. I wanted to see the place for myself first. So with Little Albie in his pushchair, I strolled down Redriff Road and onto

Rotherhithe New Road, before turning into the Old Kent Road.

I reached the shop after checking down several wrong streets, and stood outside, feeling nervous all of a sudden. The shop itself had a large glass window with the door sitting to the right of it. There was a sign saying, 'Frying Tonight' and another saying, 'As British as Fish and Chips!' It looked clean and tidy. I peered through the glass and saw gleaming, white-tiled walls and a large counter with jars of pickled onions and vinegar bottles lined up in regimental formation.

It was just past 4 p.m. and despite the fact it was obviously closed, I tried the door. To my surprise it opened and I pushed my way inside with mounting trepidation. At that moment a slim, dark-haired man appeared from the back.

'Can I 'elp you, dearie? I'm not open till five, so there ain't anything I can do if you're 'ungry.' And with that he gave a chuckle. His face was kind-looking, his eyes twinkling as he spoke.

The muscles in my throat relaxed enough so I could get my words out: 'A friend of mine told me you're lookin' for an assistant,' I said, with more than a few flutterings in my stomach.

'I certainly am, an' who wants to know?' The man came to the front of the counter and leaned against it, all the while beaming at me.

'Oh, sorry, me name's 'ilda an' I'm lookin' for a job. I'm a good worker. I'm never late an' I'll work as 'ard as you need me to. I've packed biscuits for Peek Frean's an' worked fillin' shells in a munitions factory during the war ...' My voice trailed off.

'Sounds like I've found me girl, then!' replied the man. He was wearing a white coat with smears of batter on the front. 'Been rushed off me feet these past few weeks. Seems like everyone in the borough wants a fish supper an' a smile from me an' me missus! Me name's Wally, pleased to meet you.' With that he wiped his right hand on his coat and held it out to me.

I grasped it willingly and we shook hands with mutual delight. 'Wally's a funny name, though, ain't it?' I asked, shyly.

'It's me nickname. No one knows me real name, an' that's 'ow I like it,' he replied. 'I named myself after the pickled gherkins for a laugh. After all, I spent me days in 'ere, dishin' em out to 'ungry punters, so why not be named after 'em?'

I laughed at that. The slang word down our way for a gherkin was a 'wally'. I liked him for that fact alone. What a funny chap he was. 'You don't look like you're from these parts, though ... ?' I said, cautiously. Wally had a look of the exotic about him. Possibly Jewish, though I didn't know the polite way to ask him. People weren't so forward about these things so close to the war. We'd all read about the terrible treatment of the Jews in the concentration camps, with people reduced to walking skeletons by the cruelty of the Nazi regime. Somehow, it didn't seem right to ask too closely; you never knew what people might be trying to forget.

No such shadow passed over Wally's face, though. He had dark hair greased back off his face, and his voice carried a slight accent that I couldn't place, even though he spoke with the broad South London twang. But there was definitely something different about him. Strange when he'd chosen to open the most English shop imaginable! 'Oh, don't you go tryin' to find out anything about me, young miss.' He winked, and his teeth flashed white against his olive skin as he smiled.

'Mrs,' I corrected primly.

'I beg your pardon, *Mrs*! I'm a mystery! Even me own

wife, Betty, don't know where I'm from!' He laughed. I couldn't tell if he was joking or not, but I decided it was none of my concern anyway. 'Now, when can you start, an' what will you do with the littl'un?' he said, at once businesslike.

'Golly,' I replied. 'As soon as I've told me 'usband an' saved a few pennies for me neighbour. I could start in a week's time – 'ow about that?' I asked.

'Perfect! Well, I'd better be getting on. Still got the spuds to cut up. Next Friday evenin', 4 p.m. sharp. I'll be seein' yer then.' And with that, Wally disappeared through the back door with a wave as he went.

For a moment I stood in the shop, stunned by my good luck. Then I remembered I hadn't even asked about my wages! I moved over and opened the door. Immediately in front of me was a set of steps that lead down to a dark basement. There was the sound of chopping and a low humming. 'Sorry, Mr ... Wally, I forgot to ask what me wages will be ... ?' I shouted into the gloom.

'You'll get one pound, eight shillings to start with, duckie,' he shouted back up the stairs.

Grinning, I hollered a thank you, and another goodbye. I took one last look around the shop, taking in the rows of ketchup bottles, the pickled eggs, the onions and the infamous gherkins, and I smiled to myself. It suited me down to the ground.

I couldn't wait to get started.

CHAPTER 6

Shocking News

October 1949–1950

The fat sizzled as I surrendered the long, battered fillet gently down into its fizzing, golden depths. I held my breath for a moment. I could never quite trust that my fingers would remain unharmed by their proximity to the molten oil. I knew the coating of the thick batter protected me from burns, but there was always a moment when I gazed down at the slippery, oily lava and hesitated for a brief second, gathering my courage.

'Don't you worry, 'ilda, you won't come to any 'arm with me 'ere to see you're doin' it right.' Wally beamed. He was standing with his back to the counter, leaning against the blue Formica, and grinning his friendly smile. There was a queue of customers, mostly women from the nearby estates, gossiping and cackling as they waited.

'Come on, dearie, my old man'll 'ave me guts for garters if I don't get 'im 'is dinner!' laughed Queenie from the back of the queue, which reached the shop doorway. Queenie was one of Wally's regulars, and a force of nature if ever I'd known one. She had an indomitable East London spirit. She'd raised seven children, and lost three of them as infants. She and her husband Jack lived in the back of a bombed-out tenement in Bermondsey. Jack worked doing odd jobs, finding work wherever he could, which of course meant that money was in short supply. Neither of them ever complained about their lives, though they must have lived in terrible squalor. Often Jack would pop in, have a laugh with Wally and Betty on his way to laying the tar blocks on the roads or to clear out some of the slum properties destroyed during the war. Both Queenie and Jack, and their four surviving children, were always grubby-looking – we always knew when Queenie was in the shop without having to look around because of the smell of unwashed clothing that followed her around. She had black teeth with gaps at the front, and a wicked temper, but was always ready with a wink and a smile. I couldn't help but warm to her.

'All right, luvvie, it's comin'! I really can't force it to fry any faster!' I shouted straight back at her. I was equal to any of the jibes and jokes that came my way many times a day.

The truth was that I loved my job at the fish and chip shop. I'd been working six days a week now for several months, and I knew most of my regulars by name, and many of them by the stories they told about their lives. I knew the wives of wife-beaters, the wives of cheaters and scoundrels, I knew women who remained solidly loyal to their no-good men, I knew mothers of four, five and even six children. Oh, yes, I heard everything in here. There was little else to do except chat and wait to be served, and for many women it was the only real chance they had all day of some company and a sympathetic ear. Today was no different: Queenie was cackling to her neighbour in the queue, seeming not to notice that many of the customers had moved away from her because of her rank perfume. I could hear her voice, jolly and loud with a piercing laugh, as I worked.

I smiled to myself – I'd never met so many characters in all my life as I had working in Wally's Fish and Chip Shop. Yes, I loved my job, even though I worked long hours both at home and in the shop.

Every day except Sunday, I'd be up at 4 a.m. to give Bert his breakfast before he left for work. I'd snatch a couple of hours' sleep once he'd gone, then at 6.30 a.m. Little Albie would call from his cot. I'd give him his breakfast and spend the rest of the day doing my chores at home: sweeping, cooking, cleaning and shopping for that evening's dinner. I'd prepare the dinner – normally a cheap cut of meat, and two veg – for Bert to eat when he got in. Then just after 3 p.m. I'd gather all of four-year-old Little Albie's bits: his cuddly toy which was a little horse with one of its legs missing, his milk and his pyjamas, and take him next door to Vi's. Then I'd be back to the flat, where I'd pull my coat and hat on, then half-run all the way to the shop. I'd be out of breath by the time I burst through the door, apologising for being in such a tizzy. I should've been exhausted, but the work made me feel more alive than ever I did at home all day, staring at my own four walls.

When I arrived, Wally's short, plump wife Betty would throw me my white coat – Wally liked us to look clean and smart for the customers – and I'd roll up my sleeves to begin my six-hour shift. Betty, who had dark hair like her husband and that same indefinable accent, would go ahead of me to put the kettle on downstairs in the basement, then I too would make my way down the back stairs to the lower ground floor. It was in sharp contrast to the clean, white–tiled shop: the walls were pitted and craggy, with chunks of masonry littering the stone floor. It stank of damp and decay as water seeped down the walls. There were two huge bins overflowing with discarded fish heads and potato peelings. I held my nose each time I went down there, just for a second, to acclimatise to the stench of rotting fish and the debris from the busy shop. I cleared it out each afternoon religiously, of course, but the smell lingered – it got into my hair and clothes, which was the only part of my job that Bert objected to!

In the far corner was the chipper, a mechanical device that cut the potatoes into chips. Thank goodness I only had to peel the spuds, which were delivered in large sacks, and then feed them into the blades. They were then stored in vast vats of water until it was time to carry them up the stairs using smaller buckets, before being emptied into the fryers. There was also a crisp-maker that cut the potatoes into even thinner slices before deep frying them in beef dripping. The customers went mad for those crisps, and we nearly always ran out.

The day passed in a blur of activity, and by the time I stepped over my doorstep, I was ready to drop. 'It's only me, luv. I'll just get me coat off an' I'll be with you,' I called cheerily into the flat. There was no sound from any of the rooms and the lights were off. *Bert must have gone to bed already*, I thought to myself, but the first niggles of unease registered in my mind. Bert never turned off the lights before I got in, as he knew I didn't much like coming home in the dark, and he always sat up waiting for me in his chair, whether asleep or awake!

I snapped on the light in the lounge. No one was there. I felt a tiny flicker of fear. 'Where are you, luv? It ain't like you to keep the lights off,' I said, my voice slightly less sure than ten seconds ago, the possibility that something was wrong hovering just out of my mind's eye.

I opened the kitchen door, and drew in a sharp intake of breath. There was a dark figure hunched over the table. I stepped back, my hand fumbling for the door. Was this an intruder in my home?

'It's me, 'ilda. No need to panic,' came Bert's voice. It was thin, low. The shape moved, rearranged itself on the chair. The contours of his face finally stared back at me as his head lifted up slowly.

'My God, what is it, Bert? Tell me – you're frightening me,

what's wrong?' I was frozen to the spot. My eyes had become accustomed to the gloom. I could see Bert move his head back down into his hands in a position so wretched, my heart almost stopped. I moved round to him, trying not to startle him. I knelt next to his body and I could hear his muffled sobs. 'Bert, what is it? Is Little Albie alright? Please tell me it ain't my boy?' Suddenly I was seized with a violent panic. My hands shook and I waited to hear what it was that had reduced my brave soldier husband into a man clearly in the pit of despair.

'It ain't Little Albie. It's my pa.' Bert's voice was flat. 'Pop killed himself today.'

'Pop killed himself?' His words didn't register. It was hard to take in. ' 'e can't 'ave done! Who's been tellin' you lies like that? 'e luvs you an' 'is grandson – don't believe that for a minute.' I grasped Bert's hands as I spoke but he turned to me.

His face was twisted in pain, his eyes wet. 'Sorry, luv, but it's true. Ma came 'ere herself earlier. She's with me brother Frank an' sister Dorothy now. I couldn't bear to go over there. I don't think I can ever go 'ome again if Pop isn't there.'

I gasped in shock. It *was* real. This wasn't some stupid tittle-tattle gone wrong. If Dolly had been here then Pop really had died. 'What 'appened? Why? What did 'e do?' I had to ask. I had a million questions now all fighting for space in my mind.

' 'e 'ung 'imself with his belt at work. He left no note as far as I know, but 'e's dead. My pa is *dead*, 'ilda. What am I going to do?'

I stared back at Bert, the horror of the truth sinking in. I shook my head. There was nothing we could do. Nothing at all. He sunk his head into my arms, and we stayed like that for a long time.

Later, when Bert finally let me walk him to bed, he told me about Pop's father and grandfather. Pop's pa, Richard Henry Kemp, had been a violent, unstable man who'd slashed his wife, the mother of his eight children, with a boot knife to the face. They'd been married 25 years the night he struck her, after she'd fled from their squalid tenement in fear of her life. He served five years' penal servitude, dying in prison a broken man and leaving his wife to support their children, alone and penniless. But that wasn't the worst of it. Pop's grandfather, also named Richard Henry, had committed suicide at the age of 54. He'd left ten dependent children and a destitute, heartbroken wife. It seemed history was repeating itself. Pop lasted till he was 55, but the same depression and despondency that overcame his father and grandfather before him had settled on him too. There was no other obvious reason. He was a working man and had raised three children into adulthood, yet still he'd decided to take the same, tragic decision.

The next morning I watched Bert as he left the flat to walk to work. 'Don't go, luv. Stay 'ere, you're not up to it,' I pleaded with him. He needed time to grieve properly. We'd had a wretched night – we'd hardly slept a wink, but he insisted on going to work. Bert said he couldn't let people down; the subtext being, like his father had . . .

I felt a lump in my throat as I watched him go.

Pop might only have been my father-in-law but he was the closest thing to a 'real' father I'd ever known. I'd loved him with fierce pride. Him and his wife, Dolly, had loved me like a daughter. And now he was gone. Why did all the good ones die? Why didn't the bad ones, like my pa, go first, when they deserved it the most?

Pop had always been melancholy, apparently. Bert had explained that he'd sustained eye injuries from shrapnel during the First World War when he'd joined up as a soldier aged 19. He'd lost an eye and suffered from years of depression as a result. His working life had been limited due to his poor education, and the need to help support his mother and siblings, and so he'd been forced to take low-paid work as a delivery man at the local tallow (candle) works as soon as he was old enough.

It was hard to believe he had gone. And to have done it himself. I couldn't guess at the darkness he must have felt inside to be able to do such a terrible, terrible thing.

The days and weeks following Pop's death in October 1949 seemed weighted and slow. Pop was buried with little ceremony on a cold, wintry day. Dolly, who was once such a solid, dependable lady, seemed smaller than her bulky frame – shrunken somehow. Her face was drawn with grief, her eyes red from the tears she must have shed. It was such a sorrowful event. Stamping our feet on the cold ground, I wondered if any of us would feel warm again.

Bert and I both went to work, we did our jobs, and looked after Little Albie as best we could, and the cold winter months stretched on. There seemed little in our lives to give us any hope. Christmas came and went. We celebrated with a small capon and a stocking for Little Albie with an orange, some nuts, a few coins and a teddy bear inside it. We spent it alone, just the three of us. Bert couldn't bear going over to Dolly's, so I took Little Albie over there on Boxing Day. There was little in the way of Christmas cheer in Bow either, and I was grateful when the season was over and we could get on with living with some kind of normality.

I popped in to see Dolly every Sunday from then onwards, taking Albie to try to bring some sunshine back into her life, and eventually Bert too, as I recognised she needed her children around her. She seemed to have aged ten years. Her eyes looked permanently red from lack of sleep but she bustled around much as she'd always done, keeping busy and making the best of things. All three of her children supported her with gifts of money and food: Frank, Dorothy and my Bert. They did what they could to ease the practicalities of her widowhood.

I hid my feelings as I was too worried about Bert sinking under the weight of his own. There was no time for me to grieve: I had the baby to look after and my husband to feed and keep going, though God knows I spent many a night shedding silent tears into my pillow for that lovely man. I don't suppose anyone at the chippy would've guessed at the grief I felt for Pop, and for my Bert's loss. In a way I needed the escape from reality that working in the fish and chip shop gave me.

'That fish ready yet? I'm starvin', 'ilda, don't make me wait for it!' joked Old Man Bill. His feeble voice cut through my musing. I was brooding about Pop again, though it had been a couple of months since he'd gone.

Bill was a true East London character. He must have been in his eighties and he lived alone, but each evening at 5.15 p.m. sharp he'd arrive at the shop. Where he got his money from I'll never know, but each day he ordered the same thing: a meat pie and chips with a pickled onion. Every evening I'd make a fuss of him, suspecting he was lonely and needed a warm welcome and a bit of companionship, however brief. Also, there was something about him that reminded me of Pop, his sweetness perhaps, his way of being modest.

'Don't you worry, Bill, luvvie. I ain't goin' to deprive you of your dinner. I'm just makin' sure it's nice an' 'ot for you.

Now, 'ow d'you want it? Same as usual?' I winked at him. He was a dear man. He wore the same large brown over-coat come rain or shine. I suspected that he probably hadn't washed his shirt for weeks: he wore the same one every day, and I could see a rim of grime around the collar. He'd never told me anything about himself, except that he'd fought in the Boer War at the end of the last century. He'd been mar-ried but he never spoke about his wife and I presumed her long dead. He didn't appear to have any children either, so the shop was a life-line for him.

'Same as usual. You are good to me, you know, 'ilda. Are you married? If not, I'll 'ave you!' He spoke with a tremble to his voice. It was gravelly and he got stuck on some words, so I waited patiently for him to finish this, his favourite joke of all: that he'd take me for his next wife.

'Sorry, Bill my luv, but I'm spoken for, and my Bert won't take gladly to 'avin' competition!' I replied as I usually did, giving him a smile and wrapping his dinner in the previous day's newspaper. I always made sure he got the sport section so he'd have something to read after he'd eaten. 'Off you go, Bill. Don't go getting' into any trouble now!' I called as he ambled out of the doorway, clutching his warm parcel of food.

I sighed. A friendly smile and a warm dinner – it wasn't much to send the man off with, but it was all I had to offer. With that, the next customer reeled off her order, and I had to jump to it. Couldn't keep people waiting. Suddenly, I felt my stomach lurch. *Gawd, I'm goin' to be sick!* As soon as the thought struck me, I dropped the vinegar bottle I'd used to coat Old Bill's chips with and dived out the back. Taking the stairs two at a time, I raced out towards the lavvy in the filthy yard. Luckily no one was about so I banged the door open and emptied the contents of my stomach into the festering toilet bowl. *Crikey, I must've eaten something strange . . .* I couldn't think what, though. *Maybe the butter was off, but it didn't taste odd.* The thoughts vanished as I heaved yet again.

''ilda, are you alright? Wally's 'avin' kittens upstairs. 'e's worried about you,' came Betty's voice. She'd followed me outside and was standing with her back to the lavvy door to give me a little privacy.

'Don't worry about me. I'll be good as new. Tell Wally I'll be up in a second. Just came over all peculiar . . .' I said, hoping I sounded brighter than I felt. My stomach was still churning.

'Take your time, dearie, there's no rush,' said Betty. 'I'll tell Wally 'e'll 'ave to pull 'is finger out an' get workin' himself.'

I made a choking sound that I hoped passed for a laugh, then I heard her footsteps recede back towards the basement. My forehead felt cold and clammy. I leaned back against the upright wall of the latrine and closed my eyes for a second. *Just a gippy tummy*, I thought to myself, *Come on now, 'ilda, this ain't like you. Get yerself back up them stairs an' put a smile on yer face*. With that, I marched back into the shop, washed my hands thoroughly and smoothed down my white coat.

Back upstairs, the queue was now snaking out of the shop but Wally looked a picture of concern. 'I'm fine, Wally, nothing to worry about. Now, who's next?' I beamed at another of the women I recognised from my estate. 'What's that, luvvie? Two cod an' three chips? Comin' up!' And I was back in the flow, all thoughts of sickness forgotten.

Later that evening, while Wally counted the takings and I washed the floor, Betty sat watching me, sitting propped up next to the counter, her elbow resting on the steel surface. 'You look tired, dearie. Why don't you finish for tonight? Go on, go 'ome. We'll finish this in the mornin'.'

I should have refused and carried on with my chores, after

all it was what I was being paid for, but I suddenly realised I felt exhausted. Gratefully, I smiled up at Betty. 'Sorry, I don't know what's got into me,' I said, trying to stifle a yawn. 'I'll be tip top tomorrow, you'll see. I'll come in a bit earlier to make up the time.' And with that, I pulled on my coat and picked up my purse and beret and waved goodbye.

The walk back home seemed to take for ever. And when I got in, I found I couldn't eat the leftovers from the dinner I'd made Bert earlier. I didn't have the stomach for it. Bert was fast asleep in his chair, so I roused him and helped him into bed. I made myself a cocoa but had barely sipped it before putting it down on the bedside table and falling into a deep, dreamless sleep. The next day the same happened: one minute I was deep in conversation with my friend, Mavis, as I drained a large cod fillet of its molten lard coating, then the next minute I suddenly found myself face down in the lavvy again, being as sick as a dog. *Must be a bug*, I thought, wiping dribble from my chin. But I didn't feel unwell, except for being a bit more tired than usual. There was nothing going round either.

Then the thought hit me like a lightning bolt. I couldn't remember the last time I'd had my period! Since Little Albie's birth, I hadn't exactly been regular, so I had stopped counting the days between each time of the month. How could I have been so stupid? It was obvious what was going on: I was pregnant again!

Feeling slightly dazed, and more than a little anxious, I did a rough calculation in my head. I could be three months' gone – no wonder I'd been putting on weight recently. I'd thought it was the leftover chips I'd had a habit of snaffling when Wally was feeling generous! 'Oh, my giddy aunt, what timing,' I said to nobody in particular. I hadn't even felt this new child kick and I was already worrying about how we'd manage to feed and clothe it, and whether having a baby so soon after Pop's death would affect Bert and me.

What if he didn't want it?

Bert and I had always dreamed of having three children, but things had changed: life with all its complexities and tragedies had impinged on our romantic dreams, blowing them away as if they'd been made of smoke trails. Unbeknown to Bert, I'd been skipping our evening meal to make sure we had enough food for him and Little Albie, who was a growing, hungry boy of three. I hadn't wanted him to know, especially in light of his father's death. So the thought of bringing another baby into the world was alarming rather than joyful. How would we manage even with two incomes? And worse, how would Bert feel about a baby, especially now?

There was a queue of people waiting to use the lavvy this time, and someone chose that moment to bang on the wooden door. ''urry up will you? I ain't got all day!' barked the voice. It belonged to another shop owner further down the grotty, huddled row of tenements. We all had to use the same outdoor loo, and we were used to queuing in all weathers.

'Sorry, I'll be out in a jiffy,' I replied. *Come on, 'ilda, pull yerself together*, I told myself. *It ain't the end of the world. We'll be alright, you'll see, now get yerself up them stairs an' get back to work*. With that I said a harried sorry as I creaked open the lavvy door. It was falling off its hinges and wouldn't be long before it fell off completely.

Back in the shop, Betty gave me a long look. I smiled at her but she saw something in my eyes. 'Come on, 'ilda, Wally can manage up 'ere, can't you luv?' Betty nodded over to her husband. There were times you didn't argue with Betty and this was one of them. 'There aren't too many punters in this evenin', so we'd be better off peelin' some spuds for tomorrow's weekend rush.' I nodded, knowing this was an excuse and Betty was taking me to have a private word. Maybe she was fed up of me dashing out to be sick and was firing me. I wouldn't blame her. She wouldn't want the customers thinking their chips were making me ill.

Following meekly behind her plump frame as she waddled down the steep staircase to the basement, I rehearsed in my mind how I would react at being told to leave. I hoped I wouldn't cry.

Betty pulled out a chair at the rickety wooden table and told me to sit. She went over to the range at the back of the basement and put on the copper kettle. The potatoes were in two great sacks and Betty, with surprising strength, pulled one towards me.

'I'll do that for you, Betty, I ain't sick!' I leapt up.

Betty placed a hand on my arm. 'Oh no you won't, an' I know you ain't sick, you're pregnant, or didn't you know it!' she cackled. ' 'ere, take these spuds an' get crackin' – we need at least a hundred peeled tonight so we're ahead for tomorrow.'

I grabbed the knife that lay on the tabletop and started to work, moving the bucket for the peelings closer to my feet. I'd still said nothing. The news was so recent to me that I didn't know what to say.

'So, why the long face, 'ilda, dearie? A baby is a cause for celebration, ain't it? Are you an' Bert not gettin' on?' Betty peered over the table at me, her kind face cocked to one side.

I paused before I answered. I hadn't told Betty or Wally about Pop's death. I didn't want anyone gossiping about it being suicide, even though I knew them like family. 'Bert's father died recently. It was sudden, a great shock. An' we ain't got much money, truth be told. I just don't know 'ow 'e'll feel about 'avin' another mouth to feed, especially so soon after 'is father, if you know what I mean . . .' Sighing, I stopped talking. A single tear dripped onto the potato I was hacking away at.

'That spud ain't done you any 'arm! Look at the mess you've made of it. Stop that luvvie, or I'll 'ave nothing left to fry up!' Gently, Betty took it from my hand and I picked up another to start peeling it. 'Now, why didn't you tell me about your father-in-law? You poor girl. You've been copin' with that all by yerself, an' now there's a baby to think about an' all.' Betty had summed up the situation neatly. She was so kind, it broke the dam and I burst into tears. She scrutinised my face a moment longer, placing her hand on my arm in a quiet gesture of sympathy. 'Drink up your tea. I'm just goin' to talk to Wally about something,' she said, a gleam in her eye.

Lost in my misery, I nodded, sipping the hot tea to which Betty had liberally added sugar. Five minutes later she reappeared, huffing a little with the effort of going up and down the stairs. 'It's all settled. Your wages will go up by eight shillin's a week, starting tonight. Now, I know it ain't much, but it's a start, an' at least you'll be able to put your mind at rest a little.' She patted my hand as she spoke.

'I don't know 'ow to thank you, Betty. You an' Wally are so good to me, whatever did I do to deserve you?' And with that I enveloped her in a hug.

Her skin was scented with the hot smell of the lard, the tang of the vinegar and the frying fish. My tears soaked into the white coat she wore, her warm plump frame holding me till I gathered myself.

'Now, it's nothing more than you deserve, luvvie. You finish yer tea an' take as long as you need before you come back upstairs. All right, dearie?' Betty smiled at me kindly.

I told Bert we were having another baby as soon as I got home. I didn't want to wait, I was too nervous of his reaction.

He gave me the first, weak smile I'd seen since his pa had died. 'What were you worryin' about? That's the best news I've 'eard since, well since . . .' Bert didn't finish his sentence. I held his hands, sitting facing him over our small kitchen table. 'If it's a boy, I want to call him Ernest, after my pa, Albert Ernest. We've already got an Albie. I'd like that, 'ilda. What d'you say?'

'My ma always said, "One out, one in",' I replied, meaning that there was always a new baby following a death. 'She said it was God's way of makin' it all even. If our baby is meant to follow on from Pop then I couldn't be more proud.' A new life from old. A man dies, a baby is born. Simple and perfect in its way. We held hands. The night drew in, and we eventually made our way to bed. Tomorrow was another day, and even at this, the darkest hour of the night, it felt like there was a glimmer of hope, just out of reach.

CHAPTER 7

Hard Times

Summer 1950

Something slammed. I took a moment to realise it was the sound of my own front door. I rushed towards it as fast as my eight-month-pregnant body allowed me. There was Bert, kicking off his boots in the narrow hallway. 'You're back early. Are you ill?' was all I managed to say. Bert had never missed a day's work since I'd known him. I'd seen him struggle in to his delivery depot with influenza when he'd worked for Eldorado ice-cream up town.

Bert had moved to delivering meat at Smithfield Market only a couple of weeks earlier with the promise of a better wage for the same, long hours. Yet something must be up if he had left his deliveries this early in the day. I scanned his face. It was unreadable. His expression looked closed-down, defensive almost. I reached for his forehead. It was cool. No fever. I was puzzled.

'Stop fussin', will you, woman? Let me get inside an' you'll know everythin',' barked Bert at me. His voice was hostile.

I stepped back as if he'd hit me. The shock of his harsh words rendered me silent. Not knowing what to say or do, I followed Bert into the lounge. With a heavy gait, he sat down in his chair as I hovered uncertainly by the doorway. It was just gone noon. Little Albie was still asleep with his morning nap, and I had been busy making a pie for our dinner.

I wiped my hands, which were white with flour, smoothing them down the folds of my apron. I stayed quiet, sensing that anything I had to say would only inflame the situation. Bert seemed like a stranger, spiky and cold.

He dragged his hands through his hair. The Brylcreem in it picked up the light and glistened with its sticky residue. 'Listen, 'ilda, I didn't mean to shout. I'm sorry. I've got a bit of bad news,' was all he said, raising his eyes to meet mine.

'What is it, Bert?' I said, simply. My heart was thudding in my chest. Something was wrong, very wrong. Already I was running through a list of emergencies in my mind: was it Dolly? Was she ill? Was she dead, just like Pop? Or had Bert met someone else? Was he leaving me and the babies? I clutched at my throat, suddenly feeling faint.

Bert seemed oblivious to my fright, contained in his own distress. He slid his eyes away from mine. He looked shifty, uncertain. 'This is so 'ard to tell you, 'ilda,' he said.

He hadn't called me 'Duchess', I noticed. Maybe he had another lady to call that now. Maybe I was just plain ' 'ilda' after all. 'Spit it out, Bert, whatever it is, I can't stand this another moment longer.' My voice was surprisingly firm. The words hung in the air between us.

With an intake of breath, Bert opened his mouth. 'The meat delivery vans are on strike. There ain't no work today, nor tomorrow.'

I let out a sigh. No one had died. He wasn't leaving me. I almost giggled with relief. 'That's alright, Bert. The union men won't let us starve, will they? I expect it'll be over before we know it, an' life'll get back to normal, you'll see,' I said, almost light-heartedly. I made to leave the lounge and get back to my cooking but Bert's voice cut into my departure.

'No, you don't understand, 'ilda. It ain't an official strike. It ain't the union.' Bert's voice was strangled. He was a paid-up member of the Transport and General Workers' Union, and was proud of it.

I tipped my head to one side. 'What d'you mean, it ain't the union? 'ow does it affect us then?' Suddenly my certainty vanished. Bert still looked odd. I didn't like the way this was going. Surely the drivers would settle whatever dispute they'd started and get back to work? They had to, didn't they?

'It means that there'll be no pay while the strike lasts. It ain't a union strike an' so they won't be payin' strike wages. It means that until it's over, we ain't got my wages to keep us goin'.'

At last I understood his expression, because I finally felt the gut-wrenching fear he'd carried home with him: the fear of having no money. No money meant no food on the table. It meant no roof over our heads. No money meant destitution, plain and simple. 'Well, at least we've got the chip shop,' I said weakly, trying to brighten our moods.

'Not for much longer, 'ilda.' Bert glanced at my round belly as he spoke.

I placed my hands protectively over the bump, nodding in response. No money, and me off with the new baby in a month's time. I didn't even know if Wally wanted me back working there once I'd had the child. I hadn't wanted to ask him in case I didn't like the answer. Suddenly things looked very bleak indeed. 'Oh, Gawd, Bert, what will we do?' I said, gripping the handle of the door as if it could hold me up.

'I don't know, Duchess. I wish I did, but I don't.' And with that, Bert looked up at me, his face craggy with worry.

The next day at Wally's I drew up all my courage and asked to have a word with him before the shop opened. I was still walking the distance to the shop, and standing all evening, serving customers, trying not to let my tiredness show.

' 'ave yerself a seat, luvvie,' he said, as he guided me

towards a kitchen chair. 'You shouldn't be standin' about like that in your condition.'

'Don't worry about me, Wally, I'm right as rain, never felt better. But it was my condition I wanted to talk to you about,' I said. At that point I felt the baby kick hard against my swollen stomach. *My nerves must be contagious*, I thought, *even the baby's pickin' up on 'em*. 'Well, you know I'm 'avin' this baby in a month's time ...' I started.

I was interrupted by Wally's laugh. 'Yes, I 'ad noticed, 'ilda!'

'Well, I don't know 'ow to say this, but will you keep me on after it's born?' I blurted, not knowing why I felt so scared asking. I guess it was because I loved my job and I loved my bosses. I loved the friendly chatter day in, day out, with my customers. I loved the smell of the frying chips as they settled into the molten embrace of the beef dripping. I loved the tang of the vinegar and the salty smell of the fish just before it succumbed to the oily depths of the fryers Wally was so proud of owning. Some days I would sing as I worked. The customers loved that. I was always ready for a laugh and a joke as well; no one could call ever me stuffy. I'd even become friends with some of them: Mavis would pop in when her drunkard husband, Alfie, wasn't working and we'd share a hot cuppa and a chat, despite the fact she couldn't afford the chips for her dinner. I'd also taken a shine to another of my customers, a woman about the same age as me, called Doris. In looks she was as different from me as it was possible to be, being blonde and slim, but we shared a sense of humour. Then there was Phyllis, who had married her soldier sweetheart, Leonard, when he returned from the war; like me, they had a young son with another baby on the way. Leonard often worked away as he was a driver for a food company and so Phyllis would drop in if we were quiet and we'd enjoy a friendly chat over the counter. She seemed unlike my usual customers. She didn't laugh and joke. She was reserved and quite shy.

I knew I'd most probably lose contact with her, Mavis and my other friends made through the shop if I ever left so the thought of not working at Wally's was almost unthinkable, even more so given the situation at home with Bert's job. 'You will want me back, won't you, Wally?' I could hear a note of pleading in my voice.

Wally looked over at me. His white coat was stained with greasy finger prints, his hair slicked back with the hair cream all the men used. He paused for a second, the fish he had just beheaded lying slack and shiny in his hand. ' 'course we don't want you to go, 'ilda! Ain't it obvious? Bleedin' 'ell, I've got a simpleton for an assistant!' He wiped his hand, smearing his coat still further as his face crinkled into a smile. 'I won't lie an' say it won't be a bother not 'avin' you 'ere while you're nursin' the littl'un but we'll manage. We managed before you came, you know.' He laughed as he turned to carry on filleting the next fish on the table. Next to him on the wooden surface, which stank permanently of fish, was a pile of glistening fillets, splayed open to reveal the white flesh inside them. Disembowelled and ready to be dragged through the thick, viscous batter.

Relief flooded through me. 'I shan't need too long with the baby at 'ome. A couple of months at most, just till we get ourselves settled an' in a routine,' I said, slightly too eagerly.

'Now, why would you want to come back to the shop, back to work so quickly? What ain't you tellin' me, 'ilda? I've got a nose for these things an' I think you're 'idin' something.' Wally spoke as he worked, barely glancing round in my direction.

I was peeling spuds and plopping the bare round potatoes

into a vat of water to keep until I put them through the chipper. I sighed. 'Bert ain't workin'. 'e left 'is job at Eldorado to work at the meat market in Smithfield. 'e's only been there a couple of weeks but there's been a problem with the drivers. They don't think they're gettin' paid enough for their rounds so they've walked out on strike. An unofficial strike.' I knew I sounded gloomy but what else could I say? 'Until those bloody drivers sort out their pay, my Bert can't go back. I know 'e's one of them, but 'e'd rather be out earnin' a day's pay than worryin' about goin' on strike like the rest of them. 'e'll be an outcast if 'e tries to work an' breaks the strike, so it's not worth it, but it means we don't 'ave 'is wage comin' in an' I 'onestly don't know 'ow we'll manage.' A great teardrop hit the work surface. I rubbed my eyes like a small child. Suddenly, I felt very vulnerable, and immensely tired.

'I'm sorry to 'ear that, 'ilda. I don't know what to say. You can work 'ere any time. We'll keep yer place open for you. You come back as soon as you want. Life ain't easy for you, 'ilda, I'll grant you that.' And with that, Wally came over and gave me an awkward hug.

It was unusual for a man to hug a woman he wasn't married to in those days. It wasn't the done thing. Yet I knew deep in my heart that Wally meant well and was doing it as an act of almost fatherly love. The day I walked into that chip shop and asked for work was my lucky day.

'Go on, you old fool,' I said, pushing my boss away lightly. 'You'll make me cry if you do that. We'll cope some 'ow. Bert could always look for another job, an' as you say, I can come back 'ere just as soon as the baby will take a bottle. We'll manage,' I said, as if I really meant it.

Back at the flat later, after fighting my way through the nappies and pants that constituted a large batch of Vi's washing strung out on the landing, I told Bert what Wally had said. ' 'e's a diamond, that man, a real diamond,' was all Bert said, his voice sounded tight with emotion, as we sat eating the leftover chips that Wally had insisted I take home for our late supper. I kept a few over for the next day, even though they'd be soggy by then, to bulk out the beef stew I'd prepared. I had a cabbage I could add to it as well to make it last longer, so we'd be alright for a couple of days and by then, who knew, the strike might be over.

It wasn't.

The situation got worse. The army was called in to Smith-field Market to pack up and distribute the meat deliveries that lay untouched by the drivers. Bert grew increasingly restless. He set out each morning to go to the market to see if things had been resolved. Each day he was turned away. I began to dread the sound of the door opening just after 8 a.m. with Bert coming back to spend the day pacing around the living room. There was one small silver-lining: as Bert was home we didn't need to pay Vi to look after Little Albie but even so, once we'd paid that week's rent, our food money was running perilously low. I eked out what we had as best I could, but even each night's leftover chips weren't enough to bulk out our dinners.

Three weeks later, it happened. I opened the cupboard in our small kitchen and was greeted by nothing but empty space. We'd finally run out of food. There was nothing left.

I'd known this day was coming, I'd watched as our supplies dwindled, all the while thinking, *Somethin' will come up*. But nothing had. I was too proud to tell my neighbours. They had worries of their own – it wasn't like any of us were rich around here. And my wages barely covered the rent on our small flat, so there was little or nothing left each week. I sat down at the kitchen table and wept, remembering all those times as a child when I'd run in from school and look up at the shelf in the kitchen to check if there was bread. On the days there was I could relax, as I knew there was supper waiting for me; but more often than not there was nothing, except the gnawing hunger in my belly, and the knowledge there was no food to satisfy it. And here I was again. Sitting in my own kitchen this time, with nothing to feed my child. Bread rationing had ended nigh on two years ago but that meant little if, like me, you had nothing in your purse to buy a loaf with.

Suddenly there was a knock at the door. It wasn't Bert, as it was only just gone 7 a.m. and he wouldn't have left the market to return, empty-handed again, this early. If I hadn't have been so upset, I might have wondered who would knock on my door at this time of the morning. And I'd have noticed that no one round here ever knocked: we poked our heads around each others' doors and shouted, 'Cooeee, luv, it's only me!' or something similar. We were never formal with one another. It was just the way things were around our way.

I went to the door, wiping the tears away. I'd shed so many recently. First Pop dying, and now the strike. It was as much as I could bear. I opened the door and looked out. At first glance there was no one there. I peered down the landing. Again, no one. *How strange*, I thought to myself. Then I spotted the parcel on my doorstep. It was a small package wrapped in newspaper. Puzzled, I bent over as far as my bulky frame would allow, and picked it up. I shuffled back into the kitchen. *What could it be?* I wondered, unsure whether it was some kind of practical joke. I don't think I could have born it if it was.

I was reluctant to open it but my curiosity got the better of me. Slowly, as if I was opening a bomb, I drew off the paper wrapping. Inside was a loaf of bread, a tin of sardines and some Bovril. Stunned, I looked at the contents, my heart bursting with emotion. I was taken instantly back to my 12-year-old-self in Spa Road when the same thing happened.

I'd gone to the doorstep and found a package. Ma opened it and found inside it some bread and a few scrubby-looking potatoes. Everyone in our street had known our drunk of a dad was in and out of work and that times were so hard we didn't eat for days. It was at those moments the kindness of our neighbours and friends pulled us through. Several times over the years we were rescued from hunger by such packages left on our doorstep. No one ever came forward and claimed the kindness as their own. But someone was looking out for us. And it seemed that the East London spirit had followed us here, a mile or so up the road in Rotherhithe. We would eat today, thanks to one of my neighbours.

Suddenly the tears came thick and fast; I couldn't stop them. Why was it that kindness could break a person down faster than cruelty? I said a silent prayer of thanks to my secret saviour. I cut a thin slice of bread for myself and put the kettle on the cooker. We still had half a pound of tea, thank goodness, and sugar. We had enough to keep us going for another day, and for that I was immeasurably grateful.

Later that day, as I took Little Albie out for a walk in his pram, I smiled and chatted to everyone I saw, hoping that the anonymous donor was among them. I talked to Mother Edna, a widow who lived on the floor below us. She was a tiny little thing, all sharp points and skinny as anything. Her teeth were almost entirely rotten and she talked with a gummy inflection. She never let life get her down, though. She was a tough old bird – she'd had to be. Her husband had died in the First World War and she lived on a meagre widow's allowance. She'd never married again, or had children, and for that I pitied her. So many women had been left to live life as a spinster when their menfolk were culled during the wars, living on the fringes of society in almost penniless existence. I knew that I was one of the lucky ones having a soldier sweetheart who came home and married me. So many others didn't get that chance. I made sure I spent longer with Edna, and with Vi and several of the other housewives whose names I knew but hadn't had the time or opportunity to get to know better, until then.

When I returned home, Bert was in a fluster, telling me I'd be late for work but I didn't regret my time spent with the women of my estate. Wally could wait for once, but my thanks to my neighbours needed to be said, albeit anonymously.

It was while I was laughing and blushing at a particularly rude joke told with ribald good humour by Violet that I felt the first tightening sensation across my tummy. I bent over, with a soft 'Oh!' and grabbed the counter for support.

'Look 'ere, Vi, you've gone an' sent 'ilda into labour!' joked Wally.

'You alright, 'ilda, luv?' said Betty, in her practical way. She'd ignored the joke and was concentrating on me as I pushed myself back up.

'Nothing to worry about. Just the baby givin' me a kick,' I replied.

Violet raised her eyebrows at that but, unusually, had kept her silence. If she knew the truth she didn't let on, to her credit.

I wasn't sure why I'd lied. I didn't want a fuss, or to put anyone out, so I pretended the baby was lively when really I knew it was the signs of labour starting. Later, I walked home slowly. Wally and Betty had insisted on walking with me in case the baby was coming, but I laughed off their suggestions, saying I needed the exercise. Betty had given me a knowing look. Despite the fact she'd never had a child herself, she knew I wasn't being entirely truthful. But I was firm in walking alone. Babies took hours to come – I just needed to get back to Bert and I'd be happy.

Every now and then I stopped and held on to whatever was handy: a set of railings, a lamppost, until the contraction had passed. They were still far enough apart not to worry. As long as I got home, Bert would look after me. It took me nearly an hour to get back.

Bert was frantic with worry, and had been on the verge of putting Little Albie into his pram and coming to find me.

'Don't worry, it's just the baby comin'.' I placed my arm on Bert's shoulder to reassure him, but it had exactly the opposite effect.

'The baby! The baby's comin'! Oh, Gawd, 'ilda, you just sit there an' I'll get John to go an' call for an ambulance. Don't you worry, it's all in 'and!' Bert flung open the door and disappeared into next door's flat.

I sighed. Men always got so terrified when it came to babies. I was nervous, of course I was. Every birth went differently. But my ma had birthed five babies with no problems, and my Little Albie had come out into the world with no more than the usual fuss and pain, so I was as relaxed as a woman could be before the ordeal of labour.

I let Bert take my hand and walk me gingerly down the stairs to the estate entrance where the ambulance was waiting to take me to the hospital. Violet and John had accompanied us too, as if we needed the extra help. Like I said, you didn't get much privacy around the estate, but I knew it was kindly meant. Little Albie was deposited with Vi.

An hour or so later, Bert left the hospital to go back and look after him. I sent him off, saying the baby would be hours yet and to come back after he'd had a sleep. Things didn't go quite to plan, though. My second little one had decided she would make her appearance rather faster than her older brother. Within an hour of Bert leaving I was in full labour, panting on gas and air and shouting curses at Mother Nature for making women suffer so. By the time Bert would've been up, washed and eating his bread and marg for breakfast, I had a beautiful baby girl wrapped up in hospital blankets placed into my arms.

She was a bonny thing, weighing more than eight pounds. I sank into that dreamy state all mothers go into just after the birth as Bert arrived, his eyes popping out of his head at the sight of me resting with our new daughter.

'Blimey, Duchess, you don't waste yer time,' he said, amazed at the speed of the night's events.

I smiled and looked down at the scrunched-up little face of the mewling baby in my arms. 'Come an' meet your father,' I said, lifting her up into my beloved husband's grip. His face melted at the sight of her. 'She'll be a real daddy's girl, I bet.' I giggled, and stretched back carefully. Everything ached, and this time I'd had some stitches.

'She's a beauty, just like 'er mother,' was all Bert said, looking down in wonder at our little girl.

'Yes,' I added, 'she's our littl' princess.'

'Not even the royal baby will be loved as much as ours.' Bert chuckled, referring to the fact that Princess Elizabeth was due to give birth to her child in a month's time.

'But what will we call 'er, Bert? We didn't think it'd be a girl, we only 'ad a name for a boy,' I replied, lying back against the pillows, feeling suddenly very sleepy. It was warm in the ward. There was a hush even though several women nursed newborns. The matron was so strict that I suspected even the babies knew how to behave. Sunlight streamed in through the windows that lined the ward and I felt drowsy and spent.

As my eyes closed I heard Bert say, 'Brenda, we'll call 'er Brenda. An' she'll be our littl' angel.'

CHAPTER 8

Slum Girl

1951

There was a scream and the sound of glass shattering on the cobbled side street outside the chip shop. A man's rough cockney voice hollered insult after insult. A woman was yelling, her voice shrill with fear.

I hesitated in the back of the shop. I'd been happily listening to the latest episode of *The Archers* on Wally's wireless while I was cleaning the floor of the chippy when I heard the calamity. I put down my mop, unsure for a moment what to do. Should I intervene? I'd been at the receiving end of many a hard fist and vicious punch from my pa. I knew what it felt like to be frightened, to be cornered like the prey of some vicious animal. I also knew that it was considered wrong in East London to get in between a man and his woman, even if they took their violence into the streets for all to hear and witness.

The woman shrieked again. It was high-pitched, a kind of wail. I couldn't stay where I was a moment longer. I ran out into the road, not caring who saw me, and was greeted with a terrible sight. The woman was one of Wally's regulars, a good-looking young woman called Mabel. She had long fair hair, blue eyes and a slim figure so unlike my own, which had been shaped by my two babies. I'd always felt envious of her. She was so pretty with her pink cheeks and delicate features, how could I not step in?

She was kneeling on the ground, begging the man to stop.

There was blood splattered across her face, oozing down her cheek and soaking into her blouse, making a sodden mess.

The man was spitting and slurring, one fist raised, a shard of glass from a beer bottle contained within it. His face was level to hers, and he shouted, covering her face with spittle: 'You fuckin' whore, I know you've been at it with another man. Come on, you floozy, tell who it was an' I'll get 'im. I'll teach 'im a lesson 'e won't forget in an 'urry!'

Mabel moaned and swayed on her knees. 'Roger, you don't know what yer sayin'. There ain't another man. It's God's 'onest truth. Now let's just go 'ome, I'm beggin' you . . .'

She'd barely finished when I shouted and ran over. 'Get off 'er!' was all I managed to say. I grabbed Mabel's thin shoulders and dragged her forcibly back from the man I presumed was her husband.

His face was wild. He seemed barely able to focus. I knew she had recently married a casual docker and as I took in his threadbare trousers and his hobnail boots, it felt like history repeating itself. He was a good-looking man. He was handsome with dark hair and high cheek bones. He almost looked foreign, but I couldn't find him attractive, not in the least, not with his scowl and his temper, and the fear I saw in his wife's eyes. He'd have been a real heart-stealer had his face not been screwed up with drunken rage.

'Go on, get away. Go an' sleep it off and leave your poor wife alone.' My voice was authoritative, commanding. After all, I'd stood up to my bullying father a thousand times and more during my lifetime. I knew I had to help or he might kill her.

The man seemed all at once to collapse in on himself. He wiped his brow, cutting himself with the glass. He stared at it as if he'd never seen it before, then dropped it as if it was suddenly scalding hot.

'Get away, Roger. Go an' sober up. Mabel is comin' with me for now.'

The man looked at me, his face crumpling. 'I'm sorry, I don't know what 'appened. Mabel! Oh, Gawd, Mabel, what 'ave I done?'

His wife was crying in my arms. She lifted her head and spoke: 'Go on, Roger, go an' get your 'ead clear of the grog.' And with that, he grabbed his head with both hands and stumbled away, without looking back.

Mabel was weeping softly now. She seemed to have collapsed like a rag doll, floppy and unmanageable in my arms, so I half carried her, half dragged her inside Wally's shop. I got her inside and down the back stairs. I made sure the 'Closed' sign was up at the window so we wouldn't be interrupted.

I'd only been back at work for a couple of weeks after taking six months off to nurse my new baby girl, Brenda. The strike that had put my Bert out of work had ended just after she was born, before I'd even left the hospital, and so life had gone back to normal, much to everyone's relief. Vi had Little Albie, who was now four years old, and Brenda, with her each evening I was at work. I'd cut my hours down so I only worked four days a week. My half-sister Val was also staying with us for a while: I'd convinced Pa that she could have a little holiday to play with Little Albie and the new baby. In reality I wanted to give four-year-old Val a break from his drunken violence. I'd asked again if we could have Patsy with us for a while, but Pa had refused. Patsy was growing into a beautiful young woman of 14 years old and would soon be starting work. I could see that Pa wanted to keep her, and her wages, close by him and so I'd had to accept I couldn't help Patsy yet again.

'Come on now, let's get you cleaned up. A nice sweet cuppa will see you right.' I chattered as brightly as I felt able as

I busied myself making tea, and finding some clean linens to wash Mabel's cuts. 'I can't do nothing about your pretty blouse, but at least we can sort out your face,' I said, carefully dabbing the gash on her cheek. The slash made by the bottle was, thankfully, superficial, and would heal by itself. 'No need to go up the 'ospital – you'll be right as rain in no time, it's just a scratch,' I added, placing a steaming cup of tea in front of Mabel as she sat in a shrinking huddle at the table. Her eyes refused to meet mine so I chatted away, hoping that the warmth of my voice would relieve the terrible shame and upset she was so clearly suffering. 'No customers are due 'ere for a while so we've got time to 'ave a proper chat an' get ourselves ship shape.'

I'd gone into Wally's early that day. I'd been getting the shop ready for the weekend rush when I'd heard the commotion outside. Wally and Betty lived above the shop, but they knew I came in early now and then, especially if we'd had a lot of customers the night before. I liked keeping a clean shop, and making sure we had enough spuds for the fryer. The oil had to be strained, to get rid of all the bits of leftover fried fish, and the batter had to be made. I knew I was trusted to let myself in, and get on with some work.

'Thank you, 'ilda. I don't know what to say. My Roger, 'e ain't never like that normally. 'e's never 'it me before.' Mabel's voice was small and brittle. I raised an eyebrow. I'm not sure I believed that but I wouldn't dare tell her that to her face.

At that moment the door at the top of the basement stairs burst open and Wally appeared. 'What was all that hullaballoo outside? Did you 'ear it, 'ilda?' he stormed, then just as abruptly took in the sight in front of his eyes.

'As a matter of fact I did, Wally. You know Mabel – no need for introductions. We was just 'avin' a nice cup of tea.

Can I 'elp you wiv anything?' I tried to keep my voice as light as possible.

Wally looked from Mabel's bloody blouse to her swollen face, then back at me. He looked like a rabbit caught in the hunter's snare. 'Oh, well, if there's anything I can do, you just shout, alright ladies?' He gave us both an awkward nod of his head, and turned on his heel and went straight back out of the door.

Mabel and I gave each other a knowing look. It wasn't that Wally was uncaring, it's just that he was unsure of how to cope with the truth of Mabel's plight. It was considered women's business. Men just didn't get involved. I clicked my teeth, in slight irritation, and we smiled a grim smile at each other. ' 'ave a biscuit,' I said. After all, what else could I offer my friend?

Eventually, Mabel, who must've been a young woman of 25, came out of her shell and started telling me about her life. She was one of seven children, born to an alcoholic mother and a lay-about father in a slum tenement in Rotherhithe. During the war the family had been evacuated to the Midlands and she'd lost contact with her father. Her mother had died in the bombing raids after returning to London in search of work. After the war had ended, Mabel had come back to London with five of her siblings; her elder brother had met a girl in Wolverhampton and had decided to stay. Mabel did whatever she could to make ends meet but it had been a struggle. When she'd met Roger, a dashing, charming man, she'd thought her troubles were over. He was so good-looking and so loving. He'd offered to take in her and her siblings, and so Mabel thought she'd met the man of her dreams. She hadn't minded that his work was casual, or that he never had much money: it was love she craved.

It wasn't long after they were married that the violence

started. First a slap, then a bruised wrist where he'd held her down during a row, then it escalated to a punch in the face or a kicking, depending on how drunk he was.

It was a story echoing across wartime Britain: families wrenched apart; loved-ones killed in the raids; orphaned children left destitute and vulnerable; young women prey to the charms of men who turned out to be monsters. And now Mabel was stuck with him. She could leave him, but where would she go? Her story retold my mother's plight so succinctly that I felt the old feelings of helplessness and anger well up in the face of such abuse. There was nothing I could do to help Mabel, except offer her a sympathetic ear. Her life was set for her. She would stay with him as long as she could then, maybe, one day she'd have enough, unless he killed her first, and she'd flee with her siblings into the pitiless, cruel world. Alone, vulnerable, desperate.

I couldn't see a happy ending for Mabel and I so desperately wanted one for her. That night I prayed with extra force for her and for all the young women out there who'd been forced by fate and circumstance to stay with men who beat them, who stole their dignity and shattered their souls. I prayed that Mabel would find a way to leave and would be, one day, safe and happy, and, most importantly, free.

The next day, I was daydreaming again as I stood by the shop window and waited for the first customers of the afternoon. I was smiling to myself at Bert's reaction to the news we were having another baby: he'd nuzzled into my neck and held me round my plump waist. He'd sworn he'd guessed that we were pregnant, and he patted my tummy gently as he smiled at me.

The only thing that qualified my happiness was wondering about Mabel and whether her no-good husband had sobered up enough to realise how badly he'd behaved. I'd packed Mabel off home just before we opened, knowing she wouldn't want to face any of our regulars looking like a casualty from the war, but I'd worried about her all evening, hoping she'd escaped another beating. There was nothing I could do for her, of course – the same for my regulars at Wally's. Mavis had been in again, yesterday, and I'd managed to sneak her in an extra scoop of chips, but it wasn't much of a help.

Suddenly the bell above the door clanged as my first customer came in. It was Reenie from the same estate as Bert and I lived on. Londoners like us would rather walk the extra mile to go somewhere we knew a friend or neighbour than take our custom to a closer shop. 'Alright, Reenie, 'ow's life with you, eh? I 'aven't seen you in 'ere for a while. Yer 'usband keepin' you chained to the hob?' I joked, giving her a smile.

Reenie laughed with a throaty sound from the cigarettes she continually rolled herself through the day. Her fingers were stained yellow, and her teeth were black, but she was always cheerful and up for a laugh. ' 'ow's your Bert?' she cackled, wheezing as she spoke.

'My Bert's alright. 'e's workin' today. They offered 'im overtime an' 'e jumped at the chance,' I replied, as I dished out the thin crisps that Wally's customers loved into grease-proof paper envelopes. I always knew each customer's order – they never veered from what they liked, and I found that endearing. 'Hake and a portion of chips with that?' I said with my back to her, scooping chips from the warming tray and onto the newspaper sheets to wrap into hot bundles.

'That's it, 'ilda, an' plenty of salt an' vinegar,' replied Reenie, leaning her thin frame, which swaddled in cardigans that looked like they'd seen better days, on the counter.

' 'ow's your Fred?' I asked, as I wrapped her steaming hot

dinner after covering it in liberal amounts of tangy vinegar and salt.

'Oh, 'e's alright. Same as ever. I can't complain, 'ilda, an' if I could, what would be the point? There ain't nothin' I can do about anythin'!' Reenie laughed again. She was always cheerful, always looking on the bright side of life even though her and Fred barely had two shillings to rub together. 'Fred's lumbago is playin' up but apart from that 'e's the same as ever.'

'Well, give 'im my best, won't you, Reenie,' I said as I handed her the two parcels containing her meal. Once again, I marvelled at the resilience of people like Fred and Reenie. The couple must've been in their late fifties but they looked older. They'd lost their only son, Fred, a bright boy of 20, in the war, yet they never complained. They must've been through such grief and such misery, and, if truth be told, it was etched on Reenie's face, but she never alluded to it. She never once broke down or shed any tears that I knew of. People like us just wiped our eyes and got on with life, whatever it threw at us. Losing your only son would be the worst thing a mother could go through and I thought about Reenie and the sacrifice she and countless other mothers had made during the war. Yet she never showed her feelings, she kept them private, and I admired her for that. I always liked seeing Reenie, and occasionally Fred if I happened to bump into him on the estate. They were both shabbily dressed with threadbare clothing and shoes that were barely holding together, yet they were always polite, always cheerful and ready with a quip and a joke to say hello.

By now the shop was steadily filling up with customers. The rest of the evening went in a flash. We had people queuing most of the time we were open. Weekends were always busy which is why Wally and Betty needed me to work on

Saturdays. I loved it though. We shared jokes, had a laugh and a bit of a sing-song as we worked.

By the time it came to closing I was even more tired than usual but happy, and looking forward to getting home to Bert. I smiled again to myself. We'd always said we wanted three children. I could scarcely believe that our dreams had come true so completely. If anyone had said to me that everything that we talked about while courting would come true then I'd have said they were lying. I grew up in a slum. I was raised to survive from one day to the next. We had no idea there was a future waiting for us outside our tenements. Even now, I had moments when I thought I must be dreaming. I had a good man, a neat little home, a job and two children of my own, with another on the way. I may not have had cars or jewellery but I had what mattered the most: I had love, and I had it in abundance.

I sang as I walked home, feeling the velvety night air on my face.

CHAPTER 9

Hilda's Sacrifice

1952

'Oi, mine! My bread!' Brenda's little baby voice was indignant.

'It's mine, give it 'ere!' shouted Little Albie in response.

'What's all this racket?' I asked, bustling over to the table.

'Mum, it's Brenda! She's pinched me piece of bread an' eaten it,' wailed Little Albie. He was pointing at his younger sister Brenda, a lively girl of two years old who was clutching the remains of a slice of wholemeal bread and grinning.

I sighed. 'Brenda, 'ave you stolen Little Albie's bread?' I asked, knowing I wouldn't get a straight answer. Brenda, who was a dear little thing with blonde curls and grubby cheeks, scowled back at me and shook her head. Her plate was empty. She'd eaten every morsel of the stew I'd made from the scraps of the meat I had left, eking it out till tonight's supper.

At this, Little Albie stared crying. 'She *did* take it. It's not fair. I'm bigger than 'er an' I'm starvin', Mummy!'

I looked at them both and knew with a great swooping sensation in my belly that they were hungry, which was why they were both acting up. I also knew I had one slice of bread left, and I'd been saving that for my dinner. Of course I'd give my son the slice, though it would leave me with nothing to eat. As if on cue, my stomach growled. 'Go on, you 'ave this slice, Albie. Make sure you eat it all up now, I don't want you goin' 'ungry, darlin',' I said. He held out his hand and took the bread with a murmured 'Thank you.' I sat and watched them as they finished their meal. Albie was so grown up now. He was only six years old but children grew up fast down our way. They had to. Our third child, Christine, was still only a babe-in-arms at a year old.

When they'd finished their meal, Albie and Brenda raced off into the tiny lounge to play with the train set that Bert and I had proudly saved up for last Christmas. They both loved it and it kept them occupied for hours.

I scooped up both of their plates, balancing Christine on my hip as I worked, and, hovering by the sink, I used the last heel of the bread that Albie had left to wipe up the last traces of gravy. Just as I popped the food into my mouth I suddenly realised I was being watched. I looked round.

Little Albie was standing behind me. He may only have been a little boy but his face registered my shock at being caught. There was a moment's silence. My cheeks flushed hot and red. Then Albie's little voice piped up: 'You said you'd eaten earlier.' His face was cocked to one side, and he was scrutinising me.

I flushed an even deeper red. I was speechless. I couldn't lie to him – his innocent little face stared up at me as he pro-cessed what was taking place. Immediately I was transported back to a much earlier age in my mind: I'd finished my dinner and had raced out to play but decided to go back into Ma's kitchen for something, I can't remember what. I had caught my own mother in the act of wiping the remains of our dinner off our plates so that she had something to eat that day. It was a moment that crystallised in my mind for ever. I would never forget the look of shame and guilt on her face as she realised she'd been caught lying about having eaten. It was the shame of not having enough money to feed your own child, and it hurt like hell, as I was now discovering.

Once again I was reminded of the sacrifices Ma made for us kids, and now, in a sickening twist of fate, I was repeating it.

I stepped forward to say something. Albie's face had gone through several expressions: one of confusion, then dawning realisation, then the inevitable upset. Before I could say a word he turned from me and ran outside, through the front door and into the estate.

The sight of his skinny little legs fleeing the flat was too much to bear. It was exactly what I had done when I caught my mother in the same act: running to escape feelings of such pain, and such fear. Suddenly the world had felt an even harsher place, and one where not even a meal could be taken for granted. I felt sick at the thought that my own boy was now feeling that same terrible emotion.

Tears stung my eyes and I leaned back against the counter, half wanting to race after him, half knowing that he would come home when he was ready to face me with the truth that we didn't have enough food between us.

I put Christine down for a nap in the cot and waited for Albie to return. Time moved on until eventually I heard the sound of the door opening and his little footsteps. Snot was smeared across his face and his eyes were red from crying, but he looked at me with defiance it made me shiver. I knelt down and scooped him into my arms. He resisted for a moment and then sank into me, a little boy needing reassurance that the world wasn't such a confusing place. 'There, there. Things will get better, you'll see. We'll manage, an' I promise you I won't lie to you again.' I kissed his white-blond hair. (Lord knows where he'd got that from. Bert always joked he was the butcher's son. Our local butcher in Bow had had the whitest blond hair I'd ever seen and he'd always tipped me a wink on his delivery rounds.)

That night, in the lounge, I told Bert what had happened.

To my surprise, he hit the roof. 'How could you 'ave been so stupid? Lettin' 'im see you. An' what the 'ell are you playin' at, missin' meals? If you ain't got enough money then you should bloody well tell me an' I'll be the one to worry about it!' He was furious.

'Shush, Bert, you'll wake the children,' was all I managed to stutter, shocked by the turn of events. Then a wail came from the children's room: Christine had woken up and was screaming. Probably Albie and Brenda would now both be awake too. ' 'ow can I ask you for money if we ain't got any?' I said sharply. I didn't like being called stupid: it was too reminiscent of That Man and his put-downs. Mind you, he'd called me much worse than that. He'd even called me a 'whore' once or twice, but my Bert had never said anything so remotely nasty, whatever our differences.

'Bloody 'ell, 'ilda, I don't care if I wake the children! This is important. You don't go missin' meals ever again, d'you 'ear me? I won't 'ave it under my roof! I won't 'ave people say I can't provide for me own wife and kids!' Bert was beside himself. He raised his arm and for one awful moment I thought he might strike me.

'Stop it, Bert! Just stop!' I cried. Christine was sobbing in the other room. I pushed Bert out of the way and hurried into the children's room. Christine was holding on to the bars of her cot and wailing. Brenda and Albie shared a double bed next to it. Both were huddled together, looking terrified; Brenda was weeping softly. Their eyes were like saucers, big and round with fear. 'Now, now, there's nothing the matter. Just your father and me 'avin' a ding-dong. Sometimes that's what mums and dads do, but everything's alright. Now come an' cuddle up an' we'll 'ave a story to get us all nice an' sleepy again.'

It took nearly an hour to settle them all back to sleep. I

closed the door quietly and tiptoed into the lounge. Bert was still in his chair, his face like stone.

'Bert...' I said, but my voice trailed off. He wouldn't even look at me. I was turning to move to the kitchen when he spoke.

'It ain't right, 'ilda. I don't want yer ever to go through what yer mother went through, missin' meals an' the like. I 'ad no idea, no idea you 'ad to do that for us all.' Bert's voice was low, his face full of sorrow, and something else, something that looked like guilt. 'I'll get more hours drivin' the vans. I'll do whatever it takes to put food on the table. Just promise me you'll never give up your own dinner again. I'd rather it was me who starved...' Bert's voice cracked with emotion but he stayed staring ahead.

I supposed that was as close to an apology as I was likely to get. His words had stung me, but I realised it was his pride that was hurt. He'd always been the breadwinner, and the thought of not being able to feed his family had cut him deeply, especially after the strike which so nearly left us destitute. I told him I promised I wouldn't miss another supper, then I sat out in the kitchen, the dim glow of the light keeping silent vigil. I sipped sweet tea, begging my tummy to stop betraying my hunger and stay quiet. I couldn't have eaten, though, if there'd been fried steak and chips in front of me. I felt troubled and heartbroken in equal measure. I was upset that my son had witnessed what I had as a child, and Bert's angry outburst had left its mark.

Eventually I went to bed, leaving Bert in his chair, the only time we'd ever gone to bed separately. Suddenly there felt like a chasm at the heart of my marriage and my life.

The next day things seemed to have calmed down, but Bert had left with barely a word and returned from work in the same, distant mood. I tried to be my usual, cheerful self but the heart had gone out of me. I was grateful not to be working that day. For the life of me, I don't think I could've been happy-go-lucky ''ilda' for the customers. Later, Little Albie was caught by a neighbour playing in the bombsites that lined Redriff Road, pretending the exposed basements and piles of rubble were mountainous terrains filled with dragons' caves and terrifying wizards. I tensed up when I heard the news, fearing the worst that Bert would shout at him, given his dark mood. Bert was cross with Albie but nothing like he'd been last night. He banned our son from playing on those dangerous sites, and told him to keep away from the dockside. His manner was tough but he didn't raise his voice. And Little Albie seemed to take it well.

Despite the Blitz decimating the docklands, there was still some trade going on there, even in the timber yards, which had sustained such heavy bombing. Albie liked chasing down to the riverside to watch ships coming and going as it was always such a spectacle. Just as Les, Ron, Joanie and I had done as children. There were people from all over the world docking and unloading, even meeting locals and getting married. But it was the transient nature of the dockyards that made us locals fear that children could be whisked away. There were always rumours circulating about children disappearing after playing down there, though I'd never heard of it happening to anyone we knew. Little Albie took his telling-off on the chin and skipped out to play.

I sighed with relief. I hadn't realised how affected I'd been by Bert's angry outburst. *He isn't Pa*, I said to myself, over and over again, like a mantra. *He isn't Pa*.

Days later, I was shovelling chips into the warming pan when I heard the shop door open. 'Be with you in a minute, luv, just gotta sort out these spuds an' you'll 'ave something to eat!' I said with my back to the entrance.

A familiar voice replied: 'Well I never, if it ain't my Duchess runnin' the shop!' I turned on my heel to see my husband Bert grinning at me.

'What are you doin' 'ere? You're meant to 'ave picked up the kids from Vi—?' I instantly jumped to the most important aspect of our shared lives: the welfare of our children.

'Keep yer 'air on! I'm just poppin' in, won't take a second, but I've got some news, Duchess, an' I'm afraid it ain't good,' Bert said. His face fell into a frown. Puzzled, I asked what was wrong. Luckily he'd arrived during a quiet patch and there were no other customers in the shop. 'It's Bill and Flo,' he said, simply.

Flo and Bill (not to be confused with Old Man Bill from the chippy), were our friends from Bow. They lived in the same building as Dolly and Pop. They had a single floor of the tenement as their own, living and sleeping in just one room with a separate kitchen/scullery on the side. I had got to know them a little when I first moved to Bert's parents, but it was only after leaving and starting my own family that we grew close.

Bill and Flo had seen their share of tragedy in their lives. Their five children had all died from rickets. It was a common illness in the East End. The lack of sunlight in the foggy, dirty docklands, and the diet of meagre soups and bread meant that children developed bone deformities. It wasn't an unusual sight to see children with curved spines or leg braces hobbling around the cobbled streets. Somehow, all four of my siblings and I had escaped the ravages of it, though my half-sister Val had to wear leg braces as a child.

It was this tragedy in her past that drew me to Flo, in particular. As a mother I could not fathom how any woman could go through so much pain and be as kind and as gentle as she was. Bill was a character. He was a rough East Ender: he smoked cheap tobacco continually, and spoke in cockney rhyming slang with such a broad cockney accent I could hardly understand him at times. But he had a big heart, and they were both carved from the tragic deaths of their little ones. They had a single photograph of their youngest child, a boy wearing his leg braces with a crooked smile on his little face. It was taken a year before he too died. I had held that photograph many times, stroking it and wondering how Bill and Flo kept going in the face of such painful memories.

'What about Bill and Flo? Tell me, Bert, what's wrong?' I said, feeling the first fluttering of alarm.

'It's cancer. Bill has cancer of the lungs an' 'e ain't goin' to be long for this world,' Bert said.

I stopped and stared at him. For a moment I couldn't make sense of it, then I sat down on the stool that Wally kept near the counter. I let out a long breath. 'Well, we knew there was something wrong with 'im. Gawd, why is it the good ones that seem to cop it?' I answered at last.

Bert held out his hand and I took hold of it. It was a moment of togetherness, but at such a terrible price. Our beloved friend, who was more like an uncle to our children, was fading fast.

'It's Flo I feel for,' I said, as I looked up at Bert. 'She's the one who 'as to go on without 'im.' With that, Bert gave my hand a squeeze.

'Look, I must go, 'ilda, but I wanted you to know. It was Frank who sent me the message – 'e'd been down there with me mother when they 'eard the bad news.'

'Alright. Thanks, luvvie, for tellin' me. I'll see you later,' I said as Bert left.

What a shock. Even if the news had worked like a magic

salve and brought Bert and me back to each other, it was the news we had feared. Bill had been coughing and complaining of pain in his chest for years and yet he'd only just seen a doctor. It was a remnant of the fact that GPs used to charge, and poor people like us and our friends would never have had the money to afford such a luxury as doctors and medicine. Now that there was a National Health Service, we could actually have doctors come out to us for free. What a marvel that was, at least.

Our marriage troubles forgotten, Bert and I took the children over on the next Sunday to see him. Little Albie and Brenda clattered up the stairs to greet the couple, who were now in their sixties. Usually Bill met them at the top of the staircase with a laugh and a coin from his rough workman trousers, while Fluffy, Bill's little dog, would scamper along the hall-way, excited at the prospect of playing with the children. Bill always dressed in the same outfit: a greying shirt, a pair of black trousers shiny from wear, and a pair of braces that he hooked his thumbs round.

Today he wasn't there.

I glanced at Bert. He'd registered Bill's absence, as had the children.

'Come on, you lot,' I joked brightly. 'Let's see if we can't find Bill. 'e's probably 'idin' somewhere to jump out at you all.'

Flo called out for us to come up and we shuffled into the main room of their flat. The room was dark and smelled of unwashed linen. There was a washing line which acted as a curtain through the centre of the room, with an iron bed behind it serving as the couple's bedroom. There was the sound of a cough and Bill's voice from behind it.

' 'e ain't well today,' said Flo, as she came out from behind the curtain. She looked pale and worn out, with a black dress and faded apron. Her long brown hair was streaked with grey and pulled back into a top knot. 'It's 'is lungs. 'e can't breathe all that well, but 'e's been lookin' forward to seein' the children.'

I was carrying Christine in my arms, a warm, heavy bundle smelling of talc and soap. I was suddenly taken with the urge to smother her in kisses. Life was so precious. I didn't need to remind Flo and Bill of that. And yet they were so cheerful and sweet in the face of such adversity. I loved them for it, and I know Bert felt the same.

'Now then, what's goin' on 'ere?' I said, laughter in my voice. 'Bill's in 'is bed, is 'e? Must be nice to get a proper rest, eh, Bill? 'Bout time you 'ad a lie down – I reckon you deserve it.'

His response was a laugh and a hacking cough. 'That's right, 'ilda, don't I just.'

I poked my head round the curtain. Bill's white face was propped up on his pillows. There was a bowl with putrid-looking phlegm in it next to his bedside. His beloved tobacco was on the bed as well. I raised my eyebrows and Bill chuckled.

'Me doctor says they 'elp a bad chest,' he said, before a new burst of coughing racked his frail body.

'You stop talkin' and give those lungs of yours a rest. Bert'll roll you up a ciggie to 'elp you breathe,' I said, rather sternly, figuring the only way I could deal with his debility was to bustle around and make him more comfortable.

The doctor was calling later on in the day and I wanted Bill to be spick and span, as my ma used to say. 'I'll get the kettle on,' I said to Flo, and marched into the tiny kitchen.

We stayed for a couple of hours before Bill fell asleep, a line of drool reaching down his mouth and onto those musty sheets. 'I'll be back next week to give you an 'and with yer washin',' I told Flo. 'No buts, I'm comin' to 'elp, and that's that.' I would ask Wally to spare them a hot pie and a portion of chips to take round. Wally was all heart, and when I explained their predicament I knew he'd want to help. Dolly would pop up most days to check they were coping so I felt reassured that someone was keeping an eye on them. Still, I wanted to do what I could as well. Our lives were centred on family and community. From the day Little Albie could talk, he'd referred to them as 'Uncle Bill' and 'Aunty Flo'. They were family even if they weren't blood relations, and so we stuck together through thick and thin. That's the way it was in London. We looked after our own. We helped each other, even if it was just a cuppa and a hot pie. It all helped. We had no one else to look after our interests. We were poor, working-class people. We had pride in our community but we also knew it was up to us to help each other. Who else would?

Leaving Flo was a wrench, but the time came for the doctor's appointment and we didn't want to be there when he arrived. We left with promises to return.

I would never tell them, or Wally, or Dolly, or anyone, for that matter, that Bert and I were struggling, but I would do everything I could that was in my power to do right by our friends. That was life round our way. That was the East End.

CHAPTER 10

Hooray Hilda

1953

There was a whine from the shop basement. I stopped dead. *I must be goin' mad*, I thought to myself, before carrying on with the task of sweeping the grey-tiled floor. But, no, there it was again. There was definitely an animal making a noise downstairs!

I'd only just got in to work, on a mild sunny day in June. I'd changed into my coat and was starting to clean up from last night's business. *What the 'ell is goin' on?* My thoughts raced. A dog couldn't have got inside the chippy, could it?

I marched down the stairs, feeling a little nervous as I wasn't sure what I'd find. Sure enough, as my eyes adjusted to the gloom I found myself staring into the black eyes of a thin, wiry dog looking up at me from inside a newly created partition in the basement of Wally's shop. 'Well, I never!' I said aloud.

There was a snort of laughter behind me. 'You've found 'er then,' chuckled Wally, as he descended the stairs. 'She's a beauty, ain't she? Got 'er from a mate of mine. She's fast and rarin' to go – I've got 'igh 'opes for 'ooray 'ilda.'

I barely had time to splutter my response when I registered the name he'd chosen for this beast, who was now licking her paws and gazing up at me with doleful eyes. ''ooray 'ilda? That ain't 'er name, is it? Please tell me you 'aven't called 'er after me!' I said, indignantly.

'Of course I 'ave!' Wally laughed again. 'Who else would I name 'er after? She's a fast worker, loyal an' always likes a tickle under 'er chin. She's practically your twin!' With that Wally gave a great 'Ha!'

'You cheeky so-and-so! 'ow dare you call a dog after me! You wait till my Bert 'ears about this,' I bantered back, half in jest and half deadly serious. I wasn't sure what to think about a racehound named after me. But suddenly I saw the funny side and burst into laughter. ' 'ooray 'ilda! Well, blow me, it ain't every day a girl gets 'er name in lights. I expect you'll be racin' 'er then?' I said at last, wiping the tears of laughter from my eyes. 'Look, you've made me cry and it ain't even time to change the pickled onion jar!'

'Oh, yes, she's a goer – beggin' yer pardon! An' she'll race nicely down the Stow. As she's your namesake, why don't you an' Bert come along for 'er first race?' Wally's kind face twinkled at me. 'I might even shut the shop as it's a great occasion. Could be the start of big things, eh?'

'What d'you mean, the Stow? What in Gawd's name is that?' I replied, bemused. Was it one of Wally's cockney slang words?

'The Stow? It's Walthamstow Stadium, where all the dog racing 'appens! 'aven't you 'eard of it? It's famous down our way!' And with that Wally made his way back upstairs with a jaunty whistle.

I looked down at the dog. She looked back at me with a resigned face. 'Oh, well, we'd better get to know each other, then. I'm 'ilda, 'ow d'you do!'

The stadium was lit up like a Christmas tree. Wally's car slowed as we entered the parking area. There were several other cars already there but the majority of people were arriving on foot. There were peals of laughter and the occasional shout as people mingled together in the anticipation of a night at the races.

Wally had driven to Rotherhithe to pick us up. I chuckled to myself at the thought of my neighbours' eyes boggling at the sight of Bert and me being whisked away like royalty. I don't suppose many of us in the Redriff Estate had ever been inside a car, let alone being picked up by Wally's shiny Ford Prefect!

I'd spent longer than usual getting ready that night. I had one 'best' dress: it was navy blue and cut to hide the curves I was always so self-conscious of. Even so, it fitted me like a glove and I felt several inches taller on the rare occasions I wore it. I had powdered my face and applied a thin layer of pink lipstick, rolling my lips together to even out the pigment. I brushed my hair and put on my watch and the necklace I always wore with a picture of my Bert inside the locket, and stood back to look at myself. I wasn't a beauty. I was resigned to that. My eyes shone brown though, my hair had a few tiny streaks of grey even though I was only 32 years old, but my face was friendly looking and pleasant. I smiled back at my reflection. *Not too bad*, I thought to myself. *You'll do for a night at the races, 'ilda Kemp.* When'd I stepped into the lounge, Bert'd given a long, low whistle and said, 'Well, I never, you look like a proper duchess tonight. No, you don't – you look more royal than the Queen did on 'er coronation!'

The new queen, Elizabeth II, had been crowned exactly a week before on 2 June before a jubilant nation, including us Londoners. We'd had a week of celebrations on the estate, organised by the Redriff Estate Coronation Committee, with races and games for the kids and a firework display as the finale. Little Albie, who was seven years old; Brenda, three; and Christine, who was now a plump toddler of two years old, had all joined in and been given certificates to mark their attendance at the party. They had been pleased as Punch, and truly lived up to the certificates, which declared: 'We her children, rejoice and celebrate this Royal Occasion, with all its historic splendour and pageantry.' Wally had even put bunting up around the shop to mark the occasion. We'd got the bus across Tower Bridge and over the river on the coronation day itself. Little Albie had clutched his Union Jack flag, Bert carried Brenda and I pushed Christine in the perambulator. We almost didn't make it on board the crowded bus but Bert gave a shove and we crammed inside.

We disembarked into a huge swell of people, all heading for the coronation route, which circled the centre of the city. 'Blimey, I 'ad no idea there would be this many people!' exclaimed Bert, looking rather worried. 'Stay close to me, an' don't wander off anywhere.' I gulped, also feeling concerned about the sheer volume of people. It was a happy bunch, though. The atmosphere was one of excitement and high spirits. People waved flags and homemade bunting, and there were a few rounds of 'God save The Queen' sung spontaneously as we all walked in unison.

We quickly realised we would have to have camped by the eight-mile route that the soon-to-be-Queen would travel in her coach, in order to get a view: people were standing in rows eight or nine lines back from the edge of the procession. We got almost as far as The Mall but the crush was too great and so we hung back, watching the sights and colours that swamped the busy streets. Buildings were hung with flags. There were long banners with 'ER' emblazoned upon them. People huddled in blankets from the night they'd spent sleeping on the kerb of the coronation route. Women were applying make-up, chattering and laughing as yet more people gathered. I gasped as I spotted the tops of the busby hats the Guardsmen wore as they lined the route, standing to attention in anticipation of our young Queen. We kept Brenda and Albie close to us.

A couple of hours after we arrived, suddenly there was a ripple of cheers in the crowd. The wave of sound moved towards us and we craned up on the tips of our toes to try and get a glimpse of the oncoming procession. A carriage passed to enthusiastic cheering, then the sounds grew even more overwhelming. 'This must be the Queen!' shouted Bert. He put Little Albie on his shoulders and we shouted up at him, 'What can you see? Can you see the Queen from up there?' Little Albie shook his head but waved his flag anyway.

The emotion of the crowds was infectious, and I felt a great soaring in my heart as the procession drew closer. I swelled with pride at the pomp and ceremony, and for being such a little island that had so recently won two terrible wars. I shouted and waved with everyone else and we kept cheering even after the carriage had passed by. I was so proud to be British. I was proud to have a Queen who would bring new life into our country. I was proud to call myself an English-woman that day, by goodness I was.

'You'll always be my queen, 'ilda,' Bert said later, as we got ready to go out for the evening, kissing my neck as he passed me. I blushed a little. He never failed to be kind to me but I still felt like a slum girl inside and so I always felt uncomfortable with his praise, as if somehow I didn't deserve it. 'Get off you silly 'a'porth!' I exclaimed, batting off his advances. I knew that I hadn't left my past behind me, despite being a married woman with a new life. Whenever I thought about myself, which wasn't often, admittedly, I saw a dirt-streaked ragamuffin who ran wild through the hive of activity that was the dockside, but equally I saw a girl old before her time, helping to bring up her siblings as her ma's right-hand woman.

It made me dizzy knowing that the nice-looking woman with a husband and three healthy children, staring back at me in the mirror, was in fact the same as the girl who dwelt inside me. That wasn't to say that I was living like royalty now: I still lived near the docks in a tenement, in an estate that was over-populated, with washing hanging down every passage, in every block. I wondered if I'd ever really leave my past in the slums behind me. There were dirty, skinny children running to and fro like feral cats. Housewives still stood outside their doorways, wearing their faded aprons, their hair in the turbans we all wore, gossiping about their husbands and the other mothers on the estate. Little had changed. And yet everything had changed. My life was in stark contrast to the life Pa was still leading, which carried on being strangled by drunkenness and violence. My sister Patsy must have struggled to live with Ted and his moods. My heart bled for her. Her childhood had been lost in different ways to mine, with the death of our Ma, but lost all the same. Did she have a chance of living a good, decent life?

'Come on, 'ilda! Wally's outside – I can see the car. Get a move on or we'll be late!' Bert's voice cut through memories of the past. My heart had sunk to the soles of my feet thinking about Patsy and her future. Had I done enough to care for her? Could I have done more? The questions stayed with me as we drove through the streets of East London and into Walthamstow.

It was a Tuesday night. Wally had shut the shop in order to take Bert and me to see his new greyhound race for the first time. The children were staying with Vi for the night and Bert and I were having the first night out we'd had since getting married. As such it was a big occasion for us.

Wally, too, was beside himself with excitement. Betty was seated next to him in the front, her plump figure swathed in a fur stole even though it was a mild summer evening, and clutching a pink bag. I couldn't believe how luxurious it felt being in their car. I felt like a Hollywood actress!

Once the vehicle had pulled to a stop, Wally got out to open Betty's door, and Bert did the same for me. He held out his arm and I took it, feeling a heady mixture of nerves and excitement. The sun hadn't set yet, and the lights from the stadium entrance were soft in the evening glow.

Bert and I looked at each other in wonder at this, the latest turn of events in our life together. We both laughed in shared delight.

'Come on, follow me, an' don't forget tonight's on me. Don't even think to put yer 'ands in yer pockets. I'm payin' for everything!' Wally beamed.

'We can't let you do that,' said Bert.

'Yes, you can. I won't 'ear another word about it. Come on, follow me, or we'll miss the fun!' With that, Wally and Betty led the way, Wally eventually stopping and turning to me. 'Take this, as I'm off to check on 'ooray 'ilda. You stay 'ere an' keep tight. I'll be back before the race starts.' Wally strode off to find his dog and whoever was looking after it before the race started. I looked down at the leaflet Wally had thrust into my hand. It was a race programme. We were in the three-shilling enclosure, which was one-up from the two and six stand. 'Blow me, we really are royalty tonight!' I exclaimed, clutching Bert's arm even tighter. The noise in the stadium was incredible. There must have been thousands of people there, chatting, drinking, milling about, joking and shouting. I glanced down at the programme. Hooray Hilda was listed in the first race. 'Not long to go,' I shouted above the hullabaloo. Bert grinned a response.

'Better get us a drink,' he said. 'Betty, what do you want?' At that moment I wondered how on earth we were going to afford to buy each of us a drink. I gulped but couldn't say anything – it would make Bert look foolish and I didn't want to hurt his pride.

Betty shook her head. 'It's all on us tonight. Wally gave me some money. Come on, let's find the bar an' order some drinks.' Bert looked like he might argue, but Betty took charge and led the way to the crowded bar. 'What'll you 'ave, 'ilda?' she asked.

'A port an' lemon, please!' I mouthed over the din.

'Bert, what'll you 'ave?' Betty added.

Bert's face was mutinous. He obviously didn't like being bought a drink by a woman. It wasn't the done thing in those days but, bless him, he didn't kick up a fuss and I was grateful for that, especially as we only had a few shillings left after the rent to last the week. 'I'll 'ave a brown an' mild, if you please,' said Bert. He managed a weak smile.

Betty turned to the bar, and while she waited we had a chance to look around. There were men in trilbys and ladies wearing glamorous dresses; there were rough-looking working men in groups wearing caps and their docker boots and trousers shiny with wear. Alongside the track were the bookmakers – gambling was still illegal off-course, but the bookies always did a roaring trade 'at the dogs', legally or otherwise.

I pursed my lips and turned my head away. I didn't approve of gambling. I'd seen my pa spend his wages on illegal betting, and I knew the empty bellies that were the consequence of a run of bad luck, which always seemed to be the case. All in all, I thought the world would be a better place without more ways for a working man to spend his hard-earned money.

' 'ere are yer drinks – now let's find a table an' wait for Wally,' said Betty with a smile. I clasped my drink and followed, feeling rather overwhelmed by the sights and sounds of the frenetic racecourse. ''ooray 'ilda is up first. Wally 'ad better get a move on or 'e'll miss the race,' she added, looking round for his familiar dark hair.

Moments later, as if by magic, Wally appeared. 'She's all set. I've got a good lad down there at the track who's lookin' after 'er. Just one last thing to do.' And with that he leapt off again, this time in the direction of the track. I laughed at that. Wally was such a character. He always knew how to have a good time. I felt great fondness for him and his wife. Seconds later he returned, clutching a handful of betting slips. 'I've put a shilling on 'ooray 'ilda to win, for all of us!' he declared, looking pleased with himself.

'You've put a bet on?' I asked.

'I 'aven't put one bet on, 'ilda, I've put four bets on, luvvie. Now come on, drink up – they're about to start the race an' I want to get down to the track to see my girl come in first!' Wally's face was a picture. He was absolutely sure the dog would win. I couldn't help but be carried away by his infectious optimism, and I suddenly felt excited.

'Yes, let's go an' watch my namesake win!' I countered, bursting into laughter. We made our way through the throng of people down to the trackside. We managed to get a good view, gripping onto the rails. A great booming voice was heard across the stadium announcing the race.

'Look, there she is!' shouted Wally excitedly. Sure enough, there were the dogs being lead round the track. Their coats bore different colours and numbers. 'We're lookin' for number three,' Wally called out and, squinting, I saw the dog in the middle of the pack.

The dogs were lead to some small boxes, in which they were contained until the start. There was a moment when the race course went quiet – if that was possible – and then they were off.

Wally was leaning over the railing, almost falling into the track. 'There she goes!' he bellowed, waving his betting slip as the shutters clanged open and five dogs looking like streaks of grey shot out after a fluffy rabbit which whizzed round the track in front of them.

There was a roar from the crowd and a frantic waving of programmes and betting slips.

'Come on, 'ooray 'ilda!' shouted Wally.

'Come on, 'ilda!' hollered Bert and Betty.

It felt bizarre shouting my own name so I let the others do the honours.

Wally beat the sides of the railing, Betty was flushed and jumping up and down. Even Bert was shouting as if his life depended on it. Then, suddenly, it was all over.

'Where did she come?' I panted. 'Did she win?'

Wally had collapsed in on himself and was bent over. His face bobbed up and, with theatrical effect, he slowly ripped up his ticket in front of us. 'Last! She was bloody well last!' His face was a mixture of disbelief and tragedy. Then, all of a sudden, he threw his head back and howled with laughter. 'Me beautiful dog was last, can you believe it?' He was holding his sides, guffawing at the disaster that had befallen his racehound. 'The bloke who sold 'er to me swore she was a winner an' I believed 'im. What a silly sod I am.'

Betty was laughing. Bert was giggling beside me.

Suddenly I felt affronted. 'You mean, 'ooray 'ilda is a duffer?' I stated, crossly.

With that, Wally laughed even harder. 'Stop it, 'ilda! You're goin' to do me an injury! Yes, she's a duffer – a real duffer – by the looks of it, an' I fell for it!'

'Time for another drink, I think,' said Betty and we couldn't disagree.

Later that evening, as we watched the rest of the races,

Wally announced that he wouldn't give up on his dog yet and would train her for another race in a month's time. He believed in her.

'I thought you said she was a duffer?' I said, sipping my second port and lemon. I was feeling a bit woozy with the alcohol, which I wasn't used to, and I wasn't sure I liked the sensation. Wally had been as good as his word: we didn't open our purse or wallet the whole night long.

''course I am, 'ilda, duckie. I ain't beaten for long, you know that. I'm goin' to train 'er up an' make 'er into a winner. You watch me.'

Betty raised her eyebrows and said nothing.

I giggled in response. 'Well, good luck to Wally and 'is greyhound!' I said, lifting my glass.

'Good luck to 'ooray 'ilda!' we all chorused, and chinked our glasses.

Later that night, when Wally and Betty had dropped us off at the entrance to our estate, and we'd thanked them both for a thrilling evening, Bert and I snuggled up in bed and reflected on the evening. It had been an eye-opener to say the least, but neither of us was keen on repeating the experience, despite Wally's protestations he would take us back there for the next race.

'Once is enough for us,' said Bert, planting a kiss on my forehead and pulling the blankets up higher. His body was warm and comforting lying next to me. Soon his breaths became longer and more even.

I lay awake for a while, reliving the crowds and the cheers. Once was enough, but what a night it had been. It wasn't every day a woman had a greyhound named after her – even if it had lost.

'oppin'

1954

'We're goin' on 'oliday,' announced Bert one morning, over his breakfast fry-up. For a minute I thought he was joking. We didn't have the money to go away as a family. We barely had enough money to feed ourselves, let alone pay for a holiday. I turned round from the cooker where I was making Bert some fried bread. He was grinning back at my puzzled expression. 'We're goin' 'oppin' down in Kent. I've sorted it all out. We're goin' on a workin' holiday and that's final.'

I opened my mouth to object. Even though hop-picking was paid work it still meant there were expenses such as the train journey and food while we were away. As I opened my mouth to argue the point, Bert interrupted.

'I've sorted it, 'ilda. I've been savin' a few pennies 'ere an' there an' I've saved enough for our train journey there an' back.' With that Bert whistled and returned to his breakfast. 'Now where's that fried bread you promised me?'

'Well, I never!' I exclaimed, torn between feeling cross at Bert for keeping something from me, and delighted that we would get a chance to go away together as a family. Then I thought about Wally and Betty. I couldn't possibly go away – they needed me at the chippy.

'Did I mention I've spoken to Wally an' 'e's fine about you 'avin' a week off work?' said Bert.

Well, I was stumped – he'd thought of everything!

*

A week later and I was finishing off the last of our packing. We needed to take everything we'd use while hop-picking. I made sure we had blankets, a small paraffin stove, some pots, soap and enough clothes to keep us all warm. Even though it was late August, it was starting to get that creeping autumn chill in the evenings.

'Is there anything I've forgotten?' I asked nobody in particular.

Bert had arranged a week off work from his deliveries. He'd been making up the time by working weekends recently, and now I knew why. The children were as excited as could be. Eight-year-old Little Albie was wild with delight at the thought of playing in the countryside. He'd never experienced wide open spaces except to gaze over the Thames from Tower Bridge or on the dockside. He was more likely to be found playing in the bombed-out buildings around the docks, despite the many warnings he was given by Bert, so this trip would be heaven for him.

By noon, everything was ready. Our belongings were packed in big suitcases borrowed from Wally. Bert dragged the cases to the bus stop, Little Albie had responsibility for keeping four-year-old Brenda safe and I carried Christine, three, in my arms.

By the time we reached Victoria Station on the bus from Rotherhithe, I was on the verge of turning back. The children were over-excited and bickering. Bert looked exhausted at carrying our things. It didn't feel like a holiday at all! It was only when we'd found a seat on the train, shushed the children and settled down for the two-hour journey into Kent that we started to relax. It was the first time the children had been on a train. Little Albie was beside himself with delight. He was too excited to stay sitting down, and kept bobbing up to point out of the window or exclaim at the speed we were travelling.

Bert and I gave each other an indulgent look. Perhaps this was a good idea after all. It was the first time we'd been away as a family and it felt special. 'We're goin' on our first 'oliday together,' I whispered into Bert's ear, smiling. He patted my hand by way of a reply and we both gazed out of the window at the city that was rapidly disappearing before our eyes. Soon the tenements and the bombsites, the factories and the houses, were replaced by lush green fields, tiny villages dotted here and there and the growing feeling that we were going somewhere special.

This wasn't the first time I'd been hopping. I'd been with my family when I was a young woman, at the start of September 1940. We'd been delirious with excitement, driving down in Pa's mate's van with my siblings Ron, Les, Joanie and me in the back, alongside Ma and Patsy. It'd felt like a whole new world. I'd never been out of my borough, let alone outside of London, and seeing the big skies uncurl as we left the city scared me as much as it delighted me – my own children must've been feeling that same mixture of trepidation and delight, seeing their world expand from the city into green fields and country lanes. A few nights later, when we were picking hops in the fields, the first wave of German bombers had appeared overhead, heading towards our beloved city. It had heralded the start of the Blitz, which destroyed everything in its path: a lean, terrifying killing machine. I'll never forget that night, when the darkness settled over us, and we stood watching the orange glow of the fires that devastated our city, wondering if we'd ever see our home or our friends and neighbours again.

I could hardly believe I was heading down to the same place, to Faversham, this time a married woman with a young family. So much had happened since those days. Ma was alive then, and I would always remember her lovely smile as she watched the younger children frolic in the fields with the wild ecstasy of gazelles. Suddenly I felt a lump in my throat. Any sudden memories of my mother would cause me to blink with the grief that never really went away. She'd been dead ten years this summer, and there wasn't a day I didn't think about her, and wish with pointless fervour that she was still with me, looking after my babies, setting the world to rights, and making everything 'spick and span' as she liked it.

'You okay, Duchess?' said Bert. I turned to him, my eyes full of tears and nodded.

He wiped away one of those treacherous tears that had spilled onto my cheek. 'Memories?' he asked gently.

I nodded my reply and tipped my head onto his solid shoulder.

Later, we arrived at the farm, the great hop bines looming over us. There was a line of tin huts at the far end of the field and we trooped towards them, tired now from the journey.

Our cabin was allocated to us by the foreman. It was nothing more than a simple wooden hut with a flattened earth floor, a hook for our gas lamps, and an earth pit out the front for our camp fires. It couldn't be described as luxury by any stretch of the imagination, but it was our home for the week, away from the smog and bustle of city life.

The children squealed with delight, especially when we told them they'd be sleeping on hay. Their excited chatter accompanied our efforts to unpack and settle in. We filled our paliasses with straw from the adjoining farm, and set them onto the pallets which were known as 'duck boards'. I set about sorting our belongings and making the hut as homely

One Lord, one faith, one baptism.

Albert Leslie Kemp

was baptised

at *St Mark's Church, Victoria Park, E.9*

on *Sunday 18th August 1946*

by *William H Ford*

Vicar

(*left*) Albie's baptism certificate, 18 August 1946.

(*above*) Little Albie, aged around 18 months, at East Street Market in 1947.

(*below*) Brenda's baptism certificate, 14 January 1951.

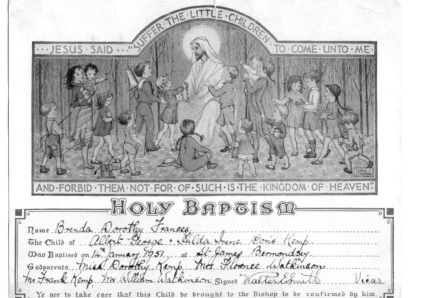

···JESUS·SAID··· "SUFFER·THE·LITTLE·CHILDREN TO·COME·UNTO·ME·

AND·FORBID·THEM·NOT·FOR·OF·SUCH·IS·THE·KINGDOM·OF·HEAVEN"

HOLY BAPTISM

Name *Brenda Dorothy Frances*

The Child of *Albert George & Hilda Irene Doris Kemp*

Was Baptised on *14th January 1951* at *St James Bermondsey*

Godparents *Miss Dorothy Kemp. Mrs Florence Watkinson.*

Mr Frank Kemp. Mr William Watkinson Signed *Walter E Smith* Vicar

Ye are to take care that this Child be brought to the Bishop to be confirmed by him.

HOME WORDS NO. 321

Having fun outdoors.
From left to right:
Christine, Albie and
Brenda.

This booklet contained
Children's Coronation
Party certificates for
Brenda, Christine and
Albert, 2 June 1953.
There were sports events,
a grand balloon race, a
fancy-dress parade, a tea
party, a talent competition
and dancing to celebrate!

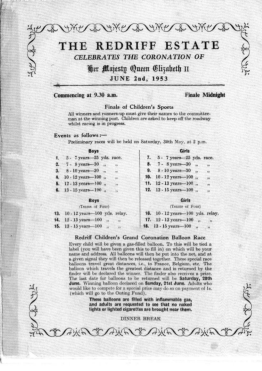

THE REDRIFF ESTATE

CELEBRATES THE CORONATION OF

Her Majesty Queen Elizabeth II

JUNE 2nd, 1953

Commencing at 9.30 a.m.   Finale Midnight

Finals of Children's Sports

All winners and runners-up must give their names to the committee-
man at the winning post. Children are asked to keep off the roadway
whilst racing is in progress.

Events as follows :—

Preliminary races will be held on Saturday, 30th May, at 2 p.m.

Boys		Girls	
1.	5 - 7 years—25 yds. race.	7.	5 - 7 years—25 yds. race.
2.	7 - 8 years—30 ,, ,,	8.	7 - 8 years—30 ,, ,,
3.	8 - 10 years—30 ,, ,,	9.	8 - 10 years—30 ,, ,,
4.	10 - 12 years—100 ,, ,,	10.	10 - 12 years—100 ,, ,,
5.	12 - 13 years—100 ,, ,,	11.	12 - 13 years—100 ,, ,,
6.	13 - 15 years—100 ,, ,,	12.	13 - 15 years—100 ,, ,,

Boys		Girls	
(Teams of Four)		(Teams of Four)	
13.	10 - 12 years—100 yds. relay.	16.	10 - 12 years—100 yds. relay.
14.	12 - 13 years—100 ,, ,,	17.	12 - 13 years—100 ,, ,,
15.	13 - 15 years—100 ,, ,,	18.	13 - 15 years—100 ,, ,,

Redriff Children's Grand Coronation Balloon Race

Every child will be given a gas-filled balloon. To this will be tied a
label (you will have been given this to fill in) on which will be your
name and address. All balloons will then be put into the net, and at
a given signal they will then be released together. These special race
balloons travel great distances, i.e., to France, Belgium, etc. The
balloon which travels the greatest distance and is returned by the
finder will be declared the winner. The finder also receives a prize.
The last date for balloons to be returned will be **Saturday, 20th
June.** Winning balloon declared on **Sunday, 21st June.** Adults who
would like to compete for a special prize may do so on payment of 1s.
(which will go to the Outing Fund).

**These balloons are filled with inflammable gas,
and adults are requested to see that no naked
lights or lighted cigarettes are brought near them.**

DINNER BREAK

"oppin" in 1954. From left to right: Little Albie, Brenda, Christine and Hilda.

South London Crematorium

THE GARDEN OF REMEMBRANCE
ROWAN ROAD, STREATHAM VALE,
LONDON, S.W.16

The Cremated remains of the late

Brenda Dorothy Frances Kemp

are laid to rest in the Garden of Remembrance, Plot CN/25

A PLAN IS EXHIBITED ON THE FLOWER LOGGIA
OF THE CREMATORIUM

No. 62

(*left*) Brahms' 'Lullaby' played as Brenda was cremated in 1957.

(*below*) On a day out to Canvey Island after Brenda and Pop had died. From left to right: Bert, Albie, Christine, Dolly and Hilda.

A picture sent to Auntie Dorothy from Albie and Christine in 1958.

(*below*) Bert and Hilda standing strong and smiling in the late 1950s.

(*above*) Happy and proud, Bert and Hilda together at Little Albie's wedding, 17 August 1968.

(*top right*) 'My one true love.' Hilda wrote this about Bert after he died for an event at the W.I.

(*right*) Hilda's precious locket – Bert on one side and Brenda on the other.

26·3·20 — 18·5·99

THIS IS MY WONDERFUL
Husband. A TRUE SON OF
HIS FATHER: ALBERT GEORGE
HE FOUGHT IN WORLD WAR
TWO OVERSEAS FOR 5 years
HE WON 6 MEDALS WHICH
I PROUDLY DISPLAY IN OUR
Home.
I FOUND A CARING LOVELY
MAN WHO WORKED HARD
FOR HIS WIFE + 2 REMAINING
CHILDREN, WE NEVER WENT
WITHOUT.
HE IS MY ONE TRUE LOVE
SADLY HE DIED ON MAY 1999
ALBERT GEORGE KEMP.

To, My dearest

Son Albie)

My heart is so full of love for you, that I'm ????? and want you to know how I feel,

The day I married your dad was the happiest of my life then, to think that the very hand some boy wanted to make me!! his Wife, But then what, you were going to be born to us + wonderful News! everyone was over joyed we fell in love with you instantly, you were our first born son from our Toe's, we had a Rocky

stat for a few years, but worked hard at our Marriage and Thank God it Survived for 54 years, I must confess I am more in love now than ever with my Albert + Albie,

Then came Two beautiful Girls, and we had a wonderful 6? years with Brenda and forty Nine with Chris. I was God Rest their souls why they were taken I'll never know, only God can answer

allways afraid to show any favour ism, so might have come across a bit cool? Harsh?? I don't know, then you moved away to Rainham because of your work, so that made a family break, then you married and had your own family So that doesnt mean you are any less than my first born Toely Baby Boy

From my Heart.

ALL My Love

Mum XXX

'My heart is so full of love for you.'
A message left for Albie in Hilda's address book.

(*above*) Laura (aged 5), me (aged 8) and Nan in 1979.

(*below*) 'We Love You'. Hilda died in 2003 and this card
to 'Boot Brush Lil' is from brother Ron.

*In Loving Memory of
My Dear Sister*

To Hilda
(BOOT. BRUSH LIL.)
We Love you.
BROThEr Ron e Blue
(AUSTRaLia)
XX

as I could. Bert went out to collect firewood for the campfire outside our hut, and to buy some eggs and bacon from the farmer's wife. I laid out the blankets and pyjamas while the children, all screeching with the happiness of animals released from captivity, went exploring.

That night we all huddled together, telling stories by the light of the fire and watching people come and go as they too, settled into their cabins.

We started work at 7 a.m., stripping the bines and filling the carts with hops, their sweet smell coating our hands and clothes. We were paid by each bushel we filled, and each bushel contained a backbreaking eight gallons of hops. It was tiring work but it was such a sharp contrast to our daily life in the city that we set to it with cheery enthusiasm. Our hop carts slowly filled, bristling with the hops and their stalks. The foreman logged our bushels in his small hopping book, written in his tight hand.

As Bert and I worked, the children skipped off to play with the other inner-city ragamuffins. We didn't see them from dawn to dusk, when they'd arrive back at dinner time with streaks of mud on their faces and knees, ravenously hungry from a day spent chasing each other through the rows and rows of hops, and exploring the woodlands, fields and meadows.

And then, one evening, disaster struck. The sun was setting across the field, and I realised that neither Little Albie nor Brenda had returned yet from their day playing in the fields and vines. Christine was sitting beside me, playing with her favourite doll – one I'd knitted for her from scraps of wool. Just as I registered alarm, I saw the skinny frame of my eldest child bob through the hop bines. I saw him and my heart sank. I knew before he told me that there was something terribly wrong: Brenda was nowhere to be seen.

Little Albie saw me and burst into tears. I ran over to him and shook his shoulders. 'Where's Brenda? Where is she?' Little Albie's skinny body was shaking with sobs. My heart had frozen inside my body. Had something dreadful happened? Who knew what strange people or animals were out there among the endless fields, woodland and streams? 'Albie, tell me, where's Brenda?' My voice was sharp with fear.

Bert looked over at us, dropped the piles of leaves that he was clearing, and ran over. Little Albie looked up at me. His voice was reedy and small. 'I don't know, Mummy, I ain't seen 'er for ages. We was playin' down by the stream an' then she weren't there anymore. I've been lookin' for ages, Mummy, I promise.' And with that Albie's body convulsed with great choking sobs.

Bert and I looked at each other. We didn't need to say a word. My heart had become like ice. 'There, there, you did the right thing in comin' to tell us. Now you go an' take Christine into the hut and get her changed into her nightie. Can you do that for me?' My voice wavered only slightly.

Meanwhile, Bert was running up and down the bines, telling everyone to form a search party. It was already getting dark. Men and women threw down their hops and, with grim faces and barked instructions, set out to look for our little girl.

'You stay with the children. Don't worry, we'll find 'er, I promise,' shouted Bert over to me. My heart felt like it would burst from my body, my hands felt cold. There were miles of fields. There were streams where Brenda could've slipped and fallen. Rumours had been circulating of a loose Alsatian dog being seen in the locality: could it have hurt my daughter? My head was racing. I felt my teeth chatter with shock. They *had* to find my little girl, they *had* to.

An hour passed. There was no sign of the search parties except for the occasional shout from a long way away and the bobbing of the lanterns which normally lit the site, but which the men had taken as darkness had fallen. I read Albie and Christine a story, reassuring them that Brenda would be home soon. Even as I read the book, I felt breathless with fear. It took all my strength to say the words. All I wanted to do was fling the bloody book to the floor and scream with desperate fear.

Then there was a shout.

It was Bert's voice. I tore out of the hut to see him carrying a little dark shape in his arms. The shape was wailing. Relief rushed through me. She was alive. She was safe. I grabbed my daughter and checked her over – there were no signs of injury. I held her tightly in my arms, shushing her and rocking her, though she was a big girl of four. Finally her body stopped shuddering, and I could unfurl her.

She was clutching an old, misshapen coat hanger as if her life depended on it, holding it to her body like a comforter, and my heart overflowed with love for her. Gently, I prised the metal hanger out of her clutches as she hiccupped away the last of her distress. I wiped back her hair – it was damp with sweat and I smelled the sharp tang of fear. I kissed her forehead and took her into the hut, nodding to some of the men from the search party as the only way I could thank them for finding my precious daughter.

Little Albie started crying when he saw his sister. Just then, Bert burst through the hut door. 'Albert, where are you? I've got a mind to give you a right good 'idin' for what you've done today. You don't ever take yer eyes off yer sister when yer out together, d'you 'ear me?' Bert's voice was harsh with fear and anger. It was the first time I'd seen him shout at one of our children. Albie recoiled in shock, staring up at his dad, his blue eyes wide with terror. 'She could've died, she could've drowned in the stream or been snatched from us by passing tinkers. 'ow could you 'ave been so stupid? 'ow could you?' Bert hit the makeshift cabin door with his fist. His face was wild with anger and the terror of thinking his child might have died.

'Bert, come on now, you've made your point,' I said, trying to pacify the situation. 'We've got our Brenda back. There's no point creating more upset. Come on, luvvie, let's be thankful our daughter is back 'ere with us, safe an' sound.'

But Bert wouldn't calm down: he was furious, though I suspected it was driven more by terrible fear for his daughter's safety than anger at our son. He turned to me. 'Keep outta it, woman,' he said, in a voice I didn't recognise. 'Albie 'as to learn 'e can't mess about and expect everythin' to be okay. We could've lost our Brenda for ever!' Bert's voice cracked. The emotion of the day was painted across his face.

I stepped back, unsure what to say. I'd never seen my husband so angry.

Bert turned to our son. 'You don't move from this cabin tonight, d'you 'ear me? You can eat yer dinner in 'ere as punishment. I don't want to 'ear another word from you, except to say sorry for what you did.'

I looked over at Little Albie. He was staring up at his father with an expression of pure shock. 'I'm sorry, Daddy, I didn't mean to lose Brenda. It'll never 'appen again.' He sniffed as tears rolled down his cheeks.

'We've got Brenda back an' that's that,' I said firmly. 'The matter's closed.' I placed an arm protectively around my son. Brenda was still clinging to me; her sobs had become snuffles and I could feel her warm body start to relax and become heavy. I didn't like seeing Bert shout at Little Albie: it brought back too many memories of my pa screaming at my siblings, Les and Ron. I wouldn't have that in my family, by God I wouldn't, even if it meant standing up to Bert in all his rage and upset. 'Bert, why don't you stoke up the fire? It's low, an' we need our dinner cooked. Albie, why don't you 'elp me get Brenda into 'er nightie an' we can put her to bed.' I looked around my family. 'What we all need is a good dinner, an' an early night.' I glared at Bert. I'd never faced him so brazenly, but if he carried on shouting at our boy I was scared I'd lose faith in him completely.

Bert rubbed his hands through his Brylcreemed hair. 'I was frightened we'd lost 'er.' He exhaled, and his body seemed to droop with the effort. 'I didn't mean to shout, 'ilda. I thought we'd never see our girl again.' His voice was low as he tried to make his apology.

'Well, we ain't lost 'er. She's safe an' sound an' it's time for our dinner. Go an' stoke the fire, Bert, an' we'll talk about this later,' I repeated stoutly. I would brook no argument. I was tired and I wanted to keep the children in their routine of dinner, bath and bed to minimise the fallout from the day's events.

Bert turned on his heel and left the hut, while Albie and I exchanged a look. I knew that Bert adored his children and would do anything to keep them out of danger but I hated seeing him attack his son, even if Albie had been careless.

As an exhausted Brenda slept nearby, I chatted away to Albie in a quiet, bright voice until eventually he told me what had happened. He and Brenda had been playing down by the stream that intersected the fields at the far reaches of the farm's land. Albie had been trying to race sticks and leaves down one stretch of the water course with another boy from the hop-pickers, and had been so absorbed with his game that he'd forgotten to watch his younger sister. That was the moment Brenda had wandered off. But he hadn't realised his sister was missing until much later, and then, fearing he would be punished, Albie had spent the next few hours calling for her until he gave up and came back, dreading the moment he had to tell us the truth. As he expected, he was right to fear it.

'Well, all's well that ends well,' I said, ruffling Albie's blond hair and getting up off the paliasse. 'I'm goin' to put the dinner on. You get a wash an' put your pyjamas on an' it'll be cooked an' ready to eat.' I forced myself to grin at him to reassure him, though I was still deeply shaken by the evening's events. My response masked the primal fear that only a mother can feel at the prospect of losing a child.

Albie gave me a weak smile and headed out to the hut that served as the camp's bathroom. It contained a single tin bath and a jug of water. I sidled up to Bert who was coaxing the fire into life.

'You don't 'ave to tell me I did the wrong thing,' Bert said gruffly.

'So why did you, then? It weren't Little Albie's fault – 'e's only eight years old. An' Brenda is so independent, it was bound to 'appen, if you think about it.' I spoke calmly: I didn't want another fight.

Bert sighed, rearranging the bundle of firewood he had carried in, then looking up at me from his crouching position by the flames. The light from the fire flickered against his face, casting shadows behind him. 'I really thought we'd lost 'er. I couldn't bear it, 'ilda. I couldn't bear losin' my littl' girl! I know I shouldn't 'ave shouted at Albie the way I did – I'll go an' 'ave a word with 'im. I'll make it up to 'im, I promise. I don't know what came over me, I just felt like everything inside me twisted up.'

I sat next to him, listening. Bert had always told me he had a hot temper if he was pushed but, thankfully, I hadn't ever seen it, till now. I watched his face as he spoke, searching for any sign that he was like my pa. All I could see was a father feeling remorse for his reactions. That was as unlike Pa as it was possible to be.

I sighed and moved away. I needed to get the dinner on and get my little ones into bed.

Later that evening, as the children settled onto their straw-stuffed beds, I sat with them, singing their favourite lullabies like they were tiny babies again. The ageless words comforted us all and I promised them everything would be better in the morning.

I knew my Bert loved his children and loved me.

That night I took a long time to fall asleep and I know Bert did too. We lay awake, not speaking, absorbing the day's events, and hoping that the next day would be better, as I'd promised.

CHAPTER 12

The Tallyman

1954

'Oi, 'ilda, watch what yer doin'! You'll set the place alight!' guffawed Wally, reaching over to take the searing hot pan of oil from me. I'd kept it too long in the hot pan and it looked close to catching alight. 'What's got into you, girl? You ain't sloppy usually!'

'Oh, Gawd, Wally! I'm sorry, I don't know where me 'ead is today! I'm alright, I promise. I'll take more care next time,' I replied, trying to smooth over my mistake with chatter. I knew I wasn't very convincing though, and I gave him a falsely jaunty smile hoping to cover my tracks still further.

Wally stopped what he was doing and looked at me. His gaze was sharp and knowing. I averted my eyes, hoping he'd leave it at that.

Several of my regulars had commented that I didn't seem myself. I was trying to be 'Hooray Hilda' as Wally kept calling me, but my heart just wasn't in it.

The hop-picking holiday still weighed on my mind. We had only been back a few days and I still couldn't get over that feeling of fear that I'd lost my daughter, and the fallout with Bert. On top of that were the rekindled memories of my ma and me hopping when I was a girl. Suddenly the grief felt just as fresh again as it had when I received the letter from Pa telling me she'd passed away. Ma had gone quietly, with no fuss one afternoon, sitting by the fire. It was Ron who spotted she'd gone, and it was he who was sent by Pa to fetch the woman who washed and laid out the bodies in Braunston.

Every night now I would trace her outline on the photograph I had of me and her in the fields near the cottage where we stayed in Braunston. That photograph sits on my bedside table and it is the last thing I look at in the evening, and the first thing I see every morning. When Ma died I was living at Bert's parents' home in Bow, East London, while he was away fighting. When I got Pa's letter, I took a train up to Coventry and Pa met me at the station and took me to Ma's funeral in the village church. She was so modest, so worried about the cost of things, that she had insisted before she died that she was to lie in an unmarked grave. I laid flowers there to remember her. The place was peaceful and I remember feeling grateful she was out of Pa's clutches and could suffer no more brutality at his hands. I missed her terribly though, and the time spent hopping had brought back so many memories of her that I felt bereft, as if she'd died only a week ago.

'Come on, 'ilda – yer mopin' again. I need six cod and three 'addock filleted and battered an' up 'ere for fryin'.' Wally's voice was jovial, but I knew he was getting cross with me and I couldn't blame him. He prided himself on giving his customers the best service in town, which is why people flocked to Wally's Fish and Chip Shop from as far north as Rotherhithe and as far west as Brixton. Wally's was famous in south-east London, and he wasn't going to let a dopey assistant like me stop his customers getting their dinner.

'Alright, Wally, I'm comin'. So that's three cod an' six 'addock on its way,' I replied, my face falling at the sight of Wally shaking his head.

'Betty'll do it, don't worry. Why don't you pack some chips up for Mrs Collins 'ere? She's got two 'ungry boys an' an 'usband all waitin' for their dinner, so get yer skids on!' Wally said, before proceeding to holler down the stairs to Betty for the correct fish.

' 'ow are you, Mrs Collins?' I managed to ask, as I shook the excess oil from the golden chips before tipping them onto the news pages.

'All right, dearie,' she replied. 'Nothing to complain about – well, nothing more than usual, eh?' Pat Collins was known as being a bit of a gossip so I knew I had to keep my guard up around her. She had a hard life, though, with two growing boys and a husband who worked on the roads, repairing bomb damage. They ate her out of house and home, and she often said that she only had one pair of underpants between the boys which they had to wear on alternate days, they were so poor. Whether it was true or not, I didn't know, but life wasn't easy for most people round our way – Pat's worn shoes and ripped apron was enough of a sign to know that new clothes of any description were a rarity for her family. 'Did you 'ear about Mrs 'arris's problem with 'er legs?' Pat started on her favourite topic: other peoples' health problems. I couldn't see why they were any of her concern, but I humoured her anyway, nodding and smiling intermittently while throwing a sly wink to Mavis who was next in the queue. I had to make it up to Wally for being clumsy earlier.

Just as Mrs Collins was about to leave I told her to wait, and threw an extra scoop of chips into some paper, wrapping it deftly and pushing it into her hands. Her look of shock was replaced by gratitude. I glanced over at Wally. He'd seen what I'd done, and even though he shook his head he was smiling. He knew I couldn't bear to see people go hungry, and I knew the comforting power of a good, old-fashioned plate of chips to ease hunger and restore faith in the world.

For a second I thought back to a time during the Blitz when we'd survived yet another night of bombs crashing on the docklands, and Pa had gone out and found the only food not rationed: a supper of fish and chips. Oh, my giddy aunt, I could still recall the salve of that taste of hot crunchy chips and fluffy white fish with crackles of batter, coated in vinegar and salt. It had been like having a proper family that night, with all of us in accord, sitting round the kitchen table together, eating our simple but wonderful meal. I had longed for nights like that as a child, and if my extra portion of chips gave Mrs Collins and her boys something similar it was worth the risk to give it to her.

When Mrs Collins left and Mavis stood in front of me, her lined face creasing into a smile, I smiled back, knowing I looked defeated by the effort. 'You alright, dearie?' she said, softly, touching my arm as she spoke.

Well, I wasn't used to such kindness. My eyes instantly stung with tears. I tried to bat them away but a couple slid down my face and I wiped them away with a sharp move-ment. 'Don't you go worryin' about me, Mavis. You've got enough on yer plate,' I said, and we shared a grim look.

Mavis's husband had lost his job of collecting offal from butchers' shops due to the drink he put away each night. I knew times were hard again for her family.

'We've all got our troubles to bear,' replied Mavis, patting my hand, 'but yer allowed to 'ave them as well, 'ilda. You can't always go about lookin' after other people.'

I shook my head. It had always been me looking out for my family and friends, wiping away their tears or soothing away their troubles. It was too late for me to change now. I had my Bert, so I shouldn't have a care in the world. 'I'm right as rain, Mavis. Now tell me about your Billy – ain't 'e the most 'andsome boy you ever did see?' and with that I diffused the moment of concern, not wanting to admit to myself that I sorely needed the kindness of my friend.

Later, though, I managed to restore some of my usual good humour. Old Bill came in for his supper late that evening, and I joked with him that he'd been held up by his fancy woman ... and, bless him, he blushed darker red than the tomato sauce. 'I'm only teasin' you, Bill! That'll be five shillin's, luvvie.' I took his money and handed him his warm parcel of food. *That'll keep him going for another day*, I thought with affection.

'You're back on form, 'ooray 'ilda, thank goodness for that!' said Wally with a laugh, as we cleaned up the counters and put the vinegar bottles back on the shelves at the end of the shift.

'Thanks, Wally. Sorry fer bein' a bit slow earlier. I've 'ad a few things on me mind,' I said as honestly as I could, without justifying my lack of industry.

'Anything you'd like to tell me about, 'ilda? I've always got time to listen to you, you know that. If there's anything I can do to 'elp, you only 'ave to ask,' he said, his kind face looking concerned.

I sighed and put down the cloth I had been rubbing over the same place repeatedly. 'To be truthful, it was the 'oliday. It set me to thinkin' about me ma an' it's the anniversary of 'er passin' away, so I've been a bit miserable. Sorry, Wally – you don't deserve an old misery guts for an assistant!' I chuckled, but I knew the smile didn't quite reach my eyes.

'Oh, dearie, it's 'ard losin' yer mother. I know all about that. I lost me own ma twenty years ago, an' I still miss 'er every day, God rest 'er soul. It never goes away, luvvie – the sooner you accept that, the better off you'll be,' Wally said, simply.

I appreciated Wally being so open with me; he was more than just a boss, he was my friend, but it was more than the anniversary of Ma's death. My faith in Bert had been shaken too.

That night I scrubbed the floor and the counters with extra

vigour. I wanted to make it up to Wally and Betty for my lack of attention. I knew I was also avoiding going home.

It was past 10 p.m. when Wally poked his head round the door and said, 'You still 'ere? Get off 'ome, 'ilda, we'll see you tomorrow. Go on get back to yer kids, or they'll forget who their mother is.' He gave a quick wave then disappeared to the back of the shop. I heard the sound of his feet go up the stairs to the flat he and Betty shared. All of a sudden the footsteps turned around and Wally's face reappeared in the doorway. 'Tell yer 'usband yer all invited round to watch me new television on Sunday. It's bein' delivered 'ere on Saturday. It'll be somethin' to see, I tell you. All right? Cheerio then.' Without waiting for an answer Wally vanished.

A television was a rare luxury: Wally must have saved up for months, if not years, for one. I didn't know anyone else with a television except for a burly docker, Jimmy, who lived on our estate. He was a foreman at Greenland Docks and was known locally as being very well-to-do. We'd never been invited in to see his set, even though Little Albie played with his son, John.

I headed home with Wally's strange invite making me chuckle.

On Sunday, I dressed Little Albie, Brenda and Christine in their best clothes. We all had one set of best, and one set we wore daily – I counted myself rich at having the choice of two dresses to wear! It was more than I'd ever owned in my life.

The children were told to be on their best behaviour, and given an extra scrub down in the tin bath the night before. It was rare that we got invited anywhere these days, what with Bert working all hours at the delivery depot and me working at the chippy and raising the children as best we could. It was a rare, and rather anxiety-provoking treat to take the children to Wally's flat.

We arrived at the chippy and Betty let us in. Little Albie handed her a teacake I'd made especially for the occasion. 'You shouldn't 'ave,' she smiled. 'Now, who's goin' to be the first to get a slice?' The children were instantly at their ease and we all followed Betty's plump waddle up the stairs.

I was shy at entering her and Wally's home, and worried that the children might knock something over, or break something, even if they were under strict instructions to behave. The flat was small and neat with a lounge, a kitchen, an inside lavvy and a bedroom at the back which, of course, we didn't see.

The lounge was a place of wonder. Standing in prime position between the fire place and the settee was the television set. It was a thing of beauty. It was encased in a rich brown cabinet with four legs which held it upright. There was an oval-shaped screen and several buttons. I'd never seen a television before, though I'd glanced at pictures of them for sale in newspapers. It seemed huge, though that might've been because of the size of Wally's flat.

'Don't touch, whatever you do, do not touch that set,' I whispered to my three children through gritted teeth.

Little Albie was instantly captivated, though it wasn't even switched on. ' 'ow does it work?' he shouted excitedly, making Bert and Wally laugh.

The men were already huddled round the set, Wally's voice proudly telling Bert, Little Albie and Brenda about the television's features: 'Well, it's a Motorola. Top spec. Absolutely the best television on the market.'

Betty and I exchanged a look. 'We'll get the kettle on, shall we?' She laughed, and I followed her into her tidy kitchen with three-year-old Christine pattering along behind me.

'Men, eh? They'll be fine-tunin' that thing fer hours!' said Betty, and we both chuckled at that.

I sat at the kitchen table while Betty bustled around her kitchen, pulling out a tin of biscuits and arranging them on a plate with a doily on it. *She's so posh! That's the proper way of doin' things, with a doily*, I thought to myself and smiled up at her.

Betty fussed with the custard creams and the garibaldis for a little longer. I recognised them from my days working at the Peek Frean biscuit factory in Bermondsey. 'Let's go an' see if anyone's 'ungry, shall we?' said Betty, beaming, and she led us back into the lounge where, lo and behold, the television set was working.

'Gawd, it's a miracle!' was all I could stutter. The screen glowed and a picture of a little girl appeared before our eyes. Little Albie could barely contain his excitement – he was sitting inches away from the screen, bouncing up and down on the pouffe he was perched on.

'Well, I never!' exclaimed Bert. 'Ain't it a marvel what they can do these days!'

'Who's that little girl? She's very pretty,' lisped Brenda shyly.

We all peered at the girl with long grey hair holding a piece of white chalk against a blackboard. The television picture was in black and white but it might as well have been drawn in moon dust for the excitement it gave us.

'An' there's a clown!' said Little Albie, pointing at the picture.

'It's amazin', ain't it? 'ow do they do that?' Betty added, shaking her head in awe.

Wally and Bert were still fiddling with the television dials. The picture grew lighter and darker. Betty and I sat sipping our tea, nibbling delicately on our biscuits. I kept a beady eye out for crumbs. The children were so enthralled they barely noticed the food. They were spellbound. Time ticked on. The set crackled and whined occasionally, as Bert and Wally made further adjustments. The children had settled down to gaze at the unchanging picture, utterly transfixed at the sight coming from a wooden box, as if by magic. Every now and then, Wally would ask Bert with a sense of urgency if he had seen the picture change? Did it go lighter with that turn of the dial, or darker?

Eventually, I stifled a yawn. The girl in the box was impressive but we'd been in our seats watching her for more than an hour. I shifted slightly. Christine started to fidget, but the boys and Brenda were still engrossed. I started to watch the clock that sat over the fireplace. It was coming up to dinner time. We'd been in front of that same picture for two hours!

It was at this point that I coughed and fidgeted in my seat, hoping Bert would pick up my cue it was time to go. Betty kept bringing biscuits and tea, and milk for the children, but anyone could see we'd be in danger of overstaying our welcome if we stayed much longer. 'Bert, we'd better think about the children's dinner,' I said eventually, after my hints were ignored.

'Oh, right you are, Duchess. Sorry, luv, only it ain't every day you get to see a real television set,' answered Bert.

I smiled at him, arching my brows. 'Let's leave Wally and Betty to their television, eh, an' make a move. Otherwise the children will never eat their tea,' I added. With effusive thank-yous, the children swooped out of the flat, chattering and laughing as they did.

I watched them indulgently on the walk home. They really were darlings, each and every one of them. I was a very lucky woman.

Back at home, however, they had nothing else to talk about except the television. They were completely star-struck, to the point I started getting irritable, especially when they started asking why we didn't have one. 'Yer father works long hours to feed an' clothe you, so I don't want to 'ear any whinin' about gettin' a set, d'you 'ear me?' I admonished.

They chorused a 'Yesss' in reluctant agreement before scampering off to bed, still giddy from the day's excitement.

The next day was Monday. I never worked on Mondays so I had a happy day with the littl'uns.

When Bert got in from work and had eaten his dinner of boiled sausages and mash, he fiddled in his pocket and brought out a couple of shillings. 'Last payment tonight,' he announced, smiling.

I smiled back. We'd been paying the Tallyman for months now to get us a brand new radiogram. It wasn't as exciting as a new television, but it was what we'd always wanted. Bert and I had grown close over a love of big band music, and we'd longed for a radio to tune into the BBC. Every Monday night for months, the Tallyman had come to the door collecting small part-payments, or tallies, for the radiogram. We were finally ready to pay in full, and receive our long-awaited music player!

We sat listening for the knock and when it came, we both jumped up and went to the door. Bert handed over the money, and the Tallyman recorded it in his little book. Like children ourselves, we looked at him eagerly.

He was a pleasant-enough looking man in his late fifties. He had dark hair greased back in the fashion, wore a suit which looked more expensive than anything we'd ever worn on our backs, and he carried a leather satchel with his takings and notebook inside. He was smoking a cigarette out of the corner of his mouth which jiggled when he spoke. 'You're all done, Mr Kemp, Mrs Kemp.'

And with that, two burly men appeared in the tenement passageway holding our brand-new player wrapped in a thin plastic material. They shuffled into the front room, put it down and left as quickly as they'd arrived.

I shut the door and turned round to Bert, feeling like Christmas had come early. He lovingly unwrapped the large, wooden cabinet and we both gazed at it. The radio section was at the front with the built-in speaker below it. Bert lifted up the top and propped it up to reveal the record player inside.

'It's beautiful,' I breathed.

Bert looked at me a minute. He looked like he was seeing me for the first time. 'What, Bert, what are you lookin' at?' I asked.

'You, Duchess, you look lovely tonight. I don't think I said a proper apology for shouting at Albie on 'oliday and, well, I'm sayin' it now. I love you, 'ilda, an' I promise I won't shout at any of me kids like that again.'

How did he know? How did he know I needed to hear that from him? That I'd doubted him and his love for us? My eyes filled with tears but I didn't wipe them away – I let them fall.

Bert moved over and put his arms around me and we stayed like that for a while. I breathed in the solid, male smell of him: his boot polish, his soap and Brylcreem. I thanked God for the millionth time that I was married to a man so unlike my pa.

Bert broke off the embrace, and turned to the radiogram. I left him to figure out how it worked and went to clear up the dinner pots and plates, setting the kitchen to rights. I was washing down the floor when the sound of a brass instrument called me back to the lounge. The radiogram was working!

'Shush, or you'll wake the children!' I giggled.

Bert turned the dial then grabbed my arms. 'Can I 'ave this next dance?' he said, formally.

'Of course you can, Bert. You can 'ave this dance, an' every dance that follows until the day I die,' I replied, dropping my head onto his chest and swaying in his arms as the music played.

CHAPTER 13

Rock Around The Clock

1956

ROCK AROUND THE CLOCK screamed the poster. 'So this is what all the fuss is about!' said Wally with a laugh, holding the brightly coloured notice aloft. He put it on the chip shop counter and rubbed his hands together with glee. 'We're goin' to make a fortune, you'll see. You an' me, 'ilda – we'll be able to retire early!' And with that Wally grabbed my hands and started to whirl me around an imaginary dance floor in the front of the fish and chip shop.

'Get off me you daft 'a'porth!' I laughed, tugging my arms from him. 'What if Bert saw you now, what would 'e say?'

' 'e'd say, "Thank you very much, Wally, for makin' me missus a millionaire!" ' Wally cackled with laughter at his own joke.

'So you really think you'll do well, then, just because the film of Bill Hayley and the Comets is showing at the Gaumont?'

The Gaumont was the cinema in Rosehill, Carshalton. Wally had drafted me into his other fish and chip shop nearby, and we were busy peeling a mountain of potatoes to make into the mounds of chips that Wally was expecting to sell to the crowds that the film looked set to draw.

'Yes, I know it for sure. That's why you're 'ere tonight an' that's why I've used me savin's to buy 'alf of Billin'sgate fish market. We'll make a killin' an' when we do, I shall take you an' your Bert out for a slap-up meal to celebrate!'

Wally's good humour was infectious. 'Well, I won't say no

to that, Wally. Now, where's the broom so I can brush away all these peelin's?'

The back room of Wally's Carshalton fish and chip shop was a mess. There were piles of old potato skins curled up on the floor, creating a layer of stinking mush, while fish heads poked out of the overflowing rubbish bins – the stench of old fish carcasses rotting inside them was revolting.

'Gawd, it's as if you've never cleaned this place! It's a right disgrace!' I said, my hands on my hips, my nose wrinkled in disgust. At moments like this I could see my ma doing exactly the same to us kids: standing with a scowl on her lovely face as she surveyed whatever mischief we'd got up to. I felt a wave of nostalgia overtake me again. I looked so much like her. I could see her face staring out of my own every morning as I fixed my hair in the mirror. It was comforting, thinking that in some strange way she was still with me. I drew on her fierce East End pride now as I surveyed the rotting remains of yesterday's business. 'I'll make this place spick and span in no time, but I need lots of 'ot water, a scrubbing brush an' a broom.'

'Yes, sir!' said Wally, a cheeky twinkle in his eye. 'Look, 'ere's Vera. She works 'ere Tuesdays to Saturdays. She'll definitely know where everything is.'

I turned round to see a woman in her thirties with blonde hair done up in a fashionable hairdo. She was attractive in a made-up sort of way. ' 'ello, Vera,' I said, smiling. Despite my misgivings about her cleanliness in the shop I was determined to be friendly.

'Alright,' replied the woman. She was smoking a cigarette and as she spoke, she tipped it out of her mouth and ground her heel into it on the chip-shop floor.

I stared at her as if she was from Mars. No wonder the chippy was in such a state. I had my work cut out for me.

Later, I hissed at Wally, 'What the 'ell are you playin' at, employin' Vera? She don't know a broom from a bream!'

Wally chuckled but replied, 'She's good fer business – all the young men like 'er, an' she knows all the regulars. It ain't that bad in 'ere, 'ilda. Go on, girl, do yer worst an' clean up if you fancy, but no one's ever minded before.'

I made a disgruntled sound and gritted my teeth. It was clear I was going to be busier than I thought that day, and I hadn't even finished the spuds.

In the back room I was greeted with another surprise: while I'd been out the front, Wally had brought in Hooray Hilda the greyhound and had her chained her to the wall. 'If it ain't dirty enough in 'ere, we've got the likes of you makin' it worse,' I grumbled, as I stroked her head and looked about the room. 'Right, well then, I'd better make a start,' I said to myself.

Hooray Hilda gave a small yawn and settled herself down on the floor.

The day was exhausting. I found the communal lavvy out in the filthy yard was as squalid as the rest of the shop so I gave it as good a scrub down as I could. Back inside, I washed down the floors, emptied the overflowing bins and scraped the old bits of chips and batter out of the frying vats. I emptied out the oil and replaced it with new beef dripping. I peeled spuds until my hands wouldn't hold the potatoes any more and I set the chipper to work, making a pile of chips the like of which I'd never seen. There must have been thousands of them. *I just 'ope Wally knows what 'e's doin'*, I thought to myself, the first inkling of doubt creeping into my mind. There were fish stacked up on the surfaces – wherever they could be crammed into a space. Boggle-eyed cod and hake were lying in cold submission, awaiting their beheading and then their dip into the huge bucket of batter that Wally had made earlier that day. I had never seen so much food in all my life.

Instead of making me feel hungry, I felt suddenly wary, as if all our futures rested on the limp bodies of the deceased fish. *No time for worries, you've got work to do, girl*, I reminded myself. Suddenly, I felt dizzy. It caught me off-guard and I clutched onto the table for support. I'd been having fainting spells for a while and I felt permanently cold. I'd been piling on the weight as well, and it was this that forced me to go to my local doctor.

The novelty of seeing a doctor without having to pay was still something us Londoners couldn't quite get to grips with. In the old days, even one generation before me, many of the hospitals had been workhouses, where the most desperate among us ended up. No person with a heart and soul ever wanted to end up in one of those bleak, desperate hellholes, so we always avoided the medical profession when we could, as it bought back too many ingrained memories. It was a hard habit to break – the fear of the workhouse was written into our DNA as working-class people. But, times had changed, and the workhouses were now used to treat the sick, so I guess us Londoners hadn't changed as much as we thought. Even when I'd had my babies, I'd been wary of going into hospital! It was only when I had aches all over my body and tiredness the like of which I'd never experienced before, that Bert insisted I went to the local GP.

It had felt strange seeing a doctor, but he'd taken blood and come back with a diagnosis. I had hypothyroidism, which meant my thyroid wasn't working properly and I needed an operation to fix it.

I hadn't told Wally about the time I'd need off work. I didn't like to think about the procedure, even though it was only a few weeks away. I'd been booked in to a hospital but

I was scared of going under the knife, and so I hadn't yet got up the courage to tell my boss. I knew I had to do it soon but I wasn't quite ready.

'Oi, Dilly Daydreamer, you got some of those spuds ready to go?' shouted Wally from the front of the shop.

'Alright, Wally, I'm comin'. Yer potatoes are all chipped an' ready to fry, don't you worry!' I bantered back, grabbing a spare bucket and piling in the chips.

It looked like we were ready to start our marathon of frying and salting.

Several young people had wandered into the shop. Wally had opened early for the film that had taken the UK by storm. American culture might be here to stay, but we had our fish and chips to keep the home fires burning. No matter what happened, there really was nothing that said Great Britain like a steaming hot pile of chips and fish, covered in vinegar and salt. At times like this I was proud of our humble English cooking. In a funny way, I knew who I was, and what I stood for, as I fried fish and salted chips. It was more than a meal, it was a comfort blanket to keep our collective spirits up. At that moment I remembered another time, during the Blitz, when my younger brother Ron and I had been sent out to find fish and chips for our supper. We'd been waiting in line for what seemed like ages, we'd finally given the man behind the counter our order and then, low and behold, the sirens started. Suddenly there was the sound of bombs dropping nearby, the *rat-a-tat-tat* of gunfire and explosions all around us. I had grabbed our wrapped chips while Ron panicked and ran out of the shop, heading for home. I shouted after him but, seconds later, there was an ear-shattering crash and I felt myself being thrown to the ground. The chip-shop man had pushed me onto the floor as a bomb exploded with tremendous force nearby.

Despite the danger and terror, I picked myself up, brushed myself down and legged it after my brother, finding him eventually at a nearby air-raid shelter. I remember us giggling like the naughty children we were as we ate those chips still piping-hot in the newspaper as we sheltered from the bombings. My goodness, we got a hiding from Pa that evening when we returned with nothing more than the greasy chip papers! On that occasion we didn't care, though. We'd been nourished by our sense of togetherness over those delicious chips.

Wally was already laughing and joking with his customers so I took up the chips and started steeping the fish fillets in the batter. I carried some of those up as well, hearing the gratifying sizzle of the oil as it greeted the salty bait. There was a small queue, mostly groups of boys, or a boy taking his sweetheart to the pictures, both blushing with the newness of the adventure. It reminded me of my courting days with Bert: our first cautious words, the moment he held my hand for the first time, the first kiss that sealed our fate together. I sighed again. Too many memories. I was getting lost in them today when I needed to get my head down and help Wally as best I could.

We could hear the voices and shouts of more youngsters as they gathered at the cinema, which was only a block or two away.

'It's gettin' busy out there,' said Wally, with glee. 'Come on, 'ilda, get the fish fryin'! We'll 'ave a lot of 'ungry customers once the film's finished – the cinema is heavin'!'

My face was flushed from the heat of the hot oil. My hair sprang into curls, which I tried to push back off my face as I worked. Wally kept dashing out and running in to give reports. Apparently the cinema was swamped. The film was a run-away success. Every now and then people would come in, buy a packet of chips and let us know the latest updates. All those who could get tickets were now watching the matinee, while those that couldn't were waiting for the next performance. Apparently the police had started to arrive, concerned by reports of scuffles in the queues and the sheer volume of people queuing on the street.

'The minute they come out, I want you, 'ilda, baggin' up the chips, and I want you, Vera, collectin' the money. I'll keep an eye on the fryer an' bring out more supplies as they're sold.' Wally was leading us like a general on the battlefield.

Once there was a heap of golden fish warming on the shelf above the fryers, and the chips were ready, the three of us lined the counter, waiting for the influx. 'Film should be over now,' said Wally, eyeing the clock above the door. 'They'll be 'ere any minute, you'll see.' Time ticked on. Nobody arrived. Wally's face went from expectation to bewilderment in the space of half an hour. 'I'll just pop out an' 'ave a look – see what's what. Maybe it went on fer longer than I thought . . . yes, that'll be it, you'll see,' Wally said, as he dashed out.

He didn't return for 20 minutes, by which time Vera and I looked like we felt: two women with sinking feelings in their bellies. No one had come in. We hadn't sold a single chip in the past two hours. The fish was still warming, great piles of food lay uneaten and going to waste.

Wally finally reappeared. He looked crushed. I had never seen him without a glint of playful mischief in his eye. 'It's a riot out there. There were so many people tryin' to get into the cinema the police set up a barrier which made everyone go back the other way. They couldn't get 'ere if they tried.' He sounded heartbroken, his wiry body sagging.

'But can't you explain to the policemen you need the customers to come in?' I asked, a little naively.

'I tried, but they 'ad their orders an' so they said there

was nothing they could do.' Wally gazed around the shop, looking like it was the first time he'd noticed the piles and piles of food waiting for the customers to crowd in and buy it. Except there would be no customers. 'All me savin's! I used all me savin's. What'll Betty say?' Wally looked at me beseechingly. He looked rather like Hooray Hilda did when she needed a stroke and a kind word.

'I'm sorry, Wally. I don't know what to say. It don't look like they're comin', so you'll 'ave to prepare yerself to tell Betty the truth. You took a gamble, but this time it didn't pay off . . .' My voice trailed off at the sight of Wally's face. He looked even more miserable, if that was possible, at the sound of my words. I sighed and looked round. 'We'd better pack up what we can an' see if we can give it away. I'll take as much as I can carry for the children and for some mothers on the estate. Vera can do the same for her friends. Wally, you'll 'ave to take some 'ome too. 'ave you got any neighbours you can give it to?'

Wally had his head between his hands, sitting behind the counter.

'Wally? Did you 'ear me? Come on, we'd better pack up this food an' get goin'. We can fit lots in yer car an' deliver it as well. It ain't all bad – just think of all the families who'll 'ave a fish supper this evenin' because of you. It's better than charity, it's feedin' people.'

I tried to jolly my boss along but he wouldn't have it. He drove me back into Rotherhithe and barely spoke all the way. By the time we reached my estate I was glad to get out, my string bag brimming with fish and chip meals to give out. *At least some good came out of today*, I thought to myself, *even if it weren't what Wally was expectin'.*

Wally parked his car at the entrance to the estate. 'Free fish an' chips! Go an' tell yer mothers we've got free fish an' chips for yer supper!' Wally started hollering as loud as his lungs would let him.

'Free fish an' chips! It's all gotta go – come on an' get yer free supper!' I joined in. 'Go on, Tommy, go an' tell Vi to get down 'ere an' tell all our neighbours. Tell yer pals an' all. We've got plenty to give away!' I shouted after Vi's boy.

He raced off with a portion of chips clasped in his hands.

Before long the mothers from the estate started appearing. 'What's all this, 'ilda?' said Ivy, who lived at the end of our landing with her docker husband, Jimmy, and their one son, Jimmy Junior. They were seen as relatively well-off compared to most down our way: Jimmy had regular work at the docks as a foreman and they owned a black and white television, which meant they were leagues ahead of most of us in the financial stakes.

'We made too much in the shop today – nothin' to worry about, but Wally 'ere thought 'e'd like to share it out... a bit of goodwill to one an' all,' I said, trying to shield Wally from prying questions about how we'd come to have so much to spare.

Ivy looked at the piles of chips Wally was handing out to the ragamuffin urchins who ran wild in the estate and she raised her eyebrows. I quickly turned to Mother Edna who had arrived, and stacked two piles of chips and a cod into her string bag. I didn't want any more questions from the likes of Ivy.

'Oi, Tommy, give this lot to yer mother,' I said, as Vi's son reappeared.

'Me ma sent me down to get some. She's on 'er way but didn't want to miss out,' replied the boy who gave his mother such a lot to worry about.

'I'd never give it away an' forget yer ma! What were you

thinkin'? 'ere, take this lot an' come back for some more,' I replied, piling the still-warm bundles into his skinny arms.

'Ta, duckie!' he said with a grin.

'An' enough of your cheek!' I bantered back, tutting at him as I always did.

The fish and chip giveaway had become something of an event on the estate. Hassled-looking mothers with their hair rollers tucked under turbans and their floral pinafores on came down to get their suppers, followed closely by their children.

'We've made quite a party, Wally,' I said, looking at him with a smile, hoping to cheer him up.

'Well, it looks like we 'ave.' Wally nodded and looked over at me. At last, a laugh escaped his lips.

'Don't worry, Wally, it'll all come out in the wash, an' by that I mean, it'll all be alright, you'll see,' I added.

' 'course it will, 'ooray 'ilda, with you an' me as a team. 'course it will,' Wally replied.

I looked around at the happy faces and the gossiping housewives, the children who whooped with joy at the thought of fish and chip suppers in their bellies and the men who started to appear from their day's work. As the sun went down, we gave away the last of the food and Wally got into his car with a cheery wave and a wink. I hoped he could see what a difference he'd made to the lives of those living on the estate. Wally had taken a dent in his savings, but he'd brightened many people's day, and put hot food into the stomachs of some of the poorest people in London. To me, that meant the day wasn't a total failure, and I fervently hoped he felt the same.

By the time I got indoors it was long past teatime, even though Wally had shut up shop early because of the police barrier stopping trade. Bert had arrived home and we ate our cod and chips in silence, both wondering how close Wally had come to losing his business.

Despite our worries, the balm of the meal worked its magic: the chips were fluffy and the fish was white and flaky still, even though it had long since gone cold. Wally's decision to fry everything in beef dripping as opposed to cheap oil meant they were delicious – it was why people made an extra effort to go to Wally's rather than any of the other nearby chippies.

'Well, Wally may not be the best businessman in London, but he makes a damn good fish and chip supper!' announced Bert, pushing his empty plate away and leaning back in his chair.

I smiled, not forgetting to remind Bert not to swear in the house, then we cleaned the plates away and took our cocoa to bed.

The flat smelled of fresh paint as my brother Ron had painted our bathroom for us. It was the kind of gesture happy-go-lucky Ron was known for – always there to help family and have a laugh while he was doing it. Ron's wife, Joyce, and their three young children lived in Elephant and Castle, where he'd been working as a builder. We saw Ron and Joyce regularly and it was always good to hear his chipper voice and his banter.

After a hard day's work, if not an entirely successful one, I was relieved to undress and shuffle into bed alongside my husband, despite the paint fumes. We snuggled up together before falling asleep, safe and secure in each others' arms.

The day of my admittance to hospital dawned. I had eventually plucked up the courage to tell Wally that I needed an operation. He had waved me off with a cheery 'Take as long as you need, 'ooray 'ilda. If you'd like a visit, let Bert know an' we'll be in to see you.'

I cuddled Albie, Brenda and Christine, and as I clutched their small bodies close to me, I felt a sudden wave of fear, an urge to never let them go. I held them till they fidgeted and wriggled free.

'You alright, luv?' asked Bert, sensing that something was amiss.

I nodded, my eyes suddenly filling with tears. My children were so precious. They were my life, and now it came to leaving for the hospital I didn't want to go. Bert patted my shoulder, and I reluctantly let go of my babies, as I called them still. 'I'll be home soon, I promise,' I said. 'Be good for yer father,' I added, resisting the urge to grab them and hold them tighter still.

Bert accompanied me onto the bus, carrying my small suitcase. I was going to be in for ten days, assuming all went well.

I was nervous about the procedure but more worried about how Bert would cope with the children. Vi would look after them by day and Bert in the evening. It was, at least, all worked out.

I was settled into the ward by a nice young nurse, and eventually the time came for Bert to leave. 'Give Little Albie, Brenda and Christine a kiss from me. Tell them I love them,' I said, grabbing Bert's arm as he left. I don't know why but I had a strange feeling of foreboding.

'Don't be silly, Duchess, they'll be right as rain. You just 'ave a nice rest an' we'll all be in to see you when you wake up.'

'You'll all come in, you promise?' I asked again, feeling a sense of strange desperation. Suddenly I couldn't bear the thought of Bert leaving, and having to wait to see my children. Tears sprang to my eyes again.

'Of course! Now stop all this nonsense. It's a routine operation, you'll be alright an' you'll be back 'ome with all your family in the blink of an eye.' With that, Bert gave me a final kiss, waving to me as he left the ward.

I sank back into the pillows as I watched him go, my heart feeling like it was sinking into my stomach. *Must be nerves about the operation*, I told myself, but the feeling wouldn't go away, however much I tried to quash it.

CHAPTER 14

Tragedy Strikes

1957

Panic. *Can't breathe. Where am I?* 'She's alive, thank God, she's alive. Nurse, get the oxygen mask.' *Woozy. Feel sick. My chest hurts. Where's Bert?* 'Give her oxygen – she looks like she's going again. Quickly now!' *Voices outside my head. Or are they mine? Can't tell. I'm going to be sick!* 'Quick, nurse, get a bowl! She looks like she's being sick again. Mrs Kemp, Mrs Kemp? Can you hear me?'

The voice had a cut-glass accent. I couldn't make out where it was coming from. Suddenly a bolt of nausea hit me and I struggled to lean over. I vomited violently. I heard a groan and realised it was coming from me.

My eyes started to focus. There were men in pale green outfits with masks in front of their mouths around me, and a great, bright light hovered over me. 'Where am I?' My voice was a plaintiff cry.

'It's alright, Mrs Kemp, you're safe now. We lost you for a minute but you came back to us. We're your surgeons and you're having your operation. Now, try to be calm and we'll finish up and get you back to the ward.'

The voice of the nurse was friendly. I saw her shape take on a vague presence near me. There was a flurry of activity, a man wearing a white mask, a nurse with a kind face, peering over me. 'I want my Bert,' was all I managed to say as I lay back down on the operating table. I looked up at the light and it seemed to drift over me, away from me, disappearing into itself as I watched with fascination. 'You're going back down,' came a voice from the far end of the room. I tried to nod but my head felt heavy, my mind disengaged from my body. I turned to smile in the voice's direction but realised I couldn't now move my head. I started to have a thought, but the room went dark.

I went dark.

Hours later, or maybe it was only minutes – who could say? – I found myself lying in a large, quiet room. The ceiling was white. As I came round I started to distinguish voices, low murmurings. I tried to look up but I still couldn't move my body. 'Water,' was all I could say, 'need water.' My voice came out small and cracked.

'Duchess, you're awake! I'm 'ere, don't you worry. 'ere's your water . . . now, just 'ave a sip.' Bert leaned over to me and attempted to hold the glass to my lips.

I swivelled my eyes to Bert, drinking in the sight of him. 'I'm alive!' I said. 'I thought I'd died. It all went strange and then dark. But there was this light . . .'

At that point Bert interrupted me. 'Now don't get yerself worked up, Duchess. No need. You 'ad a funny turn during the operation; in fact, the surgeon told me that you died for a few minutes but they revived you . . .' And then his voice drifted off, or maybe it was me.

I felt woozy again, disorientated. *I died for a few minutes?* I could hardly take in what Bert was saying. 'I died?' I croaked, my voice coming out like a whisper. My throat felt sore and bruised.

'Let's sit you up. That's better,' said Bert, ignoring my question as he shuffled the pillows behind my head, propping me up so I could better see him and the ward. 'Now, drink up, there's a good girl.'

He held a glass of water to my lips but I shook my head. My throat felt swollen after the surgery. I managed to swallow but refused the drink. I looked back at Bert and realised by the look of tiredness and relief on his face that he'd been through the mill emotionally, and decided not to pester him with questions. I was alive wasn't I, and that would have to be enough for me. Whatever happened on that operating table was over now.

The ward was clean and bright, and nurses were tending to other female patients. Even though it was busy, there seemed an air of calm about the place, which made me feel safe. 'I died . . .' I said, trying to make sense of things as I looked over at my lovely Bert's face as he peered at me.

The memory of something was hovering just out of reach.

There had been a pale, glowing light that had pulled me towards it. It had seemed to soak up my body and drench me in goodness. But there was something else. Something more troubling. I was sure I saw a little girl, she was very ill, very poorly indeed . . .

'Come on, 'ilda, drink up. There's a good girl. We don't want you bein' sick again, do we?' said Bert as he leant over me with the glass. His face looked pale, his lines more pronounced. In fact, he looked dreadful.

I wrinkled up my face as another fleeting memory swam past me. I'd seen a young girl, I'd swear it. She was lying in a white bed in a white room, not unlike this one.

Oh my God. I suddenly remembered what I'd seen. I'd hovered above my body. I'd followed that strange light as it took me into another ward where a little girl was lying, barely breathing, still as death, in another hospital bed. 'Brenda! It was Brenda! Bert what's 'appened to our girl? I saw 'er in 'ere, I swear it! I saw 'er when I floated out of my body! I'm not goin' mad, Bert, I know what I saw! 'as something 'appened? Tell me.' My voice became shrill with fear. I knew something was terribly wrong.

Bert's face only confirmed my deepest fears. He had gone even paler, the colour draining from his face as he stared at me, shuddering as I spoke. There were dark circles under his eyes but right now he looked frightened, wary of me, even.

''ow the 'ell did you know? 'ow could you possibly know? I've been comin' in to see you an' leavin' by a different door so that you wouldn't see me go to the children's ward.'

'It was while I was under, Bert. I swear, Bert, I floated up an' drifted into Brenda's ward an' I saw 'er there, lyin' still as anythin'. What's wrong wiv 'er? Tell me she ain't 'ere. I'd rather be goin' mad than that . . .' I was gripping Bert's arm. There was a heartbeat's pause, a silence that I felt rather than heard.

Bert took both my hands. Something was terribly wrong and, God knows how, but something strange had happened. I don't know whether I really had travelled out of my body, or if it was instinct but, as Brenda's mother, I knew my daughter was here in the same place. And, hand on my heart, I was sure I'd seen her lying still and pale in her hospital bed. Her head was bandaged. I could feel that she lay between the states of life and death. I had looked over her and felt overwhelmed with love. Then the illusion vanished. The light and the darkness left, and I had been cast back into myself, vomiting onto the floor.

'Now, be brave, Duchess, because I've got something to tell you but you 'ave to be brave. Can you do that?' Bert's voice was low.

I nodded, desperate for the news, and yet hoping that somehow this was all part of the delirium of the operation.

It wasn't.

Bert's mouth made the sounds and shapes of words I did not want to hear. I made him repeat them, even though I couldn't bear to listen. 'Brenda was out playin' with the swings an' she was 'it on the 'ead by one of them. She was brought in to the 'ospital an' is bein' looked after. She's very poorly, 'ilda, very poorly . . .' Bert's voice trailed off. He'd spoken slowly to me, like he was talking kindly to someone who wasn't quite there in the head. There were tears running down his cheeks. I'd only ever seen him cry when his father died, and the sight of his tears chilled me far more than his words ever could. Something must be very wrong for him to break down.

'I want to see 'er, Bert. When can I go an' see my little girl?' I wailed, feeling at once utterly helpless.

'Now, don't you go rushin' out of bed – you've 'ad an operation an' we nearly lost you, so I don't want you upsettin' yerself, 'ilda. I don't want you goin' down there, not yet. Will you promise me you won't try and get out of bed? I'll be 'ere every day, an' I'll be with Brenda, an' I'll let you know when she's well enough for you to visit.'

'But I want to see 'er! She's my daughter,' I said mutinously, using the last ounce of my strength. I lay back on the pillows, openly crying now as well. The ward was full of patients and their visitors but I didn't care who saw my tears. I felt the same urgency and sharp fear as I had when Brenda had gone missing while on our hop-picking trip. I wanted to see her now, and her to be safe in my arms.

'Now, listen 'ere, 'ilda, I don't ever say no to you, do I?' Bert's eyes were pleading with me. 'On our wedding day you promised to love, 'onour an' obey me, d'you remember?' he said. 'And now is one of those times I need you to obey me as yer 'usband, who loves you more than 'is own life.'

'But . . .' I started to say, but Bert interrupted: 'Promise me you'll wait a day or two until you're better before you go an' see Brenda. I don't want you upsettin' yerself. Promise me, 'ilda. I need to 'ear you say it.'

I nodded my head. A single tear stained my pillow. 'I promise,' I said, my voice now a whisper. 'Will she be alright?'

' 'course she will, luvvie. We just 'ave to pray a littl' 'arder than normal. It'll all be alright, I'm sure of it.' But Bert didn't look sure. He looked as far from certain as I'd ever seen him.

We looked at each other in silence. I realised from Bert's manner, and from his insistence that I didn't go and visit Brenda, that she was fighting for her life.

The anger at the promise that Bert had made me make evaporated and I was left with the creeping beginnings of grief; the kind of emotion that stalls, waiting in the wings, just out of sight of my mind's eye. I hoped it would stay there, and Brenda would recover back into the bonny, bright little girl that she was.

That night, hours after Bert left my bedside, I prayed to my mother. I held the picture that I always had with me, of Ma and me in a field in Braunston, laughing into the camera on a rare day of peace with Pa. Wherever I was, I had that black and white photograph with me. It had become my talisman, keeping me safe, protected by her love even from the grave. I stroked her face as I spoke to her, feeling my love for her warm my heart. 'Ma, please look after my baby girl, Brenda. She's so young, she's barely even 'ad a childhood. Just make 'er better, Ma. I know you're up there, lookin' over me an' my family, so please take care of 'er for me, 'cos I can't get there to see 'er myself.' I wondered why Bert had been so insistent on me not visiting our daughter. I'd given him my promise and so I would no more break it than run for prime minister, but something inside me felt it was like a warning. Things must be bad if Bert was keeping me away. Or else I was being morbid and things were not as bad as they seemed. He wouldn't keep me away from Brenda if he knew her life was in the balance, would he? I lay back, breathing heavily, feeling confused and desperately worried. I called a nurse over and told her my daughter was in the hospital and would she go down and see her, and give her my love? The nurse, who was a pretty, plump girl with brown, curly hair and a posh Home Counties accent looked at me like you might at a stray dog in the street. Was that pity in her eyes? Or was I just tired and muddled from the sedatives I'd been given for the operation?

'Of course I will, dear. Don't you worry yourself. I'll make sure your sentiments reach your daughter,' she eventually said, patting my arm. I noticed she didn't quite catch my eyes as she spoke.

I watched her as she walked towards the matron's table at the end of the ward. I saw her take Matron aside and speak to her. They both looked over at me before returning to their conversation. The plump nurse eventually bustled off.

Matron shuffled the papers on her desk then got up from her chair and walked rather slowly over to me. She put a smile on her face and said: 'Now, Mrs Kemp, we need you to concentrate on recovering from your procedure today. Your daughter has the best possible care in this hospital. Maybe tomorrow we can check on Brenda's progress and let you see her.' With that she gave me another stiff smile and turned away to the sound of another patient calling for her.

I wanted to scream at her. All of a sudden I felt a huge jolt of fear. I knew, as if it had been written down for me, that Brenda lay gravely ill somewhere in this place. I wanted to see her. I wanted to be there with my daughter. But the scream wouldn't come out. My throat was bruised and painful. The emotion seemed to lodge somewhere above my heart. I wanted to shout and rage against the world that was keeping me from my daughter. Yet all I did was lie there, my heart pounding with the fear that seemed to have become liquid and was shooting through every cell in my body. My Brenda. My beloved girl. Would tomorrow be too late? There was nothing I could do except pray with renewed fervour. I pleaded with God to stay with her, to save her life. I offered mine in exchange and I asked why hadn't He taken me instead of my girl while I was on that operating table? I asked why all this tragedy hung over my life and I received no reply, none at all. I sank back into my pillows and began the business of waiting for news.

CHAPTER 15

Saying Goodbye

1957

'Brenda's gone? What do you mean she's gone?' Bert and the nurse looked at me. There was sorrow written on both their faces. I looked from my husband to the woman who had been looking after me for the past few days.

Nurse Gladys – I never knew her surname – was the first to speak. Her eyes were kind but I couldn't bear her kindness, not now, not when my Brenda had disappeared without me having a chance to see her.

I'd been much, much sicker than I'd realised coming round from the operation. My body's reaction to the procedure had made my recovery frustratingly slow. I hadn't been well enough to go down to see my little girl, and now it seemed I'd lost the chance to stroke her hair and tell her everything would be alright.

'Your daughter was too poorly to be looked after in this hospital, so she had to be moved to Great Ormond Street to have specialist care.' Nurse Gladys looked over at Bert and he nodded back at her. 'There's something else we probably should have told you but you've been so poorly yourself, we didn't feel we could upset you, as it might have hindered your recovery, Mrs Kemp,' she added – defensively it seemed to me.

'What is it? What haven't you told me?' My voice was a whisper, partly from the operation on my thyroid, partly from the terror that seized my throat.

Bert dropped his gaze. Even he couldn't look me in the

face. He put his head into his hands as he sat in the chair next to my hospital bed.

'What is it? Tell me!' I demanded, finding my voice, despite the pain.

'Mrs Kemp, you must keep calm. Getting agitated won't help you or Brenda.' Nurse Gladys sighed.

I stared at her, unable to speak, waiting for her next words. 'I am calm, I'm very calm, now will you please tell me what is wrong with my daughter?' I could barely keep a civil word in my head.

'Brenda was hit on the head with a swing, that much you know.'

I nodded, trying to keep my temper, biting my lip until I heard the truth they'd been keeping from me. 'Well, when we did scans of Brenda's skull we found something else. We found a brain tumour.'

A brain tumour. I heard the words but I was desperate for them not to be true. There was a moment's silence, broken only by the sounds of the ward as visitors started arriving to see their loved ones. 'What's goin' to 'appen to 'er?' I asked, feeling too shocked to register the enormity of what the nurse was telling me.

'They may operate if the tumour can be removed. Whichever way, we'll know within the next couple of days. As soon as I hear back from Great Ormond Street I will let you know.' With that, the nurse threw Bert a look and left us.

I turned to him. The man I loved had lied to me. Every day as I lay here in this damn hospital bed, feeling as powerless as any human being can feel, he'd said that all was well and Brenda would soon be up here to visit me. I'd chuckled at that, and had been counting the hours till I was well enough to be back on my feet and down in that ward with her. But Bert had lied. None of it was true. If what the nurse said was correct, then my darling girl was very sick indeed. At that moment I had the first real inkling that my daughter could die. Now I knew the reality of the situation, and with it I felt red-hot anger at Bert for keeping me out of the most vital information of my life.

'You lied to me.' My voice was choked with emotion. 'I don't know if I can ever forgive you,' was all I managed to say before the tears came, hot and fast, down my cheeks. I made no attempt to wipe them away. I was beside myself with the terror only a mother can feel when her child's life is threatened.

'I'm sorry, Duchess, I 'ad to. I didn't want you sufferin' any more than you 'ad to,' Bert replied. He tried to hold my hand but I snatched it away from him.

'Don't call me Duchess. I don't know if I ever want you to call me "Duchess" ever again. You lied to me, an' I never got a chance to say goodbye. I'll never forgive you for that, Bert, I swear I won't.'

Bert's face was a pool of misery. 'Don't say that, 'ilda, you don't mean it. It's been a nightmare keepin' the truth from you. Don't you think I wanted to tell you? It's been the worst few days of my life, knowin' 'ow ill Brenda was an' seein' you both at death's door.'

'So she's at death's door?' I said, harshly.

Bert looked at me with such agony that the wall my fury had temporarily built around me suddenly crumbled. I was Bert's girl again, and the sight of him in such pain at what he'd had to do, filled me with remorse. 'Oh, Bert, I'm sorry, I didn't mean to say that. I can't bear it though, I can't bear knowin' there's nothing I can do to 'elp our littl'un!'

Several days later I was taken to convalesce in a nursing home in Margate. Bert came to visit with the news that Brenda was no better but she was receiving the best possible care in London. I cannot describe how I felt, knowing I couldn't be with my girl – just to touch her hand and stroke her hair from her face. I felt bereft, like part of me was already missing, and at times I wondered if I was preparing for worse to come.

Bert took me on a boat trip one day as my recovery time came to an end. We held hands and watched the shoreline as it rose and fell with the rocking of the boat. We hardly spoke. After all, what was there to say? Our hearts were in that hospital with Brenda, and there was nothing we could do to help her.

Back on the landing strip, we strolled along the seafront and came to a booth with a hand-painted sign saying: 'Fortune Teller – Consult The Best'. I don't know what prompted me to go in, as I'd always dismissed mystics as charlatans and con men, but something made me go inside. Perhaps a desperate need to know what would happen to my girl?

The booth was small, cramped and dark. An ordinary-looking woman was sitting inside at a small table with a deck of cards laid on it. She looked up as I bent my head to enter.

'Come and sit down, dearie. You look like you need a friend,' said the woman, which struck me as strange. I had lots of friends, but at the same time I desperately needed someone to talk to, someone who didn't know my life or my troubles, whom I could open up to and free myself of the terrible burden of worry that weighed down my every waking moment.

Bert stayed outside and I could hear his feet shuffle as he waited for me.

'Show me your hands,' commanded the woman, and I obeyed, holding out both hands in front of me. She gripped them both tightly and, with an intense gaze, looked them over, muttering a little to herself.

'What's there? What can you see?' I asked, feeling nervous now. I shouldn't have come, this was a silly waste of time. 'I want to know what will become of my children,' I said suddenly. It was the reason I was in this odd little wooden hut, after all.

'One of your children will be big in business – oh, yes, I can see success and a good life,' she said. 'The other will help others, she'll do something with health.' And then she stopped. 'What about the other of my children?' I said, feeling alarmed all of a sudden.

'The third is blank,' was all she said.

I looked up into her face. Her eyes peered at me in the gloom. Her brown hair was thin and her eyes looked sad. I could see sympathy on her face and I stood up with a jolt.

'It's all rubbish!' I said sharply and dropped her money on the table. The lady smiled a sorrowful smile. It was too much to bear. I bolted out of the doorway.

Bert looked up, startled by the speed of my exit. 'It's all a load of nonsense,' I said and he shrugged, taking my arm and leading me back to the nursing home. I couldn't rid myself of the agitation, though. One of my children was a blank. What did that mean? Was she just some crazy old woman, or had she really seen the future?

I arrived back home a week later, still feeling groggy and unsettled, but glad to be back in the flat and in our borough, and seeing my children: Little Albie, 11, and Christine, who was still my baby at 6 years old, for the first time since my operation. I held them tightly and openly wept, telling them I'd missed them so much. They were giddy with excitement at having their mother home. I couldn't help but think that I'd left three children and returned home to only two. Life was so precious, so fragile, and none more so than the lives of my beloved babies, who were desperate for news about their sister.

Bert and I kept up a happy front, telling them she was very poorly but that she would be better soon. I went back to work at the fish and chip shop because we needed the money after my time off. Everyone was glad to see me. Wally brought a chair up to the shop so I could sit and chat to the customers if I was feeling tired. Then the inevitable moment came . . . Betty asked about the children and how they'd coped, and it was at that point that I had to tell them about Brenda.

I don't know how I said the words. They choked me.

I saw Wally and Betty's faces change from their usual chipper selves to horror and sympathy as the realisation sunk in. 'Oh, Gawd, 'ilda, I don't believe it. You were both in the same 'ospital at the same time, both critically ill. What were the chances—?' Wally said.

'You poor dear, I don't know what to say except that you can take as much time as you need. You don't 'ave to come in to work, we'll manage,' said Betty.

'I 'ave to work, an' I want to work. What will I do at 'ome except mope about gettin' myself into a stew about Brenda?' I said. 'It's best I'm 'ere keepin' meself busy an' getting' on with normal life. I can't 'elp 'er, an' all the worryin' an' cryin' won't 'elp 'er either . . .' My voice trailed off. I kept getting sudden bursts of emotion that threatened to overwhelm me. It was best to stop talking and do some work, keep my mind busy so I didn't dwell on the terrifying turn our lives had taken.

My mother-in-law Dolly had been told the news by Bert and she was adding her prayers to mine. Every night I asked God why my Brenda had been taken so ill. I pleaded with God to make her well again, to remember our suffering and to help us in our desperate plight. I hadn't told any of my brothers or sisters. Their lives were going on and I didn't want to worry them, and part of me couldn't bear people knowing as it made Brenda's illness all the more real. So I carried on as best I could, serving fish and chips and pretending it would all be alright in the end.

It had to be, for all our sakes.

Every evening Bert arrived home late after he went in to see Brenda in the city centre; each night he returned home with the same, ashen expression on his face.

Then, 'She's comin' back,' he announced one evening.

I looked up from my knitting, expecting to see a huge smile on his face, but if anything it was more grave. I stood up, my half-knitted scarf falling to the floor, and I grabbed his hands. 'But that's good, Bert! She's comin' back to us, she must be well enough...?' I scanned his face, but there was no change of expression.

'She's very poorly. They operated on 'er brain but couldn't remove the tumour. Our lovely girl is now in a wheelchair, the doctors say she's paralysed. They say there's nothing else they can do, that's why they're bringin' 'er back. An' she ain't comin' 'ome. She's goin' to the 'ospital so we can at least see her before...' Bert stopped talking abruptly.

'Before...? Before what? What do you mean?' I urged, gripping Bert's hands tighter.

'Nothin'. I meant nothin'. Now go an' put the kettle on, Duchess. I'm parched,' he said, his voice rattling. I saw the look of stubborn resolve on his face and knew I'd get nothing more from him that night.

Inside, I felt the shock of all this new information. My Brenda was in a wheelchair and her doctors were saying she'd never walk again. I could hardly take it in. All I could see in my mind's eye was my boisterous, confident little girl skipping through the hop fields and across our estate. How could all that life and vitality have left her? I felt like shaking Bert until he spat out exactly what he was thinking and feeling. Something told me that wasn't the end of it. My mother's intuition told me things were worse than even he was letting on. I felt a sob well up and I choked it down.

Reluctantly, I went out to the kitchen and lit the cooker, placing the kettle onto the flame. My hands were shaking as I worked. I put out the cups and sat there, waiting for the water to boil, my mind racing. *Well, Brenda's comin' back, that's got to be a good thing*, I told myself sternly. *I can go round an' see 'er at last.* The thought of setting eyes on my daughter again cheered me up despite the bleak warnings on Bert's face. I almost didn't care that she was paralysed – I just wanted her back home with us so I could look after her myself.

By the time I'd brought Bert's tea and two garibaldi biscuits into the lounge on a tray, I was almost calm again. I said nothing as I placed the tray in front of Bert. We sipped our drinks in silence, the biscuits lying untouched.

A week later, and almost a month since I'd left hospital, I busied myself getting our dinner cooked before leaving for my shift at Wally's. Bert had left as usual, saying he'd be back early so we could go to the hospital and see Brenda. We planned on getting there and back before the children were out of school. Bert had taken Albie and Christine to the hospital while I was convalescing as they'd pleaded with him to see their sister. In those days, children weren't allowed inside hospitals as visitors so Bert had arranged for the nurse to wheel Brenda to a window so the children could see her. Bert told me later, his voice breaking, that Brenda had looked small and frail. The nurse held her hand and waved. She gave no sign that she recognised her siblings but she was a little too far away for Albie and Christine to realise how poorly she was.

Bert arrived home and we set off, getting the bus. We were both silent for the length of the journey, lost in our thoughts and ill at ease with not knowing how our girl would be when we saw her. I'd brought Brenda's favourite toy, a plastic dolly with a sweet little yellow dress that I'd knitted for her, and half a sponge cake to give her if she was up to eating.

Arriving at the hospital, I let Bert steer me towards the children's ward. There were bright pictures painted on the walls, cheering the place up a bit. We found the nurses' station and Bert spoke to a nurse. Instead of guiding us to where our daughter lay, she asked us to wait in a side room as she needed to fetch Matron.

Bert and I cast an uneasy look at each other but let ourselves be led into the small room, which contained a single chair and a basin. Bert signalled for me to sit down and I did, placing my handbag on my knees in front of me in a protective gesture.

Seconds later, a stiff-looking woman with pale red hair scraped back under her headwear arrived. She closed the door behind her and stood in front of us. We both looked at her and it was then she spoke. The words have haunted me ever since. They came out of her mouth and sort of settled into me rather than being something I heard. I felt like they were coming from a great distance away. 'I am very sad to say but your daughter Brenda passed away just after 12 p.m. today. The severity of her condition was simply too much for her to bear. Please accept our condolences – we did everything we could to try and revive her but it was not to be. I'll leave you both in here. Take as long as you need. If there's anything you need to know the nurses are here to help.'

The matron backed out of the room, leaving us staring at the closed door. Our world collapsed. I felt like the earth beneath my feet had vanished, and there was nothing to anchor me to myself and my life any more. My daughter had died. My beloved girl Brenda was dead, and I hadn't seen her.

I hadn't said goodbye.

I doubled up as if in tremendous physical pain. The hurt was emotional but my body seemed to crumple in on itself. I was lost in grief and love and anger against the forces of the universe that had conspired to rob me of my first-born girl. There was the sound of a woman wailing. She was me. I was her. I wept and I raged, and I felt Bert's warm, solid body hold me. We rocked together in mutual pain as the terrible truth sunk in. We would never put Brenda to bed again, never wrap her up warm against a winter chill. We would never make her cocoa and read her a story.

Our losses were nothing compared to hers, though. She would never become a woman in her own right. She would never learn to think and feel for herself. There would be no suitors for her hand, no wedding to plan, no children to birth. She would remain a child of seven for ever, and there was nothing, absolutely nothing we could do about it.

Our hell seemed vast and fathomless. Bert wept and it was my turn to hold him.

'I want to see 'er,' was all I managed to say and Bert nodded. We walked out of that room like victims of a holocaust, our bodies and minds irreversibly altered, flayed open.

We found a nurse and told her what we wanted and she smiled a small, grim smile and told us she was in the hospital morgue. We said we wanted to see her wherever she was, and so, clinging on to each other for support, Bert and I followed the nurse down into the bowels of the building.

She spoke to other nameless nurses and we were taken into

a cold room with white stone floors. The wall was made up of compartments. There were empty slabs and sinks nearby. I shuddered but there was no way I would leave this place till I saw my girl for the last time. We were told to wait and taken behind a green curtain that was pulled around us, like our grief was too raw, too real to be seen.

We stood waiting, clutching each others' hands until a nurse appeared. 'She's here, if you still want to see her?' she said.

We both nodded. The curtain parted and there was my seven-year-old daughter on the mortuary slab. I walked over to her, slowly, expecting at any moment that my bright girl would jump up and shout, 'Surprise! I got you, Mummy!'

There was no surprise. There was only my girl, pale and cold.

I stroked her blonde hair, feeling the tangles snag my fingers. There was a large cut on one side of her head – the bandages had been removed, I guess where the surgeons had tried to save her life. I moved round her; she was still dressed in her nightie and I was glad of that. She at least had died wearing her own clothes; it was some kind of tangible link to our lives. Her eyes were shut and I leant over and planted a kiss on her ice-cold cheek. She felt clammy and her skin looked like fine porcelain, almost translucent, underscored by blue veins. I kissed her again, wanting her to know, even in death, that she was deeply loved.

I sensed Bert had stepped back. He seemed stunned. I drew him towards Brenda. 'You must say goodbye to her, darlin', or you'll regret it for ever. I know it's painful but she's still our daughter, even if she's 'ere like this. You 'ave to tell 'er 'ow much we loved 'er, an' will always love 'er.' My words were a murmur. Bert came closer, gently holding one of her little hands. His voice was charged with emotion. He said a few words that are too private even for me to tell. When he'd finished he broke down into tears. I moved to comfort him but he gestured for me to stay with Brenda while he went to regain control of himself.

I stayed chatting to Brenda and stroking her body for a while longer. It wasn't unusual then to spend time with the body of a loved one. It was the tradition of the East End to embalm the body and then have three days where the person would be laid out in their coffin in the parlour at home so that friends and family could gather to pay their last respects. Dolly had done the same thing with Pop. Bert and I had been able to go to Bow and pay our final respects to the man who'd brought so much love into both our lives. It was how things were done then.

I wanted to stay with my girl for as long as the hospital staff would let me. I wanted to remember every little detail of her, soak her up so that I could always picture her in my heart for the months and years to come. I talked to her as I held her cold hand. I told her how loved she was, and how we'd always love her. I said that her daddy and I always tried to be the best parents we could be, and I hoped she knew that everything we'd done for her was done with love at its centre. I stroked her blonde curls off her pretty face. It was still chubby, her puppy fat had not quite come off her yet, and I traced the outline of her eyes and mouth, whispering words of love as I did.

I tucked a hospital blanket around her body, knowing she was far away from feeling the cold, but as a way of reassuring myself, I suppose. I wanted to say goodbye properly, as I hadn't had the chance to do before God had taken her from me. I asked Ma to stay with her 'up there', and for them both to watch over the rest of us until whenever God saw fit to reunite us.

Eventually, I realised that time had marched on. Little Albie and Christine would have been home from school for at least an hour, if not longer. Bert and I had better make a move. I fussed with Brenda's nightie, doing up the top button on her white cotton garment, and kissed her forehead for the last time. Now it was time to leave, I couldn't bear to go. I heard a noise behind me and Bert was standing there. He placed his hands on my shoulders and, without a murmur, he lead me quietly from the morgue.

It wasn't until we were both outside that the tears came. Bert held me as I sobbed, feeling the finality of my goodbyes to our elder daughter.

In a strange way I was comforted by the bizarre experience I had had when I 'saw' Brenda in hospital during my operation. That, at least, was a connection with her before she had died. I hoped she'd sensed my presence, watching over her, my maternal love covering her like a blanket made of the softest down.

Bert would not speak. He only shook his head, and together we turned and headed for home, back to the children, back to our lives that had been torn into shreds.

Somehow, we made a silent pact not to tell the children until the next day. I don't think either of us could cope with any more emotion that night. Without a word we settled the children that night, read them a story and tucked them both up in bed. Albie and Christine were so used to Brenda being in hospital that neither of them asked when she would be home, and for that, at least, I was grateful.

CHAPTER 16

The Brightest Star

1957

'What's 'appenin', Mummy? Why are all these people 'ere?' Little Albie stood at the kitchen doorway, rubbing his eyes. It was gone 9 a.m. on a school day and my son obviously realised something was up as the kitchen was full of people.

Dolly and her neighbour in Bow, Flo (Bill's wife), Vi and I turned to look at him. I had no words for him. Instead, I knelt down on the kitchen floor and scooped him into my arms and held him against me tightly. He didn't squirm to get away as he usually did when I embraced him.

'I've got some bad news to tell you. It's your sister, Brenda. I'm sorry to say that she's died, darlin'. She's gone to the angels,' was all I could say.

There was a brief moment's silence, then Little Albie pulled away from me and looked into my eyes. He nodded, his face grave. ' 'ow are we goin' to tell Christine?' is all he replied.

My heart swelled for my courageous boy of 11. He was grown up beyond his years. By the looks of his little face he'd known his sister wasn't long for this world.

There was a yawn from the doorway and I looked up to see Christine. Before I could move, Dolly bustled over to her and marched her into the scullery to wash her face.

'Now then, you, yer mummy 'as something she needs to tell you an' she needs you to be very brave, Christine. Do you think you can manage that?' Dolly said when they'd finished their wash and returned to the crowded kitchen. Dolly's voice was soft as she peered down into her face, a plump arm now on both Albie and Christine's shoulders.

Christine blinked up at her, suddenly quiet. I swallowed. This was the moment I'd been dreading. It was time to tell my daughter that her best friend in the world had gone to heaven. I'd been dreading this moment from the second I laid eyes on Brenda's body. The only thing worse than seeing her lying cold and still on that mortuary slab was the prospect of having to tell her siblings the tragic truth that their sister would not be coming home. She'd never be coming home. I clutched the locket I wore round my neck with its picture of Bert on one side, and I drew in a big breath. The time was now, I couldn't keep it a secret from my youngest a moment longer.

Bert and I had discussed what I should say before he left the house at six that morning. We had sat in ghastly silence, curls of steam rising from the untouched tea in front of us. 'It's best you tell 'em the minute they're awake. I'll be bringin' me mum and Gawd knows who else back to be with you, so they'll know somethin's up. You'll 'ave to find the courage, 'ilda. I can't do it. It'll kill me to say them words.' Bert looked up at me. He looked like a broken man. He'd scarcely said anything since we left the hospital only 12 hours before. It seemed like we'd stepped into a nightmare where everything was the same and yet deeply, strangely different. Our lives had been stopped mid-way, and nothing would ever bring back the happiness we shared as our family had grown. We had changed irrevocably and for ever. Now we had the worst part to get through. The final insult to add to the injury we felt so acutely in our hearts. Telling Christine that her sister was gone. How would we find the courage? 'I'll do it, I know it'll be too 'ard for you, Bert,' I said, laying my hand over his. 'We 'ave to see this through together, no matter what 'appens.

We're a family an' I love you. We will get through this. One day we will be able to speak of our girl without tearin' our 'earts to bits. I know it sounds a million miles away, but we will find peace again one day, I promise you.' With that I wiped away yet another tear. I closed my eyes for a second, sending up a silent prayer for courage, then I heaved myself up off the kitchen chair.

Everything seemed so difficult, so heavy. My body felt like it had aged a thousand years in one, sleepless night. I washed up our plates and set the kitchen to rights. Bert sighed a long, terrible sigh. He reached for his cap and his coat, even though it was late summer and still warm, even in the mornings, and he sloped out of our home.

I watched him go: the sight of a man weighed down by the tragedies of life that can strike anyone at any time. There was little comfort in knowing there were parents the world over who had witnessed a child of theirs die. In that moment I didn't care that others had suffered similar fates to ours. I could only see our life through the dark prism that had descended upon us. Final. Absolute. The light in our life puffed out as if it had never been.

I only felt anger now, pure rage, at God for letting this happen to me. Wasn't my bleak childhood suffering enough? But that pain wasn't enough for my God – there had to be more. And now He'd done his worst. He'd taken my child. And I couldn't see how I would ever find my way to forgiving God for that.

Bert had left early to walk to work to explain he couldn't drive for a few days, and he would then get a bus over to Bow to collect Dolly and Flo, who lived in the same house as Bert's mother. Flo's husband, our great friend Bill, had died only a few short months since we'd learnt of his illness. There'd been a lot of tragedy in our lives, and it didn't ever seem to stop. Dolly already knew that Brenda was gravely ill but Bert would be imparting the news that she was gone from us, and I didn't envy him that a bit.

Just before eight o'clock, Dolly and Flo arrived with Bert. My neighbour Vi had realised something was amiss and had come in, gasping with shock when I told her of Brenda's death. It was the custom to gather close family and friends around when a loved one died, especially a child. It was a support mechanism, and a way of showing respect to the bereaved family. Dolly had brought with her a couple of loaves of bread and a joint of ham and was busy boiling it on the stove. Flo was slicing bread for our breakfast and making sure the kettle was hot for the gallons of sweetened tea I would be made to drink over the next few days. It was our way of counteracting the shock. Bert left again, this time getting the bus to Walworth to see Pa and Phoebe to tell them the tragic news. I didn't envy him that either. We hadn't had much contact with them over the past few years. I'd wanted to stay as far away from Pa as I could, and unfortunately that had cut me off from the rest of my family. I knew that Joanie had moved back to Braunston with her Sid, and that Ron was thinking of emigrating to Australia with his wife Joyce and their three children. Phoebe might well come back with Bert, but I hoped That Man would stay away, even though it was expected to have immediate family close by during a bereavement. The last thing I wanted in my life at this moment of ultimate grief was his presence. I prayed he would be too hungover to come, or still out boozing and committing adultery with the floozies he now flaunted in his second wife's face.

My thoughts were interrupted by Christine's little voice. She was six years old, but she was the baby of the family and had seemed so much younger than Brenda, even though there was barely a year between them. 'But why aren't we at school?' said Christine with a little lisp, looking up at Dolly. She looked confused, and a little frightened, at this unexpected morning with its strange beginning.

Dolly looked over at me. It was my cue. I gently herded Albie and Christine into my bedroom, as somehow it felt safer to talk about the terrible news in bed, away from the others and away from their own bedrooms. I didn't want them associating their own room with the tragic news. Slowly, I framed the words, hearing them leave my mouth as I held both of them tight to me. 'You know that your sister Brenda's been very poorly.' I started. Christine nodded, remaining silent. I held them closer still. 'Well, when the doctors had a look at Brenda's head they found she was even poorlier than they thought. They tried to make her better but it was impossible.' I gulped again, feeling sick at what I had to say next. 'Well, God decided that it was best if Brenda went up to 'eaven an' lived with Him instead of us.' I looked at Christine's face. It was clear she didn't understand.

'Brenda's with the angels?' she said, as the truth started to dawn.

I nodded my head, trying to smile reassuringly at her. She was too young to hear news like this, but what else could I do? 'Brenda's gone to live with the angels an' with God in 'eaven. She's gone away from us as she was too special to stay here on earth,' I said as firmly as I could manage. I felt a wave of grief building inside me and I willed it away. I didn't want the children to see me fall apart – anything but that.

'Brenda's dead,' said Albie, matter-of-factly.

'Yes, luvvie, she is. She died yesterday in the hospital, and later on today your daddy will take you to see her, if you want to. She's dead like yer father's pa, Bill, is dead. Gone off to 'eaven as well – d'you remember when Bill passed away?'

We'd mourned Bill as a good friend and a lovely man who was more like family to us.

There was a moment's silence, then Christine burst into tears. 'I want my sister back! I don't want God to 'ave 'er, it ain't fair!' Her voice became a wail. 'But you said she'd get better! You said it would all be alright!' she added.

'I know I did, an' I'm sorry I said that, because in the end she was too poorly to live an' so we 'ave to get used to the fact that our Brenda won't be comin' 'ome to us.' At that my voice cracked.

Christine was crying, but I wasn't sure she really understood that Brenda was gone for ever. Little Albie, who was an intelligent boy, seemed to understand, but I knew it would take time for them to come to terms with the loss of their sister, as it would for all of us. 'Go an' sit with Dolly in the kitchen. Your daddy will be 'ome shortly. 'e's gone to tell the family our sad news, but 'e'll be 'ome soon, so you'd better 'ave yer breakfast an' get dressed so 'e can take you up the 'ospital.'

Dolly took charge. She gave the children their breakfast and wiped away their tears. She brought me hot tea with so much sugar I could almost stand my teaspoon up in it. By ten o'clock word had got out on the estate and a series of housewives – some I'd never even spoken to before – dropped by with condolences and food. It was the tradition to bring food to feed all the visitors that were expected to descend on a family in mourning, and to help us out so we didn't have to worry about money or practicalities during the initial shock. When Bert's father had committed suicide, Bert and I had gone round to Dolly's with a pot of stew and a bag of scones. We'd stayed until it was late, and returned each day until the funeral was over. It was our way of showing our love and our fierce community spirit. Whatever happened to working-class folk like us was shared with our neighbours, for good or for bad. On one hand there was no privacy – everyone knew what you were doing; but on the other hand, there were moments of pure grace, when the love and support of a community could literally save our lives with food parcels and support in crises, such as the one that had imploded in my family.

On top of all this, I was worried about Bert. He had not slept a wink the night before, lying awake all night. I kept waking up and trying to soothe him, telling him we would get through this, that God had chosen this for us, and our job now was to find a way to bear this tragedy. He barely acknowledged me. He had withdrawn inside himself so completely I felt like I may never reach him again. For me, the tears wouldn't stop flowing. I had no idea how I was going to live and breathe through the next 24 hours. I literally felt like the world should have ended, and yet it went on turning. It felt so cruel that it should be like this. The world carries on, and somehow we had to make sense of our loss and move with it, or remain forever in the shadowy hinterland of grief.

When Bert returned, I asked the children if they wanted to see Brenda. Only Little Albie wanted to go. I didn't pressurise Christine. The situation was already traumatic enough, without adding to it. She stayed with me, fretting and settling into playing with her doll, then remembering Brenda wasn't there. It broke my heart to have to keep comforting her every time she realised who was missing.

An hour or so later Bert returned. Little Albie trailed in behind him, looking very pale. 'Oh, darlin' boy, are you alright?' I pulled him into a cuddle but his body seemed stiff, unresponsive.

'Albie 'ad a funny turn when 'e saw ... when 'e saw ...' Bert couldn't finish his sentence.

'What 'appened?' I asked.

'Albie wouldn't kiss Brenda's lips like I asked 'im too. Instead, Frank got 'im to kiss 'er forehead but it made him go into shock. 'e's not feelin' right. I'm sorry, 'ilda, it's all my fault. I thought it was the best thing for 'im to say goodbye...' Bert looked anguished. 'Best thing'll be a tot of brandy, that'll sort 'im out,' he added, reaching up onto the kitchen shelf for the bottle kept for medicinal purposes.

Bert's brother, Frank, who had been to see the body with Bert and Albie, poured out a shot for Little Albie. When he'd downed it, Bert tipped the bottle and poured it all down the scullery sink.

'What the 'ell are you playin' at?' I gasped. 'That bottle cost a small fortune!'

'I won't 'ave brandy in the 'ouse ever again. I don't want nothing 'ere that reminds us of today. Nothing.' Bert walked out, shutting the door behind him.

I watched him go, feeling my heart bleed and knowing there was nothing I could do to take the pain away from any of us.

Later that night, I tucked Little Albie and Christine up in bed. It was a clear, starry night, and for once we had a good view of the skies above our normally foggy, dirty city. Neither child had been able to fall asleep at their usual time; both were too upset, and Christine couldn't stop crying.

It was late when I went to shut the curtain, at which point both children climbed out of bed and Albie pointed out of the window, up to the heavens. 'Our Brenda's up there, she's with the angels.'

Christine and I looked up, almost expecting to see our lovely girl's face in the night sky. Christine turned to look at Albie, her face cocked to one side, puzzled.

'It's our Brenda, she's become that star up there, the bright-est star in the sky,' said Albie, with his little-boy logic.

'The brightest star,' repeated Christine, with wonder in her voice.

I felt a lump come to my throat and I swallowed it down. I had to remain strong for my living children. 'That's beautiful, Albie. You wait till I tell yer daddy about that. 'e'll like that.' I smiled as I guided him back to bed and tucked his blanket round him. 'Good night, God bless, see you tomorrow, please God,' I said with feeling.

I wouldn't ever take the thought of seeing my children each morning for granted ever again.

Days later and Brenda's cremation was held in Streatham Cemetery. I could never work out why she had to be held there, but Bert tried to explain that it was something to do with the council.

Dolly helped us hire a car to carry Bert and me to the ceremony. Children rarely went to funerals back then. It was seen as too upsetting for them and so Little Albie and Christine stayed at home with Vi.

The funeral passed in a blur. I could no more describe the flowers or the readings than I could read a foreign language. Both Bert and I were in shock. All I remember was the red curtain being pulled by an invisible hand across the coffin. Such a small coffin. It looked so lonely up there at the front of the room. A great lament sprung from the recesses of my soul. I felt like I'd received a wound that gaped open for all to see. The curtain started moving, and it was then I realised my daughter was leaving me for good. I heard myself scream, calling out, 'My baby, my baby.' Bert had hold of my arm or I might have clawed my way up to that little wooden casket. I sobbed and shouted my grief until I was moaning that same mantra over and over: 'My baby, my baby.'

At that point Brahms' 'Lullaby' played. It was the tune we played to Brenda when she couldn't sleep. It had soothed her as a baby as it was now marking her transition into permanent rest. As the first notes of the music played, I felt my heart tear apart, and I was gripped by mourning. Things would never be right again, the despair was so powerful, so all-encompassing, that it felt like it would always be like this.

All my family was there but I remember little about that day. My brother Ron had arrived with my brother Les on the back of his motorbike. Les was living in East Ham and we had rarely seen him or his wife Jean over the years, but he was there for us on that terrible day. Patsy, Joanie and Pa were there, as were Dolly, Frank, Dorothy and Flo as well as Wally and Betty. All our friends and family were around us. I remember kind words and sympathetic hugs, but it was an abstraction, a mirage. I couldn't take in the loss of my Brenda, I just couldn't believe it was really true, that she was dead, gone from us. I couldn't equate that tiny coffin with my bright young girl, skipping down the street, chattering away nineteen-to-the-dozen. I didn't ever want to think of her cold, dead body on that slab. At least I'd said goodbye, in a bizarre way, during my operation: I'd summoned up all my love for her then, and deep inside I knew she'd felt it too.

The wake was held in our home, and I recall little of that either. I could feel the strength of support with my family round me, and I thanked God for that at least. My brothers and sisters were always there in a crisis. Our family may have been broken, but we weren't beaten, and I felt the love radiating from them, which was all that got me through those dark, dark days.

Dolly popped by most days in the weeks afterwards; Vi

dropped in daily to take the children off our hands so we could have some time in peace to mourn our beloved girl.

I went back to work a month after the cremation. Bert said I was mad, that it was too soon, but I wanted life to go back to some kind of normality. I know I was still in shock, but life had to move on, or at least that's what I kept telling myself.

My children were also surprisingly resilient. They understood that this tragedy had left our family with a gaping hole at its heart and, bless them, they did everything they could to be well-behaved, good children during those first weeks. Little Albie had a key to the door and he was under strict instructions from his father not to dawdle after school but to return home with his sister and give her a sandwich while they waited for Bert to come home in the evenings. I, of course, wouldn't be home each night till much later. Some people might say I wasn't there for my children, but I honestly couldn't think how else I was going to cope if I'd stayed at home, staring at my four walls. I think I'd have gone under, and then what good would I have been as a mother to my darling Albie and Christine?

I knew, for my family's sake, I had to get through that time. 'This too shall pass,' says the Bible, and I lived by it. By God, I clung onto that mantra like it was the only thing keeping me afloat in my oceans of troubles.

Wally and Betty treated me like I was recovering from a long and painful illness. Nothing was too much for me. They fussed over me and brought me sweet tea and made me go home early most nights in the weeks following Brenda's death. I needed the familiarity of the fish and chip shop. The sizzle of the oil heating up, the smell of the vinegar and the fish frying made me think of happier times, times when families gathered together during the war in brief interludes of peace and comfort. The shop and my work in it sustained me in a way I cannot describe. Soon, my regulars were popping in to murmur their condolences. Old Bill brought me some early August flowers, a bunch of dahlias. I raised my eyes to thank him – goodness knows how he'd afforded them or where he'd even got them from – but the gesture disarmed me. I wept openly in the shop for the first time that evening. Mavis came in and held my hand.

Other women I knew only by sight nodded to me. Everyone knew what had happened and I felt, not for the first time, the balm of the community spirit we all shared as working-class Londoners. We stuck together, through thick and thin. We had nothing, we shared everything and we laughed our way through the hardships of our lives.

Most days after that I worked through a haze of tears, feeling the prayers of my friends at work within me. Each night I'd arrive home with a warm parcel of whatever was left over to share with Bert.

Bert was still struggling. He couldn't talk about Brenda's demise, much as he could never talk about the war and what he'd seen in it, no matter how many times I'd asked him to talk. All I could offer him as some sort of salve was the glistening chips, the battered fish or pie and my heart and soul, waiting for him to open up to the grief that shrouded our lives and our home.

CHAPTER 17

A Family Again

December 1957

'Deck the 'alls with boughs of 'olly, fa la la la laaaa, la la la la... 'Tis the season to be jolly...' My festive song stopped abruptly when I saw the look on Bert's face. He was frowning at me, barely disguising his feelings. 'We 'ave to carry on with life, Bert. It's what Brenda would've wanted for us. She'd 'ave been the last one to mope about. She loved Christmas an' we owe it to 'er memory...' I had started speaking with a measure of defiance in my voice, which rapidly cooled off as I saw the naked grief still etched onto Bert's face.

'It ain't right. Our Brenda ain't 'ere with us, an' I can't see any reason to be jolly, as you put it,' Bert said stiffly.

I knew his anger was the rawness of his feelings; after all, it had only been five months since our daughter had died and gone to heaven. Five months of tears, grief and shock, which had threatened to rip our family apart for ever. Bert had withdrawn into his shell, some days he felt like a stranger to me. He confided nothing and spoke little. Some days I despaired I would ever find a way back to my loving husband and the caring father of our children. Maybe he was gone from me for good? The thought made the weight of grief heavier still. I had relied on my work to see me through the hardest days, serving others so I didn't have to think too much about the pain we all felt, and my strange, isolating marriage. My children had been confused, then shocked, then tearful and angry as they realised finally that Brenda was never coming home and they'd lost their sister for good.

Steering us all through the choppy waters of our feelings, though, was Dolly. She popped over whenever she had the money for the bus, turning up, putting her apron on and, as often as not, making the dinner, or a hearty stew for lunch, 'to keep us goin'' as she put it. She was a lifeline for us in our darkest days, and it was her who I'd approached about whether to celebrate Christmas or not. I was unsure if we were ready as a family, but she gave me the kindest look anyone has ever given me, and said in no uncertain terms that we *had* to celebrate. After all, what else was life for? We had to make the good times come back, and to do that we had to start behaving like a normal family again, not four people deep inside grief and suffering.

I'd given her a grateful look. She'd been through the same darkness when Pop died. She knew better than most that life was for living, because you never knew when the next tragedy would strike.

'It's Christmas, an' it's time we started to celebrate as a family. It's time, Bert.' I put down the holly I'd bought from the market. I was using it to decorate the mantelpiece in the lounge. Alongside it were two big woolly red socks that I'd knitted for Christine and Little Albie's stockings.

Bert looked at the two stockings hanging limply by the fireplace. 'There should be three socks,' was all he said by way of an answer, turning his face away from me.

I sighed. 'Bert, we've been through 'ell an' back the last few months, but I realised somethin' the other day – none of our grief will ever bring back Brenda. It won't. So I fer one want to start thinkin' about the future, about living our lives again with our two children who are still 'ere with us. It's time they came out from Brenda's shadow, Bert. You know it's true.'

I looked at my husband beseechingly. Sometimes I thought

he'd never get over the trauma of losing our girl. He'd barely spoken three words together since she'd died. I knew he was uncomfortable with showing his emotions. It was how men were in those days – they were brought up not to show their tears or their sadness. But I knew there was more to Bert than that. He'd always told me how much he loved me and our children, he never held back from conveying his love, and his grief was just an expression of that. I just had to get through to him, somehow.

Days earlier I'd been discussing it with Wally and Betty as we sorted tinsel from baubles for the shop's Christmas tree. Secretly, I thought them extremely extravagant having a tree in their flat and in both their shops. *'ow the other 'alf live*, I'd thought to myself, as Wally brought in the plastic tree that was to be the centre of the Christmas decorations for our customers. His business had survived the near-disaster of the *Rock Around The Clock* experiment, but I was under strict instructions from Betty never to mention it again as it made Wally gloomy, and he was never meant to be a despondent man – he had too much get up and go! As we chatted and dressed it, Wally asked how we were all doing.

'We've lost our daughter an' we won't ever get 'er back. That's 'ow I feel. I love 'er still, that'll never change, an' I still feel strange tuckin' up two children into bed an' not three. I find myself makin' too many sandwiches fer tea because I forget, an' when I remember it's as if she's died again it feels so fresh, so close to me.' I took a breath in and continued. 'But I'm doin' okay. I know she's gone an' I accept that. I've made some sort of peace with God, but my Bert . . . well, that's another matter entirely.'

' 'ilda, I was goin' to ask about Bert. 'e took it 'ard when she died. I don't suppose 'e's found any peace with it at all?'

asked Betty, turning to smile at me, kindness tinged with sadness.

I'd sighed. Then I'd sighed again. I looked down at the bauble in my hand. How Little Albie and Christine would love to dress this tree. Maybe next time I'd ask Wally if they could come and help. 'Bert ain't said a word, no matter 'ow many times I say to 'im that 'e can tell me 'ow 'e feels. 'e just won't say a blinkin' word. Blow me if I don't feel 'elpless knowing I can't make it better for 'im.' I could feel tears welling up but I didn't want to cry any more – I'd done enough of that to last me a lifetime.

'We lost a littl'un,' said Betty suddenly. I'd looked up, shock registering on my face. 'Oh, nothin' like your loss, dear. We lost our baby when 'e was in the womb. The only time I ever got pregnant an' we lost 'im, but we still think of our littl' boy an' what sort of a man 'e would've become, even though it was nearly thirty years ago now.' Betty smiled.

Wally had coughed and turned away from us. Some things were hard to bear even decades down the line.

'You never told me you'd wanted children. I assumed you'd decided against it. I'm so sorry, I 'ad no idea you'd 'ad a littl'un of yer own!' I didn't know what to say. I was gobsmacked at Betty's confession.

'I lost 'im six months into my pregnancy. One day 'e was there, the next 'e'd slipped away. We'd been tryin' fer years to 'ave a child, but it wasn't to be. Then out of the blue it 'appened, an' I tell you, 'ilda, it was the 'appiest time of my life, feelin' my belly grow large an' waiting fer the day I'd bring our baby 'ome. I can still feel that warm, maternal glow in me, I swear it.' Betty's face was animated. The memory of her child was so strong, even after all this time, I felt my heart swell for her and Wally. Wally had slipped out of the room. Betty looked over at the door. ' 'e still finds it difficult, 'ilda. Men take these things very 'ard – they don't always get over it. Be patient with Bert. 'e don't mean to be difficult.'

'I know he don't, Betty,' I'd replied. 'But Christmas is coming an' I realise I want Little Albie and Christine's lives to get back to normal. I want them to be excited again, an' not be tiptoein' around Bert and me in case we get upset. I want us to be a proper family again.'

'You'll do it, 'ilda, I've every faith in you. Now come on, we're runnin' late an' I 'aven't even put the fish on to fry yet.' Betty grabbed my hand for a moment, and I clutched hers back. Two women who knew what deep pain there was in motherhood, united in our grief, and yet two women who'd survived their worst fears and gone on to live another day.

I saw in Betty the same resilience I saw in all the women of my patch of East London. Holding their families together with scant funds and getting scant praise for it. Bringing up their children, going out to work, scrimping and saving for each penny, yet keeping a smile on their faces and pride in their homes and children. It was the matriarchs of London who'd kept the country going through the war and through the austerity afterwards. They'd lost their sons, fathers and husbands yet still they kept going. And now these fresh revelations of Betty's meant I would never look at her the same again. She was a mother, as surely as me or any woman with children at her feet; she'd just never had a chance to properly express that maternal spirit.

Suddenly I had felt blessed. I had lost one child but I had two playful, naughty, gorgeous children who needed their mother and father back from the cliff's edge that grief had taken us to. That day I decided for sure that we were celebrating Christmas, and blow what Bert thought of it. It was time. Time to rebuild our lives. Time to start again, with fresh gratitude for what we'd got, rather than concentrating on what we'd lost. We had a roof over our heads, pennies in my purse, food for the table. We were the lucky ones.

That night, when I got home, instead of falling into bed I made Bert his cocoa, then said I would stay up for a while. I dug out an old red jumper of mine and started to unravel it. I would make my children a jumper each if I had enough wool to put in their stockings from Father Christmas. I had some small savings, enough for a lorry for Little Albie and a new doll for Christine. They deserved their childhoods back.

I shopped for our Christmas lunch, finding a cheap turkey down the Blue, the market in Bermondsey I'd frequented as a child, plus some vegetables. Bert had watched me with a sort of sullen, silent anger over the next few days, but I had ignored him.

Christmas Day dawned. I heard the squeals of delight from the lounge as Christine and Albie opened their presents. Bert lay with his back to me in bed but I got up and, with a determined smile, greeted them with a look of surprise at Father Christmas's nocturnal visit.

'But will Brenda get a present in 'eaven?' asked Christine.

' 'course she will,' I said, stoutly. Today was no day for explanations. It was about forgetting the past and looking to the future. 'Now, who's goin' to 'elp me with the stuffing?' I said with my hands planted on my hips.

'Me, me!' our children shouted in unison. Two excitable kids on Christmas morning – it gladdened my soul to see their pleasure. I turned on the wireless to hear the carols and started cutting up potatoes and carrots and placing them in a big pot on the cooker. The turkey went in and, while it was cooking, I placed mince pies on the table as I'd made a big batch of them the day before. I watched as Albie and Christine played with their toys.

Bert hovered close to me all morning. He said nothing but I carried on, regardless. By 1 p.m. the turkey was ready, the spuds were roasted and all I had left to make was the gravy. 'Come up to the table!' I shouted and in they all trooped.

Christine and Albie sat with their knife and fork in each hand, waiting for their lunch. Bert sat in stony silence. I dished up and handed out the plates. 'Eat up while it's 'ot!' I exclaimed, beaming at my children as they dived into their plates of food.

Only Bert sat still as a statue, not moving, not eating, just staring at his plate. 'Bert—?' I said, gently.

Then it happened. A great plop of a tear dropped onto his turkey breast. Then another. Bert was crying.

'Oh, darlin',' I said, and immediately scraped back my chair and pulled him into a hug.

'I miss 'er so much,' was all Bert managed to say.

' 'course you do, darlin', we all do. But you 'ave to find a way of dealin' with yer emotions,' I replied, swaying on the spot as I hugged him and rocked him for comfort.

'She's gone, 'ilda, an' it's so cruel that we 'ave to get on with our lives. It ain't *fair*.' His voice was gruff with emotion.

'No, it ain't fair, nobody said it was, but it's what we 'ave to do, Bert. We can't live in the past for ever.'

'You're right,' sobbed Bert. 'I know you're right. Thanks for doin' Christmas for us this year. It must've been 'ard for you,' he added.

Christine and Albie were staring at us both with wide open eyes.

'Come on, eat up I said! Yer father's just 'avin' a moment, that's all. Nothin' to worry about,' I said to them with a determined smile. 'Let's all eat up an' go for a nice walk afterwards, get a breath of fresh air to blow away the cobwebs.' And with that we all sat and ate our Christmas dinner.

It wasn't the best meal in the world, it was a simple plate of meat and two veg, but we were together as a family again and that made it more special to me than anything we could've eaten in a fancy restaurant.

After lunch, Bert drove us into the countryside in Surrey. He'd bought a second-hand black Morris Minor from work. It was an 'ex-rep' car as they called it, but Bert couldn't have been prouder of it. It was a cold day but, for the first time since Brenda's death, I had a glimmer of happiness again. Of course, I still wished she was with us, dancing around my feet as she always used to as we walked, but I couldn't keep wishing for that type of miracle. Nothing and no one could bring back the dead.

The children ran ahead into a field. On the perimeter of the land was a huddle of cows. As we entered the field the cows started to move towards us. 'Is that a bull?' I said with alarm, clutching hold of Bert's coat jacket. 'That's a bull, I swear it is. Oh my Gawd a bull, what will we do?' I started to panic. The cows were heading straight for us, the bull at the front staring at me intently as he led the pack.

'Aim for that stile over there,' said Bert, 'Oi, you two, get over that stile an' out of the field!' he shouted at the children, his voice filled with alarm. 'Come on, Duchess, run for it!' he said, as the cows started trotting to us.

'Blimey, don't leave me!' I huffed and puffed as I started to run towards the gate. Christine and Little Albie were over the other side; they looked half horrified and half delighted at the sight of their mother and father trying to outrun a bull and his herd. 'They're gainin' on us!' I shrieked.

Bert had reached the stile and had vaulted over; I didn't have time to be impressed as I was grabbing my skirt and fumbling for the wooden post. I got up on the step and swung a leg over the stile. I stopped for a second to catch my breath but the animals were charging towards me, getting nearer and nearer with each passing second. 'Blow me but I can't get me leg over, Bert! I can't get me leg over!' I repeated, panic-stricken.

Bert's face was a picture. He looked at me, then at the cows and then with a sudden shout he barked out a sound, one I hadn't heard for a long time. It was laughter! 'This ain't the time to 'ave a joke at my expense,' I said crossly, trying desperately to swing my other leg over. I'd put a bit of weight on recently – too many stolen chips at the shop before home time – and this, combined with the heavy wool coat I was wearing, obstructed my leg reaching any higher.

The children, seeing their father burst into laughter, had also collapsed into giggles. ' 'elp!' I shouted, as the herd of cows reached me, ' 'elp me, please!' I was stuck on the stile. I couldn't lift my leg and my husband and children were beside themselves with fits of laughter.

Bert just looked up at me, my face wild, the cows snorting next to me, and dissolved again into great belly laughs again. 'Duchess, that ain't a bull, it's a cow with 'orns. She only wants to be friends.' And with that, the cow that had led the stampede in my direction sniffed the air and gave my coat a big lick!

Well, that was it. I suddenly saw the funny side and doubled up, the worries of the last few months dissolving away in one precious moment. 'Oh, my giddy aunt, look 'ere Bert, I still can't get me leg up!' I said, wiping my eyes and trying to pull myself over the wooden post. By now the cows had had a good sniff of me and decided I wouldn't be good to eat and had started wandering off, their bovine breath making mist clouds in the chill air. ' 'elp me get down – I'm stuck, Bert!' I begged as we all giggled.

Bert grabbed me under the armpits and in a rather

undignified movement he lifted me over the gate post and dropped me down on the other side. I tried to brush myself down with my last shred of dignity as Albie and Christine burst into fresh giggles, cackling with delight at my expense.

'Come 'ere you lot – come on, take me arms, let's walk back together ... avoiding the bulls, of course.' I smiled broadly.

With that, we all linked arms and the four of us, chattering and laughing, made our way back to the car.

CHAPTER 18

East End Gangs

'Stop. Don't say another word.' Vi's voice sounded unnaturally harsh. 'I mean it, Wally. You don't know what they're like. They're scary people an' we don't want the likes of 'em round our way.' Vi's normally jovial manner was gone, replaced by a deep frown on her plump face. Her arms were folded over her big bosom as if protecting her from an unknown foe. 'You 'ave to be careful who you're speakin' to, 'cos they don't take kindly to gossip about 'em.'

'Alright, Vi. I didn't mean to frighten you, or you, 'ilda, for that matter, but it's the truth. The gangs are out on our streets an' we all need to keep our 'eads down an' our eyes shut.' Wally also looked stern. His face, normally creased into a smile, was serious and for the first time I noticed genuine fear in his eyes.

There had been rumours for months now that two rival gangs – the Krays from East London and the Richardsons from Bermondsey – had started falling out. And by falling out I mean taking their violence out of the seedy nightclubs and haunts they worked in, onto our beloved South London streets. It seemed no one was safe, and that we were all targets for their shady dealings and seemingly random acts of brutality.

Wally had been telling us that he had friends in the East End who ran a corner shop and who had been paid a visit by a particularly savage-looking pair of men only the other day. The owners were told to pay them 'protection money' – it seemed the practice of squeezing cash out of normal, hard-working folk was becoming more and more 'normal'. So who knew when they might start looking down our way?

'But what about the police? What are they doin' about it? Surely it ain't legal to go an' demand money from someone?' I asked, realising the naivety of my question when I saw the looks on both Vi and Wally's faces.

'The police? They don't do nothing! They're either too frightened to enter the gangs' territories or they're takin' back-'anders themselves,' said Wally harshly. 'No, the police won't 'elp you – no one will against those men.' Wally ran his hands through his black, Brylcreemed hair.

The three of us were talking just as the chip shop was opening for business, leaning on the counter while the fat heated up in the fryers. Vi had walked with me to work to buy some chips and have a bit of company. She was surrounded by various members of her large brood, and a couple of children I thought I recognised from our estate and knew for sure weren't hers. 'Oh, I'm lookin' after 'em while their ma is in 'ospital, bless 'em. She won't be comin' out for a while – it's 'er lungs, you know.'

I nodded, thinking that for all of Vi's bluster and loudness she had a big heart, and would always help out when other mothers on the estate needed her. She was a rough diamond, as Bert called her; gruff and boisterous on the outside, warm and caring on the inside. We'd chatted about several of our friends as we walked, one of whom had a husband with no work and three hungry mouths to feed. Vi was known to be a gossip so I usually told her very little about our lives but that day I'd relaxed a little and told her about how we'd nearly starved during the meat delivery strike, and it was only the goodwill of the locals that had kept us from going under.

'Oh, we all knew you was in a bad way,' Vi had winked

and, not for the first time, I wondered if it was her who'd left the parcel of food on our doorstep. She wouldn't say any more, and so we walked onwards, lamenting the troubled lot of our friend and wondering what we could do to help.

'A food parcel is always a good place to start,' said Vi, and I nodded. We could do that for them at least.

We reached work and had caught Wally in this rare, melancholy mood. When he explained why – that his friends were being stung for regular payments by the gang that haunted the capital's backstreets – he explained it would only be a matter of time before other gangs started doing the same: that it could be him next.

Now, I felt a shiver go down my spine. I'd heard newspaper reports about the gangland troubles, read to me by Bert from his daily paper while we sat and listened to the wireless with our bedtime cocoa. Somehow I'd always assumed that our lives were so uneventful we'd never attract the attention of those hard men who were stalking our streets. It seemed I was wrong. Wally seemed genuinely worried. Everyone knew Wally's Fish and Chip Shop. His crisps were legendary. People queued down the side street most nights for a bag of hot, piping chips and a piece of delicious, steaming, hot white fish covered in crackly golden batter. Wally's business was doing well, visibly doing well. And that made him a target for those men who ran rackets around our city.

'What'll you do, Wally?' I whispered, looking behind me as if there was already a hard man and his cronies waiting in the doorway.

'There ain't nothing I can do, 'ilda, except hope an' pray that they won't come callin'. An' that ain't much of a comfortin' thought, I can tell you.' With that Wally sucked in air through his teeth, making a low whistle.

My brow creased with worry. Wally wasn't normally the

praying sort. He made a point of steering clear of church and, not for the first time, I wondered if his swarthy looks meant he might be something as exotic as a Jewish man. Plenty of Jews had come to England as the Second World War broke out, so it was logical that he might be one of them. I'd never knowingly met a Jewish person before and I secretly liked having such an unusual and worldy (to me) friend, but I kept my mouth shut. Other peoples' lives were none of my business, unless they wanted it to be, so why would I pry and make a nuisance of myself?

The only antidote to the fear was a dose of hard work, I decided, so I finished tying my apron round my waist and grabbed the broom handle. 'I'm goin' to sweep up then I'll be off down to the cellar to finish peelin' the spuds. If any 'ard men come in 'ere, tell them I'm in the lavvy an' I ain't got any money,' I said, trying to inject some humour into our conversation. I felt suddenly vulnerable and afraid, much like I did when I was waiting for Pa to come home from the pub. There was always an 'enemy', always a bully to have to stand up to. I'd learnt that in my life, and I was weary of having to relearn it.

Down in the basement, Hooray Hilda – Wally's greyhound – gave a short whine, and her tail wagged in the cold basement air. However warm it was upstairs, it was always chilly down there. I sighed as I dragged a sack of potatoes closer to the kitchen table, then whispered a few words of endearment to Hooray Hilda. I threw her some of the leftover chips from the night before, then settled down to work, hoping it would calm my nerves.

It was several weeks later that it happened.

Bert and I were sitting in the lounge, our cocoa and biscuits drunk and eaten and the clock showing 10.30 p.m. Bert stifled a yawn, then stood up. 'Time for me bed. You comin', Duchess?'

'You go ahead. I'll just rinse out the cups for the mornin',' I replied, easing myself up and out of the chair. Suddenly, there was a soft knocking sound at the door. If we'd have been in bed we'd never have heard it.

'Did you 'ear that?' I said, looking quizzically towards the door.

'Probably just next door's kids,' said Bert, reaching for the bedroom door handle.

But there it was again: a soft knocking sound, barely audible above the sound of the wireless. We looked at each other.

Bert and I walked to the front door and Bert opened it. Framed in the doorway was a man wearing a black spiv jacket, a black trilby and a pair of polished shoes. I frowned. I didn't recognise him. What did he want with us at this time of night when ordinary, honest folk like ourselves were heading to their beds?

'Sidney, it's you! I didn't recognise you in that whistle an' flute,' said Bert, using the cockney rhyming slang for 'suit'.

'Yeah, it's me, Albert. Yeah, you an' the missus well?' the man said. His voice was low. I looked to Bert in astonishment that an acquaintance of his was wanting to chitchat on our doorstep at this time of night. 'Can I come in fer a minute?' said Sidney, before Bert could answer. He looked left and right in a manner that was distinctly shifty.

'Alright, in you come. This 'ere's me wife, 'ilda,' said Bert. I smiled and nodded.

Sidney made some charming reply but his smile didn't reach his eyes. Standing in the hallway, it was suddenly apparent that he had a large bag with him. It looked full to bursting with whatever was inside it. He'd been hiding it under his wool coat, which was wrapped round his shoulders.

'I know it's been a while, Bert, but I've been meanin' to get in touch an' see 'ow you were, especially after 'earin' about your girl.'

Bert nodded in reply. 'That's very decent of you, Sidney, very decent of you to think of us.'

'D'you want tea?' I found my voice at last. I wasn't going to stand here in my hallway any longer. I didn't want to invite this stranger in, but I felt I had to be polite, even if my hackles had risen with each step he took inside our flat. There was something about him I didn't like, and there was definitely something strange about his manner of visiting. 'We don't normally 'ave visitors at this time of night,' I added, my tight smile drawing over my teeth so they were bared temporarily.

'Don't you go puttin' yerself out, 'ilda. That's awful kind of you but I can only stay a minute. I used to work wiv yer 'usband on the lorries, an' we got chattin' one time an' I said I might need an 'and storing some stuff, temporary like. An' Albert 'ere said 'e'd be a diamond geezer an' 'elp me out.'

Sidney looked to Bert and smiled. His teeth flashed white in the dim light.

'Oh, yes, I remember, 'course I did. I was forgettin'. Yes, 'ilda, me an' Sidney used to load the vans together, when I got back from the fightin'. Come on in, Sidney, 'ave a cuppa. Don't stand on ceremony,' Bert said, clearly relaxing into this bizarre night-time encounter.

'I'd love to, Albert, but you know 'ow it is. I've got places to go, errands to run. What I'd love to do more than anything is to 'ave a cuppa with you and yer missus, but unfortunately I ain't got the time tonight. I'm sorry appearin' like this but I need a favour from you, Albert – I need someone to 'elp me store this bag. I just got nowhere else safe to put it an' it'll only be fer a few days, just until I get meself straight,' finished Sidney, not quite catching my eye.

'Just a few days? I don't see the 'arm in it. 'course we'll look after it for yer. 'appy to 'elp an old mate,' said Bert, and the two men shook hands before Sidney dropped the bag at Bert's feet.

'Well, keep it safe. I'll be back in a day or two. Okay to just knock an' drop by again, is it?' Sidney asked, with a crooked smile.

''course it is, Sidney mate, anytime. You're welcome anytime,' Bert replied.

When Bert shut the door we turned to face each other. My face must've showed my confusion, and my unsettled feelings about the man, because Bert made a conciliatory gesture with his hands. 'It's just for a few days, luv. Where's the 'arm in it?' he said. 'Let's just put it up the top of the wardrobe an' we'll forget all about it, eh? Now I'm for me bed.'

I could hear Bert heave the bag onto the top of the furniture as I washed up. *There must be something quite heavy in there*, I thought to myself. That night, as Bert snored softly next to me, I stared at the black, lumpy shape on top of the wardrobe. *I wonder what's inside that's so special*, I thought. *Whatever it is I can feel it's no good an' that's a fact.* But I didn't want to question Bert's decision. Our marriage had limped through Brenda's death and we were only just getting back on track. I didn't want to jeopardise what we'd worked so hard to rebuild. Yet I couldn't take my eyes off that dark shape. Eventually I drifted off to sleep, dreaming in an unsettled way of spivs with golden teeth, and bags with mystery contents filling up our small home.

Several days later – not the two Sidney had promised – I was hanging out Bert's vests and socks on the line that hung at a crooked angle along the walkway outside our flat's front door, when I heard the sound of a man's cough behind me.

'Mrs Kemp, I knew it was you,' said a voice, making me jump out of my skin.

I turned around ready to remonstrate with whoever had crept up on me. My thoughts had been miles away. It was about three in the afternoon, and Christine and Little Albie weren't back yet from school yet. I'd been thinking that Albie would need a new coat and Christine a new pair of shoes before long.

'Well, I never!' I exclaimed. 'You scared the living daylights outta me!' I continued when I turned to see Sidney. He looked as shifty as ever, and his shoulders were hunched over, his coat hanging off them as if he was trying to hide himself from prying eyes.

'Alright there, Mrs Kemp? Lovely day, ain't it? I see yer busy so I won't keep you.' He smiled but his eyes slid off my gaze, darting backwards and forwards in their sockets. He was clearly itching to be gone.

I wouldn't trust you, Sidney, as far as I could throw yer! I thought to myself, but my manners wouldn't let me act rudely, so against my will I heard myself offering him a cup of tea.

'Don't you go puttin' yerself out on my account,' he said, his voice dripping with false charm.

He really does sound like I'd imagine a weasel would sound, or a gutter rat – the types we used to see down at the docks when I was a girl, I thought, imagining a thick tail flick from under his sharp suit jacket.

I smiled automatically and he mistook my gesture for friendliness.

'Annuver time, eh, Mrs Kemp? Annuver time we'll 'ave that cuppa. But I'm a busy man an' I was wonderin' if you could see yer way to lettin' me 'ave my bag back, if it ain't too much bother for you?' he smarmed, shifting on his feet from left to right.

'Wait out 'ere, won't you. I won't be a jiffy, an' you'll 'ave yer bag back,' I replied, smoothing down my pinafore and picking up my basket with Bert's remaining wet clothing piled inside. ' 'Scuse me,' I said, as I shuffled around him. Sidney stepped out of my way and I made sure I avoided touching him as I opened my door and closed it behind me.

Quick as a flash I pulled a kitchen chair into our bedroom and heaved myself up on it to reach the bag. It was surprisingly heavy. Whatever was contained inside it felt bulky, like a big bag of books, and I struggled to lift it down from the top of the wardrobe, where it had sat untouched.

'You alright in there, Mrs Kemp?' came Sidney's nasal-sounding voice from outside.

'Yes! Won't be a second or two,' I replied, huffing a little as I pulled it down.

It slumped to my bedroom floor.

'My giddy aunt!' I puffed. It wasn't as light as Bert made it look!

But what would Bert think about me handing over the baggage? Would he approve, or should I have told Sidney to come back later when Bert was here? For a second I felt confused, but almost immediately I pushed the thoughts away. I wanted that bag, and Sidney, out of my home, and that was that. If Bert gave me a talking to then I'd just have to put up with it. This was my home and my family, and something told me that whatever was in that bag would never bring anybody any good.

With firm resolve I dragged it to the front door. ' 'ere you go,' I said, smoothing down the folds of my skirt. 'We ain't opened it.'

Sidney tipped his trilby to me in response, then looked over his shoulder. I'm not sure what he expected to find among the dank lines of washing, the drying nappies and undergarments that littered the lines that hung in jagged fashion down the walkway. He flashed me a huge, vulpine grin. 'Don't you want to know what's in the bag?' he asked.

I shook my head. I wanted nothing to do with it, whatever it was. He could have the crown jewels in there and I wouldn't care to see them. I just wanted him gone.

'Go on,' said Sidney. ' 'ave a look, it won't kill you. I can't believe I chose the most 'onest Londoners to stash me bag with but I did, an' to say thank you I'm tellin' you, you'll want to 'ave a look at what's in there.'

Before I could answer, Sidney had unzipped the bag. It fell open, with a sigh, to reveal wads of blue banknotes in pristine condition. I gasped and instinctively stepped back. Sidney laughed with delight at the effect it had on me. 'Go on, 'ave a closer look – pick one up, go on! It might be the only time you ever get that much money in yer 'ands,' he said with a leer.

As if in a trance, I picked up a roll. Sidney took it from me, ripped off the band that held it together and a flurry of £5 notes littered the floor.

Well, blow me, but I'd never even seen a £5 note in all my life, and here were hundreds of them covering my floor.

I looked at the money and all at once felt very afraid. This money wasn't mine to muck about with. This money could not be legal if it needed to be stashed at ours. This money, therefore, could bring us the kind of serious trouble that saw people in jail, or worse, ditched into the Thames with a concrete slab for footwear. The papers had been full of stories like those.

'That's enough,' I said firmly. 'Pick up yer money an' leave.' I stared at him, defiant. I knew a thing about hookey money after living with my pa. I knew when something was wrong: I could smell it. 'We've looked after yer money, an' now I wish you good day,' I added.

'Alright, keep yer 'air on. I didn't mean to upset yer,' whined Sidney as he scrabbled on the floor for the bank notes. 'I just did it fer a laugh.'

Goodness knew who was looking for that money, or whether it was even real.

My skin prickled as Sidney tipped his hat for the last time after zipping up his bag with a flourish. He'd even had the gall to offer me a couple of the notes, but I'd had the sense to refuse politely.

I shut the door with a slam. 'That money was dodgy,' I said to myself. 'If you ask me, 'e's mixed up with the gangs, by the look of him.' My anxious mind brought up another thought. ''e might even work for the Richardsons – they're the main ones round 'ere, aren't they...?' My voice trailed away into the flat. I was still standing by the front door. Suddenly our 'harmless' adventure to help Bert's old mate was taking on a whole new, and very dangerous, complexion. 'Will they know we've stashed their money? What if the Old Bill find out?' I panicked, using Bert's slang word for the police. 'Oh, what 'ave we done?' I was aware of my heart, hammering in my chest, and took a few deep breaths. 'Now, calm yerself down, 'ilda,' I said to myself, sternly. 'If anyone asks then we didn't know what was in that bag. We never opened it ourselves, which is God's 'onest truth. Anyway, we don't know fer sure it was anything to do with no gangs, and even if it was, an' if what I'm guessin' is right, then we were tiny cogs in a giant machine that has absolutely nothing to do with us,' I finished, firmly.

One thing was for sure. I would never, ever tell my husband what I'd seen that day. I knew that Bert would explode if he knew we'd harboured money. He was so moral, so upright, and I loved him dearly for it.

''e must never know, girl,' I whispered to myself, suppressing the shudder that ran through my body.

A few days later, one Sunday evening, as if he had picked up on my fears, Bert drew me by the arm into the kitchen.

'What's this, Bert?' I asked, wondering why we weren't heading for bed.

'Listen to me, Duchess. I've been meanin' to say something for a little while now, an' this seems about the right time to say it.' Bert took a big breath in and continued. 'We've lived in London all our lives, but I've been thinkin' a lot since our girl died ... We should look to move away from 'ere. There are too many memories 'ere, too much of the past. It's time to move on, 'ilda, get away for good. D'you understand me?'

'What do you mean? Move? Move where? Where could we go?' I replied, my head spinning.

'We could go out to Surrey. It ain't as far as you think, an' we all enjoyed our country walk at Christmas. You'd like it there, 'ilda. A bit of fresh air, somewhere fer the children to play.'

No gangs to worry about, I thought to myself as I looked up into his intense stare. 'You're serious then?' I answered, too dumbstruck to take in Bert's words. He really meant we should leave our beloved London. The place where we'd both been born, the place we'd grown up and lived all our married life.

It was something I'd never considered. I'd left briefly during the war, of course, when we evacuated to Braunston, near Coventry. I'd loved the countryside around the little village but I'd returned to London after a bad beating by Pa and, even now, I remembered stepping off the train at Euston Station and feeling I was home.

What if I was a Londoner through and through, and couldn't settle anywhere else?

But I had to think about my children. What would be best for them? I suddenly felt giddy. 'Put the kettle on, Bert. I won't sleep yet – my 'ead is racin'.'

'course, Duchess – but don't you see it makes sense? We could start afresh, go somewhere where we won't remember old times with Brenda, somewhere where we can make new memories...' Bert stopped talking and looked at me with such kindness in his eyes, clasping both my hands. 'Don't you see? We'd 'ave a new life together as a family.'

I thought about it for a moment longer. The incident with the bag had shown me that our part of London wasn't safe any longer. We may have got away with it this time, but I knew that Sidney and his kind would be back with more favours to ask of us, and I didn't suppose they'd take kindly to being refused. 'But I'd 'ave to leave work! 'ow will Wally manage without me?' My voice was little, almost child-like. 'They'll never manage without me, an' I'll miss them and me job...'

'You can find a new job, Duchess! We can stay in touch with Wally an' Betty – they're more than just yer bosses, they're friends. We won't leave them behind completely. But now is the time to go – I know this is right, 'ilda. It makes sense for Little Albie an' Christine. What future is there for them 'ere, with the streets not safe any more? Our London is dying, 'ilda. There's a new London growin' around us, an' it ain't fer the likes of us. Our breed is dyin' out, or leavin'. The days of our East End where everyone knew each other, an' it was safe to walk around day or night, is over. Just think about it, will you? We don't 'ave to make a decision tonight.' And with that, Bert got up, poured me a cup of tea and went to bed, leaving me staring at the wall in the semi-darkness of the night.

Memories

1981

Where the 'eck am I? I thought to myself, squinting past the rows of ethnic shops, chicken takeaways and fancy estate agents. *I was sure the shop was down this road 'ere . . .* A car beeped its horn loudly, and I nearly jumped out of my skin. I turned to see what was happening on the road. There was a cyclist shouting at the driver of a taxi. Both were making wild hand gestures and a small crowd had gathered to watch the spectacle.

I sighed. My London never used to be so busy, or so frenetic. These days, it was all petrol fumes, discarded polystyrene coffee cups and people, so many people. And all looking so busy – dashing here and there, shoving past each other as they went. I sighed again.

I'd so wanted to come back to the area to look for Wally's Fish and Chip Shop. It'd been 24 years since I had left, but I could picture that day as clear as daylight, and yet somehow I'd got confused trying to find it.

'I'm sure it was down 'ere,' I muttered to myself, avoiding a cyclist who was using the pavement and pulling my handbag closer into my body for fear of it being snatched. 'It's not like it used to be round 'ere,' I said again, a little louder.

I was attempting to reclaim my memories. It was the first time I'd been back to this part of London since we moved: despite telling our friends we'd see them regularly, somehow life had got in the way of our promises.

Within weeks of Bert asking me to leave, we'd been down to

the council offices and requested a house outside of London. With two growing, boisterous children, the flat had become far too small for us and we thought we'd do no harm by asking for somewhere bigger to live. Our request was granted to Bert's delight, and only a few short weeks later we were packing up for a semi-detached council house in Merstham, Surrey. It wasn't flash but it had three small bedrooms, so the children could have their own room at last, and a long, thin garden. Also it was opposite a large park area where they could both run free, meaning I wouldn't have to worry about the numerous cars on the road and the increasing fear of strangers preying on young children. Back in the tenement slums of Rotherhithe we'd never had to worry about strangers on the estate because everyone knew everyone else's business. The only threat were the sailors who still came from all over the world into our docks. We'd heard of children being abducted, and so Bert and I never let Little Albie or Christine play down by the docks even though we'd lived within spitting distance of them for most of our lives. But our world felt safe apart from that. We knew our neighbours and they knew us, for better or worse. That had changed though. London seemed a less friendly place. You didn't know your neighbours any more. People kept themselves to themselves. *Too busy being busy*, I thought to myself.

I caught sight of my reflection in the window of a fast food shop. I still couldn't get used to seeing the old lady who stared back at me, with streaks of grey in her hair and glasses for her ailing eyesight. I was 60 years old but I still felt like a young girl inside, dodging the bombs as the Blitz rained down on London, dancing with a Polish officer at a wartime dance, shooing off my brothers and sisters from Ma's kitchen as I helped her make the dinner. Inside I was still that young girl. I had no idea where the years had gone. How could it be that I was 60 years old and standing in 'my' London, but a London that was now completely alien? I'd been born and bred in the slums of Bermondsey, and yet there it was, even worse with the coffee shops springing up, and the old cold stores – those that had survived the bombing raids – being converted into fancy flats, unaffordable for the likes of me and any other normal Londoners. The heavy industry of my girlhood had gone, replaced with the trappings of a different, wealthier life. I shook my head.

Suddenly, a woman with a large buggy and two children perched inside it barged past me on the street. 'Sorry, luv,' she said, as she moved onwards, barely glancing back in my direction.

I watched her walk, her burning cigarette held in one hand, steering that enormous pram with the other. I sighed again. *Now, where was I? Right, it must be down 'ere*. I wandered off, stopping every few feet to check my directions. The busyness of the street, the sound of the cars and buses, the fumes and the heat of this summer's day had all conspired to confuse me. *Dearie me, I'm gettin' old*, I thought to myself. I'd entered another wrong street.

Just as I turned round to leave it, however, I had a flash of memory. It was a street like this one where I'd rescued that poor girl, Mabel, from a beating by her drunken husband. I could remember that as if it was yesterday. I'd patched her up and given her tea and sympathy, all the while knowing that she'd made her bed and would have to lie in it, and there was nothing in the world I could do to help her. And then there was Mavis, always desperate to keep her family fed while her Alfie was in and out of the many boozers that littered the docks in those days. I wondered what had happened to them both. We'd lost touch when Bert and I left London, despite our insistences that we'd write and see each other maybe once or twice a year. Well, family life had taken over and we never did meet again.

I'd left behind so many friends when we'd moved away, it made my heart swell with sadness even now. So many good people. What had happened to them all? Revisiting the past wasn't always a good thing – it brought up painful memories as well as happy ones, and I'd had enough of both to last many lifetimes.

The day I left the chip shop, I worked my shift as usual, joking with Wally and the customers. At one point I even sang a little ditty while the new batch of fish was frying. I liked to keep them entertained and happy. That was always my job in life, to care for other people, and I'd loved every minute of it. I hummed as I worked, hoping my shift would go on all night.

I'd been dreading telling Wally and Betty that we were leaving. They'd been good as gold, though, offering to help us pack and drive some of our bits to Merstham. And it wasn't long after we'd left that they moved to Carshalton, in Surrey, which meant we saw each other several times a year for a long time, up until Wally died about ten years later, followed by Betty only a few months afterwards.

' 'ooray 'ilda, bring me up some chips to fry! We're runnin' low. An' while you're at it, fetch some more ketchup,' called Wally above the sound of the wireless he had playing in the shop these days.

'Right you are, boss!' I joked as I clattered down the wooden stairs. I always had to blink when I reached the bottom as it was so dark and gloomy down there, even with the one light bulb that hung from the ceiling and was permanently switched on.

As my eyes acclimatised to the gloom, there, sitting on the

table, was a bunch of roses. 'Well, ain't they beautiful,' I said, stroking one of the pale pink petals. They reminded me of my wedding bouquet. There was a label sticking out an angle from them and, to my delight, I realised it had my name on it!

I gasped and stepped back. They were for me! 'Well, I never!' I exclaimed, then grabbed the bunch and ran up the stairs.

'Wally, Betty! You shouldn't 'ave!' I laughed as I flung the shop door open.

'Surprise!' shouted several voices, and I looked around the room in amazement. All my regulars were there: Violet with her six children; Old Bill had hobbled in, as well as Mabel with a babe in arms and two other littl'uns dawdling about her feet (and no black eyes to be seen, for which I thanked the Lord); Mavis was there with her eldest boy, Alfie (named after his father), and Wally and Betty, of course.

'For she's a jolly good fellow, for she's a jolly good fellow ...' they all sang, as I stood blushing and laughing.

'Oh, you shouldn't 'ave. Look, you've made me blush like the devil! Well, I'm blowed – I ain't known anything like it before. Thank you everyone, thank you,' I stammered, overcome with mixed emotions.

I was so sad to leave the job I'd loved and the people I'd met and served for almost ten years, but I also knew that Bert was right and it was time for us to make a new start as a family. These goodbyes were an inevitable part of that.

'Free chips for everyone, in 'onour of our 'ooray 'ilda!' said Wally, and the crowd cheered.

I could feel tears pricking my eyes. I'd been so lucky finding these good people to work for. The job had seen me through some of the darkest times in my life and I could never thank them enough for that.

'Oh, look, she's cryin'. Come on, 'ilda, cheer up, girl!

We've got some wine 'ere an' all, so we can 'ave a littl' tipple to say goodbye to you,' said Betty, putting a protective arm around my shoulders.

'Wine, eh? I don't suppose I've 'ad any of that since me weddin' day!' I laughed, delighted and sad all in one tumultuous mix.

Wally brought up some mugs from the basement along with a bottle of sweet wine. He opened it and several of the regulars whooped with joy. He poured out a little in each mug and handed it round to the adults. 'I'd like to say a few words, 'ilda, if I may—? It's been a joy an' a pleasure to know you. Now, I know you're not exactly goin' far – it ain't like you're goin' to Alaska – but you 'ave to promise to keep in touch. Will you do that?' Wally beamed.

I tipped my mug to him. ' 'course I will, Wally, you try an' stop me. I've 'ad some of the 'appiest days of me life workin' 'ere. It should be me thankin' you!' I replied.

'To 'ooray 'ilda!' said Betty.

'To 'ooray 'ilda!' answered everyone. Well, I'd never felt so special in all my life, except for the day I walked down the aisle to marry my Bert!

As I sipped my wine and watched my regulars chatting I felt another wave of sadness engulf me. I'd had happy times here, oh such laughs and such good memories. Yes, I'd seen disaster too. I gave birth to Brenda and lost her, all while I worked here. But that was life, wasn't it? You had to cling on to the good days because you never knew when the bad ones were coming. I'd never forget my little girl; in fact, I wore a photograph of her inside the double-sided locket I wore around my neck every day: on one side I had a picture of my Bert, on the other my Brenda. She sat next to my heart each day, which was where she was meant to be.

'Come on, 'ilda, 'elp me 'and out these chips, girl!' called Wally.

'Right you are, Wally,' I said, gulping down the last of my wine, savouring the sweet taste and enjoying the luxury of the giddy feeling it gave me.

I handed out portions of chips for our little party. The sight of everyone tucking in gave me a warm feeling; no one would go hungry tonight. I wanted to hold the memories of this day for the years ahead, in case I ever needed reminding that I'd had good friends and fun times. I knew life would never be the same again. I knew I'd always be a Londoner through and through, but I knew that sometimes you had to move on and leave the past behind.

The evening wore on and one by one the customers left, leaving me, Wally and Betty clearing up.

'You get off, luvvie. We'll clear this up. You can't tidy away your own party, it ain't right,' Betty said with a smile, hugging me to her.

'Well, if you don't mind,' I replied. 'We're off tomorrow an' I've still got some of me packin' to do.'

'Well, this is it then,' said Wally. He flashed me a cheeky grin but I could see he was moved by our parting.

'Thank you for everythin',' I said, feeling a lump in my throat.

'Don't be daft,' said Betty. 'We're 'elpin' you to move to-morrow, so we'll see you then. Come on, no more tears – you've cried all your tears for us. We'll stay in touch an' meet up regular.'

I nodded before taking off my white jacket, which was stained with grease after all the years I'd worked there, and hung it by the door. Slowly, I put on my hat and summer coat. 'I'll be seein' you both, don't you worry about that!' I said, and with that I picked up my handbag and left the fish and chip shop for the last time.

And I could still feel that sense of loss even now, so many years later. Musing on the feeling, I doubled back up the road, narrowly escaping knocking into a man with a parcel. 'Sorry, dearie, I'm a bit confused about where I am,' I stuttered.

'You alright, luv? You look lost. Can I 'elp you?' The man, who wore a brown uniform, stopped to help me.

'At last, the sound of a Londoner,' I said, managing a grin. 'Don't worry about me, I've just lost me bearin's for a moment, that's all.'

'You take care of yerself then. Cheerio,' said the man, and he walked off, whistling to himself as he went.

It was nice to know there were still some proper city folk about, ones who cared about people and stopped to lend a hand. It reminded me of Bert's pals from work and how they'd helped us pack up and load our van for our move out of the city.

'Different times,' I breathed, but by golly I'd never forget that day.

My heart was broken at the thought of leaving my city. I'd reluctantly agreed to the move that made Bert so glad as I'd wanted him to be happy, especially after everything he'd been through – everything we'd all been through. I'd prayed for him to look to the future, hadn't I? Yet I never thought that he'd take this drastic step of leaving our birthplace. It made sense for the children, of course it did, and I knew they'd settle in to their new schools easily. But would I settle in? Would I, a London girl through and through, be able to walk away with the same ease?

I cried as Bert and his pals from the delivery drivers loaded up the hired van. I watched from our bedroom as they heaved our furniture out of the flat, across the landing and down the stairs. I watched them with tears rolling down my face. There would be no going back, this time. It wasn't like being evacuated. We were moving for real, and I had to jolly well get used to it.

By the time Bert knocked on the door and come in, I'd wiped my eyes and was fussing about with some last bits to pack. He held out his hand to me and I took it, grateful yet again that I had such a good man.

'Time to go, Duchess. We're all packed. Wally will meet us at the 'ouse with the rest of our bits later today. Little Albie and Christine are in the van waitin' for you.' He smiled. He knew what this move was costing me, but he was adamant it was the best thing for us. Again, I was reminded of my wedding vows: to love, honour and obey. Well, it was time to obey again – not that I'd done *much* of that over the years! Bert was taking charge of this and I knew he had to for his own sake. He'd taken Brenda's death very hard, following on from the death of his father, so tragically. He needed the new start and if I knew anything about marriage, then I knew I had to go along with it and make the best of the situation for the sake of keeping my family together.

I looked around the flat for the last time, seeing the boxy little rooms as if for the first time. How had we lived in so small a space? I guess because I'd grown up in even smaller places with even more mouths to feed, clothe and bed down each night. I shook my head slowly. This had been our first real home as a family. My children had been born in this borough, they'd played on the estate, run amok in the bombed-out wreckage of dockside buildings and lived and laughed until tragedy struck, and we lost Brenda.

Now it was time to go, and part of me sighed with relief as I clicked the front door behind me, hugging goodbye to Vi and Enid and waving to some of the other familiar faces as they stopped to say goodbye...

Suddenly there was a loud *beep* nearby, and a voice shouted, 'Duchess! I'm over 'ere!'

I turned, startled, and realised I was back on the busy road, not stuck in my timewarp of memories. There was another shout: 'Oi, Duchess, over 'ere! Come on, get in the car!' Bert was frantically waving from the front seat of our Morris Minor 1000, his proudest possession and bought after years of saving up. The mists of time rolled away from the present. I was back in 1981, and my dearly beloved husband was gesturing for me to get into the car. 'But I didn't find it,' I mouthed, as I walked over and opened the car door.

'You found it in yer 'eart, though, didn't you,' he answered, not as a question, but as a statement of fact.

And I had, by golly I had. 'Come on, then. Let's get 'ome. Fancy pickin' up some fish an' chips for supper on the way?' I asked, squeezing Bert's hand.

'Can't think of anythin' nicer. Now, close the door. Time to go 'ome.' And with that, the car growled into life and we drove off.

I didn't turn to look back. I'd seen enough, and felt it had been what I wanted. I turned to Bert and smiled. 'Time to go 'ome,' I echoed, with a happy sigh.

Afterword

My nan Hilda's life was one of hardships and troubles, love and laughter. And it continued that way up until the day she died in February 2003. Four years earlier, her beloved Bert was diagnosed with colon cancer and died in May 1999 after being nursed devotedly by his wife and their daughter, Christine. I will never forget the sound of my nan keening at the funeral, as Granddad's coffin was taken away for cremation. Her love for him became pure sound, and it has haunted me ever since.

We scattered Granddad's ashes in Eastbourne by a park bench where they both used to sit together watching the sea, on their annual trips to the Transport and General Workers' Union hotel there. Tragedy, it seemed, was never far from Nan's life though, as less than a year later, her daughter Christine was diagnosed with skin cancer, aged just 49. Christine died a year later.

Who could've foreseen that Hilda would live through the death of both her two daughters and her husband? What terrible Fates decreed that she would endure such heartbreak? Despite the turmoil of those years, Nan always remained resolutely herself. She was known for her loyalty, her honour and her fierce maternal pride and instincts. She was the matriarch of my family. As a woman, I owe her, and thousands of nameless women like her of that age and time, a huge debt. She taught me the power of love over tragedy. She taught me that truth is always the only option. She taught me that we can survive anything life, or the gods, will throw at us as long as we go through it together. And she was right. She was always right.

Her life story is a testimony to the pull of survival. It is a tale of the love that glues families and communities together through the harshest of times, and the power of laughter to heal many wounds.

Nan was a legend. I hope her story speaks to women in this age, and reminds us that at the heart of life is our home and the people inside it.

Cathryn Kemp

If you enjoyed Hilda's story, read how it all began…

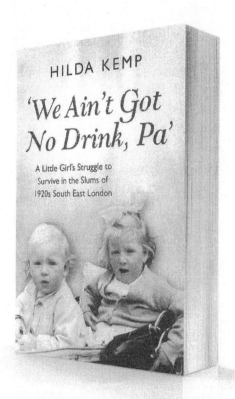

WE AIN'T GOT NO DRINK, PA
Out now in paperback and ebook

Too many children. Too little money. An abusive father too drunk to notice his family is starving. This is the true story of a little girl's struggle to survive against the odds in the slums of 1920s south-east London.

To see the whole story visit
OrionBooks.co.uk/HildaKemp

CHAPTER I

Bermondsey Slum

1928

The first we knew he was back was when we heard his key scratch on the door. It scratched again, then again, as my pa kept missing the lock. He was attempting to open the door to our dark, dingy rooms on the ground floor of a tenement in Bevington Street, Bermondsey, south-east London. The more he fumbled, the more drunk we realised he was, and so we huddled together for protection, listening to the expletives as they slurred out of Pa's mouth.

When I say 'we' I mean my younger brother, Les, and baby sister, Joanie, and me, of course. I was the eldest child at seven years old, and it was me the young 'uns turned to for protection, not that I could do much in the face of what was coming.

The three of us moved instinctively together behind the wooden table in the centre of the tiny room that served as a front room and kitchen. We had a small scullery out back where we had our weekly Friday night scrub down in the old tin bath that hung on a nail in the yard, and one bedroom with the big iron bed we all shared. So there was nowhere to hide from Pa, but God knows we tried, every time we heard our father's drunken temper as it built up outside our door.

I put my arms around little Joanie, who snuggled into my arms, her thumb in her mouth and her dark hair nestled against my shoulder. She already knew not to cry out in case she attracted Pa's wrath, even though she was just a baby. Instead of wailing, she started to cry softly. She was only just two years old, a toddler, but already she knew the fear of his fury. Les was almost four years old; a cheeky, fun-loving little boy, except, of course, when he was faced with his father's drunken rage. Then he cowered with the rest of us, his stick-thin legs curled up against him and his big dark eyes wide with fear as we huddled together for safety.

There was no one else there to protect us. My ma was asleep in the bed. Her latest illness had taken her hard. I was worried about her but right now I was more frightened for our safety.

We never knew how it would go with Pa when he got like this. Sometimes he returned home, covered in coal dust and grime from his heavy work down at the docks, and fell straight into bed, snoring minutes later in a drunken stupor. More often he would swear and rage, and then turn round to look for someone to blame for the black parts of his soul. It was always Ma and me who bore the brunt of his foul moods and raging tempers, trapped by these tiny dank rooms in this tall dark building. I felt the building tower over me, much like his temper, the danger of it frightening me to the core.

It was late. None of us had dared go to bed because Pa, or 'That Man' as I called him, often came home and he'd wake us with a swift kick, or grab one of us by the ear and drag us from the bed. He'd pull his victim into the kitchen to feed him or pour him a drink of whatever he had kicking around. It wasn't safe to sleep, we were vulnerable on nights like this.

So we stayed awake, sitting cross-legged on the kitchen floor, pretending to play games while yawning and rubbing our eyes, shivering a little from the cold as we wrapped the thin, scratchy blanket we shared around us. All the while, my heart would be thumping, knowing what might come.

We all felt the tension, waiting for That Man to come home and never knowing what state he'd be in. My stomach would feel tight, my senses on high alert, waiting for the sound of his heavy dockers' boots to announce his arrival.

Last orders would've been called nearly an hour ago. None of us would dare ask where he'd been or what he'd done. He'd probably been out earning his next evening's drink money by bare-knuckle fighting down by the docks or on the Old Kent Road or at The Ring in Blackfriars. These were the places where all the fighters would go to punch the living daylights out of each other for pennies. That money, which we sorely needed to buy medicine for Ma or for food for the littl'uns, would be thrown down his throat and there was nothing in the world we could do about it.

His key scraped against the lock. It fumbled, then scratched again. Les looked at me, his face pale. Our eyes locked for a moment, registering our terror. We heard the key turn. Then the door slammed open, kicked wide by those boots. We jumped. Joanie let out a wail and I shushed her, cuddling her close with trembling hands.

The first thing we saw were those terrible big boots. Then we saw Pa's dark frame silhouetted against the blackness of the hallway outside. For a second nobody moved. Then Pa walked in, swaying as he entered. He wiped his chin and stood surveying the room, his face a picture of mean, sodden rage. His cap had slipped to one side, making him look almost comical.

Pa was 27 years old but already he looked like a man who was disappointed with his lot in life. Despite having a wife and three healthy children, he wore the surly sneer of someone who thought he deserved more. Perhaps that was why he made such a show of fighting. It was a way of proving himself and raising himself above the men of his class and status.

I looked up at him. He was a small, stocky man, but he seemed to tower above me. I noticed that his jacket, made out of sacking cloth and tied with string round the middle, was ripped on one arm. Evidence of his fighting, if we needed it. His lip was starting to swell up and he had a trickle of blood running from the corner of his mouth, which he wiped away like swatting a fly. *More work for Ma*, I thought to myself. She would need to stitch his only jacket to hide the tear while he strutted about Bermondsey. There was only enough time to think these small, insignificant thoughts before That Man lurched into a chair, grabbing the back of it for support in his drunken swagger.

He looked around, searching for someone to take him on. He wasn't done, I could see from his gait that he wanted more violence, more confrontation, like an itch he had to scratch. I knew it had to be me. Who else was there to take his rampaging temper? As I was the eldest, I felt it was my job to protect the others, even though I was not much more than a baby myself.

I couldn't expect Ma to stand between her husband and her children as she was already poorly with a heart complaint. Her heart was always too big for her, we would say, as if knowing that made our worries about her recede. They didn't of course, and there was never enough money to pay for a doctor. The idea of calling a doctor and being whisked into hospital with medicine and clean, crisp white sheets was a fairy tale fantasy, a scenario as far from our lives as it was possible to be. So I looked after Ma the best I could and she called me her 'littl' nurse' and we pretended everything was okay, because what else could we do?

The light from the hearth cast shadows around the room.

The peeling wallpaper that had once been jolly, with faded pink roses on pale green winding stems, made awkward shapes against the gloom. Pa looked black against the shadow – prowling, dangerous. He saw us then, huddled together near the hearth, and he growled at us, 'Fuckin' move, you lazy bastards, I need to warm me feet. Go on, get out of here, you ungrateful cunts.'

The other two moved against the far wall, as if by crouching there they could stay undetected, out of harm's way. I stayed where I was. I watched Pa warily as he gripped the chair and pulled his backside down onto it. His body moved out of rhythm with itself, he stank of beer and fag smoke and there was now a line of bloody dribble running down the dark stubble of his chin.

'What are you fuckin' starin' at? Get me a drink, girl,' he snarled, running his large, dirty hands through his oily hair.

'We ain't got nuffink,' I said, cowering a little under his gaze.

His eyes were bloodshot; small pins of red in his flat face. I hated him; no, I despised him with every ounce of flesh on my skinny body. Every part of me loathed this monster. He made our lives a living hell, when they were already tough enough with the hardship of poverty.

'Well get me a fuckin' sandwich then, I shouldn't 'ave to fuckin' ask ya, 'ilda. I've been workin' down them docks all day, the least a man should expect is 'is dinner when 'e gets 'ome.' With that, he looked up at me, sniffing the air, like an animal scenting its prey. 'An' where's that lazy cow of a mother?'

'She's upstairs, Pa. Restin', like. She ain't well, Pa, 'er 'eart's givin' 'er gyp.' I trembled as I spoke, my eyes averted. There was no point giving him the means to start a fight, yet.

With that he rubbed his chin with his right hand, then

crashed it down onto the table. I jumped out of my skin with the suddenness of it. 'I don't want to know what that lazy bitch is doin', she should be 'ere, feedin' 'er 'usband. Now go an' get me a fuckin' drink NOW.' He slammed his fist down again, to make sure I understood, and by God I did.

'This bloody family. I ain't done nuffink to deserve the likes of you lot. Work me fingers to the bone I do, and what for, I ask you? To be cheeked by me own flesh an' blood.'

I looked, puzzled, at his fingers. There was no bone showing there. Instead they were thick digits, like sausages, the red veins lying under the grime of the dockyard. His fingernails were filthy and stained yellow with the tar from his baccy. I also knew he hadn't been at work today. He'd been refused work at the dockside, or so his mate Billy's wife told Ma this morning. His foul mouth and quick temper had got him into trouble with the foreman at the dock gates again, so how can he have worked his fingers to the bone?

Confused, I watched him as he launched the fury that froze me to the spot. My feet refused to move from under me, even though my mind was yelling to my legs to run away, run as fast as I could and get out and away from That Man. No good would come of tonight. The violence was coming, I could see him building up to it. I could only brace myself for the onslaught.

'We ain't got no drink, Pa.' I shook as I spoke and then somewhere inside me I found the anger, the courage to answer him back. I now knew he was going for me, so I reckoned I might as well go down fighting after all. 'We ain't got no grog cos you drank it all.'

My voice sounded shrill, sharp in the black fog of the room. I could instinctively feel the others shrink into the wall, hoping they might disappear. I wished they could. This way, he'd forget about them and focus just on me. They, at least, would be safe tonight.

'What did you say, girl? I've never 'eard such fuckin' cheek, an' comin' from a daughter of mine wiv a mouth on 'er. I'll bloody teach you for that. You don't ever disrespect your old man. What the 'ell did that bitch of a mother teach you?'

And with that he launched. I had just enough time to brace myself, then the first blow landed.

My pa was a fighter, a proper fighter. He knew how to hit so the bruises didn't show. He knew how to hurt me and I knew I would regret my cheek.

He landed the first blow as a cuff to my face. I felt the skin on my face move in shock then the saliva followed; I spat it onto the floor. I staggered sideways, almost hitting the hearth, with a surprisingly quick movement, he grabbed my hair that hung, brown, lank and dirty, and pulled as hard as he could. I tried to stop my cry, even then I didn't want to startle the babies, but I couldn't, it hurt too much.

'Let me go, Pa, I'll find you a drink, I promise,' I whimpered, only just loud enough for him to hear.

He dragged me by the hair to the door. 'Cheek me an' I'll chuck you out. I don't want you, your ma don't want you. You're no good to anyone you littl' cow.'

With that he reared his face up at me, his eyes screwed into ugly violence. His breath was as sour as the drinking holes he frequented, his skin was grey and mottled red with the booze and his latest fight.

'I'll find you a drink, Pa, I promise I will, I promise.' My voice sounded small next to the storm that was building in him. Again he yanked my hair, dragging my body after him. I felt the door swing open. My head hit the side of it and was jerked round to face the blackness of the open doorway.

I glanced back quickly with the smallest turn of my head which was in his fierce grip, tearing at my scalp.

'It's okay, I'm okay,' I mouthed to Les and Joanie. They were huddled into the grime of the wallpaper, staring at me with huge, fearful eyes. I willed them to stay there, quiet and still, so no harm would come to them.

My head burnt with the pull of That Man's thick fingers. 'I'll fuckin' throw you out, you littl' cunt. What d'you say to me, your pa? What d'you fuckin' say?'

The spittle from his reeking mouth hit my face. I tried to hide my revulsion, my pain, because I knew it excited him even more.

'I'm sorry, Pa. I shouldn't 'ave said that to you. I ain't a bad girl, I promise, Pa. I'll do whatever you say next time, won't I?'

I tried to look him in the eyes but my face was twisted round towards his body, my hands holding my head where the roots of my hair were tearing from my scalp. That must have satisfied him, because he threw me back into the room where I stumbled into the chair and grabbed the table for support. I backed off as slowly as I could, away from the babes, keeping his attention on me, wishing him to calm himself, to quieten down. For a second his eyes met mine and I almost saw something that in another man might've been regret, except it was him, that bastard old man of mine. Whatever it was, it vanished in an instant, leaving that panting, sweating, stinking brute with the remainder of his drunken anger still written on his face.

'Get me a sandwich, then,' he slurred. He looked tired now, defeated, as if the attack had drained him.

Rubbing my head, I edged towards the bread that lay under a grey-streaked piece of linen on the table top. There was half a loaf left, just enough to feed us children in the morning. It might possibly be our only meal of the day, but that wouldn't worry him. I could hardly bear to give it to him, but I knew I had no choice. As if to underline our plight, my stomach growled with hunger.

We went to bed with empty stomachs but grateful Pa's temper hadn't been worse. We climbed onto the iron bed, next to Ma's warm body. Three small children, a urine-stained mattress and a single blanket. I covered each of the littl'uns with their coats and finally settled down myself.

'No 'arm done, sleep now, it'll all be better in the mornin'.' I almost meant it.

We huddled together, not just for warmth, but for the comfort of being together, relatively unscathed by the night's events. I started telling them the same story I told them every night. It wasn't a fancy story, there were no princesses nor handsome princes to rescue them from wicked wizards.

Instead, I told a story about a family who had three children. The mother and father were always happy and loved their little ones. There was always enough to eat, and they lived in a little house that was always warm. There was no need to triumph over evil, because it simply didn't exist in that world we created in our minds. Eventually I heard small snuffles coming from the others and I knew I could finally sleep. I said my prayers. I never asked for much, just the courage to live another day under the same roof as my wicked Pa. This time though, I added a new prayer. I asked God in heaven for a proper family. One with a father who loves his children, and brings them sweets and gives them cuddles, though I knew my prayer would never, ever be granted.

hamlyn | all colour cookbook

200 juices & smoothies

An Hachette Livre UK company
www.hachettelivre.co.uk

First published in Great Britain in 2008 by Hamlyn,
a division of Octopus Publishing Group Ltd
2–4 Heron Quays, London E14 4JP
www.octopusbooks.co.uk

ISBN: 978-0-600-61861-4

A CIP catalogue record for this book is available from the
British Library

Printed and bound in China

1 2 3 4 5 6 7 8 9 10

Both metric and imperial measurements have been given
in all recipes. Use one set of measurements only, and not
a mixture of both.

Standard level spoon measurements are used in all recipes.
1 tablespoon = one 15 ml spoon
1 teaspoon = one 5 ml spoon

200 ml (7 fl oz) makes 1 average serving.
All fruit and vegetables should be washed before use.
Fresh herbs should be used unless otherwise stated.
All yogurt should be live unless otherwise stated.

This book includes dishes made with nuts and nut
derivatives. It is advisable for those with known allergic
reactions to nuts and nut derivatives and those who may be
potentially vulnerable to these allergies, such as pregnant and
nursing mothers, invalids, the elderly, babies and children, to
avoid dishes made with nuts and nut oils. It is also prudent to
check the labels of pre-prepared ingredients for the possible
inclusion of nut derivatives.